JN213867

関西学院大学産研叢書 48

# Value Research in Management Studies

Edited by **Toshihiko Ishihara**

CHUOKEIZAISHA INC

# Contents

Toshihiko Ishihara, Kwansei Gakuin University, Japan

Kenichiro Harada, Tohoku University, Japan

Koji Kojima, Kwansei Gakuin University, Japan

Bishnu Kumar Adhikary, University of Hyogo, Japan

Satoshi Sugahara, Kwansei Gakuin University, Japan

Claudio Dell'Era, Politecnico di Milano, Italy

Ochilov Bobur Bakhtiyor, Tashkent State University of Economics, Uzbekistan

Mohammad Badrul Haider, Kwansei Gakuin University, Japan

# List of figures

# List of tables

# The Editor

**Dr. Toshihiko Ishihara** is a professor at the Institute of Business and Accounting, Kwansei Gakuin University, Japan. His research areas include public policy, public management, accounting, auditing, internal control, healthcare management, university management and philanthropy. He is a Certified Public Accountant (CPA) in Japan and a Chartered Public Finance Accountant (CPFA) with the Chartered Institute of Public Finance and Accountancy (CIPFA) in the UK.

He is also the first Japanese accountant to be a Fellow of CIPFA. He is a co-founder of CIPFA Japan and is currently the President of CIPFA Japan. He was an Honorary Professor at INLOGOV of the University of Birmingham for five years from 2012. He is also currently an Honorary Professor at the University of Edinburgh Business School. In addition, he was an Honorary Professor at the University of Kent Business School for three years.

From his laboratory at Kwansei Gakuin University, 20 people have received their PhDs by FY 2024. Many of the PhD recipients have become university professors, and currently 15 full-time university faculty members are working at universities across Japan. He is also active in inviting researchers from overseas to Japan. The following researchers have been invited to Kwansei Gakuin University as visiting professors or associate professors by him as host faculty.

- Mr. Steve Freer, CIPFA, UK
- Prof. John Raine, University of Birmingham, UK
- Dr. Peter Watt, University of Birmingham, UK
- Dr. Marton Gellen, National University of Public Service, Hungary
- Mr. John Matheson CBE, NHS Scotland, UK
- Dr. Young-hoon Ahn, Hansei University, Republic of Korea
- Dr. Epameinondas Katsikas, University of Kent, UK
- Dr. Martin Jones, Nottingham Trent University, UK
- Dr. Russ Glennon, Manchester Metropolitan University, UK
- Dr. Rocco Palumbo, Tor Vergata University of Rome, Italy

- Prof. Tobias Jung, St. Andrews University, UK,
- Prof. Stephen Osborne, University of Edinburgh, UK
- Prof. Pete Murphy, Nottingham Trent University, UK

He hopes to continue to promote international joint research under an international research network based on close personal relationships. He is also actively seeking competitive research funding, including from the Japan Society for the Promotion of Science (JSPS). He is also keen to contribute to society in Japan and served as a Chief Inspection and Audit Commissioner of Nishinomiya City, Non-Executive Director of Japanese Institute of Certified Public Accountants (JICPA) and a Advisor of the Kyoto Prefectural Government.

# The Contributors

**Mr. Kenichiro Harada** is a Professor at the Graduate School of Law, Tohoku University Japan. After joining the Ministry of Home Affairs in 1993, he worked for Gunma and Chiba Prefectures, and as deputy mayor of Komono Town and deputy mayor of Miyazaki City. He has held positions as a practitioner professor at Hokkaido University and Kwansei Gakuin University.

**Dr. Koji Kojima** is a Professor of School of International Studies at Kwansei Gakuin University, Japan. He received his Ph.D. in Business Administration from the University of Washington Business School, and has taught at Kwansei Gakuin University's School of Business Administration and MBA program before assuming his current position.

**Dr. Bishnu Kumar Adhikary** is a Professor at the School of Economics and Management, University of Hyogo, Japan. Before joining the University of Hyogo, he worked as a faculty member at the business school of Doshisha University, Kobe University, and Ritsumeikan Asia Pacific University, Japan.

**Dr. Satoshi Sugahara** is a Professor of School of Business Administration at Kwansei Gakuin University, Japan. His research interests are accounting education, design thinking, impact of information technologies on business and accounting education.

**Dr. Claudio Dell'Era** is a Full professor in design thinking for business at the School of Management at Politecnico di Milano, Italy. He serves as Co-Founder of LEADIN'Lab, the Laboratory of LEAdership, Design and INnovation.

**Dr. Ochilov Bobur Bakhtiyor** is a Senior lecturer of Faculty of Finance at Tashkent State University of Economics, Uzbekistan. His academic interests include finance, corporate finance, stock market, investment, banking and management.

**Dr. Mohammad Badrul Haider** is an Associate Professor at the Institute of Business & Accounting, Kwansei Gakuin University, Japan. He previously held academic positions at Kobe University, Japan, and the University of Dhaka, Bangladesh.

**Dr. Taslima Akhter** is currently an Assistant Professor at the School of International Studies at Kwansei Gakuin University, Japan. Before joining this institution, she held positions at various public and private universities in Bangladesh.

**Dr. Naoki Inoue** is a Professor at the Faculty of Regional Management at The University of Fukuchiyama, Japan. He is a researcher on accounting, auditing and governance in the public sector, including local government.

**Mr. Shinichi Tanioka** is Ph.D. Candidate at the Institute of Business and Accounting, Kwansei Gakuin University and studies public administration and public governance. He is a Director of Toyooka City Council, Japan.

**Mr. Fumiaki Himawari** is a contributor to the conduction of the importance of balance sheets to local governments in Japan. He was previously a professor at Kwansei Gakuin University, Japan, where he taught local government accounting.

**Dr. Daisaku Sakai** is an Associate Professor of Osaka University of Economics, Japan. He was a former Japanese municipal official and held an academic post at Tokoha University. His research is focused on Municipal Performance evaluation and Public Management Accounting.

**Dr. Hiroki Sekishita** is an Associate Professor of Faculty of Economics at Wakayama University, Japan. He previously held academic positions at Fukuyama University. His research interests include local government Accounting and Financial Management.

**Dr. Ryoji Matsuo** is an Associate Professor of Department of Institute of Business and Accounting at Kwansei Gakuin University, Japan. He also works for the Kumamoto Prefectural Government as head of the Property Management Section. His research is focused on the Public governance and management, Value co-creation in public sector.

**Dr. Toshio Araki** is a Professor of Department of Tax Accounting, Faculty of Economics at Fukuyama University, Japan. He is the Head of the Department of Tax Accounting. His research is focused on the regional university management, SMEs, and Entrepreneurship.

# Introduction

The study of business administration can be categorised into, for example, management strategy theory, marketing and accounting studies. These studies are concerned with the management and governance of managerial organisational bodies, which include private companies that conduct commercial transactions as well as public service-providing organisations that provide public services. The concept of value is a very important concept in both of these disciplines. The concept of value is not only used to assess the effectiveness of businesses and transactions, but also to form the basis for decision-making and performance measurement in management organisational bodies.

Similar concepts to the concept of value include outcome, impact, cost, Value For Money (VFM) and satisfaction. One of the first goals of this book is to organise the concept of value and similar concepts. The methodology is possible from a variety of perspectives, and this book tackles the issue from the perspectives of a number of authors.

The second objective of this book is performance measurement using the concept of value. For example, arguments such as What is the value of design thinking or the value created by family businesses develop a discussion of this issue.

The third purpose of this publication is to apply Public Service Logic, proposed by Professor Stephen Osborne, the University of Edinburgh, in his work on Public Administration and Management, to the Japanese context and to examine its logical rationale. Much of the discussion in Part Two focuses on this argument.

This publication is in the form of a book with a number of authors sharing responsibility for the writing of the book. The authors' specific areas of research also vary. This diversity is in line with the perspective of "integration of neighbouring sciences" of value research in management studies, which this book advocates. The study of value in management studies is profound and does not easily yield a single answer. It would be a great pleasure for the editor if this book could be regarded as a small oasis in this difficult process.

This work was also supported by JSPS KAKENHI Grant Numbers JP19KK0034, JP23K01717, JP21K01791 and JP24K00305.

1 February 2025

Toshihiko Ishihara    Kwansei Gakuin University, Japan

# Part 1

◆

# Theory and Practice

Chapter **1**

# Significance of Value Research in Management Studies: Theory, Practice and Japanese Perspectives

**Toshihiko Ishihara**

**Kenichiro Harada**

◆

**Abstract**

The study of value in management studies should cover both quantitative and qualitative evaluation, and, moreover, should integrate the two to contribute to stakeholders' decision-making and performance measurement. In the past, value research has been conducted quantitatively, for example in economics, using concepts such as Economic Value, Value-in-Exchange and Value Added. In accounting, a branch of business administration, monetary valuation postulates have also been applied, with a history of limiting the objects of value assessment to those that can be evaluated in monetary terms. However, in accounting studies, research attempting to integrate financial and non-financial valuation started in the second half of the 20th century, and looking at the research area of Public Adimination and Management, for example, in Japanese local governments, at the end of the 20th century, introduction of balance sheets was contemplated. Subsequently, evaluation systems using qualitative performance measurement indicators were also introduced. This example shows that quantitative data alone is insufficient for analysing value, that qualitative information is needed to supplement it and, most importantly, that quantitative and qualitative data must be merged.

Methods such as facilitation and coaching are specific techniques for fusing quantitative and qualitative data among stakeholders. Design thinking is also an effective method for facilitation. The significance of value research in management studies does not lie in the pursuit of a smart framework for management studies itself, but in solving practical problems. Solving practical problems also involves, for example, the argument of value formation without cost or sacrifice, as in philanthropy, which has been attracting attention in recent years. The study of value in management science requires integration with a number of neighbouring sciences in order to solve these problems.

**Keywords**

Value, Co-Creation of Value, Value Dimensions, KPIs, Public Sector Accounting, Designing Thinking, Balanced Score Card, Philanthropy, Quantitative Evaluation, Qualitative Evaluation, Integrated Report

## 1.1 Introduction

Business administration is the study of the rational decision-making involved in organisational bodies. Accounting is a typical example of this, and management accounting, which is concerned with decision-making and performance evaluation, has been used in various aspects of business management. Cost accounting is a useful method for determining the selling price of a product. Financial statement analysis techniques are effective for analysing the management of competing rival companies. For medium- and long-term capital investment, there are economic calculations of capital investment using discounted present value.

Accounting has made a significant contribution to financial decision-making in the service sector as well as in manufacturing. Activity Based Costing (ABC) and Strategy Map have been developed for the strategic allocation of indirect costs in the service sector (Kaplan and Norton, 2004), where the rational calculation of indirect costs such as selling, general and administrative expenses is required rather than direct costs such as manufacturing costs. Costing and management accounting for the service sector has also contributed significantly to the development of public sector accounting in government and local government.

However, since the 1970s, managerial decision-making in the private sector and public sector organisations has shifted away from an over-reliance on financial information and towards the active use of non-financial information in managerial decisions. The disclosure of non-financial information has become common in financial reporting by private companies, from which new areas such as environmental and sustainability accounting have been developed. In accounting, integrated reporting of financial and non-financial information is an important research topic. Non-financial information includes not only quantitative data but also corrective data.

As financial and non-financial information is encompassed in financial reporting for external reporting and management accounting for internal management, there is a need to elucidate how this information is used in decision-making and judgement-making. Here, it is necessary to investigate how financial and non-financial information is integrated and utilised in decision-making. The concept of "value" is expected to provide a useful framework for thinking about this issue.

To begin with, the study of value in business administration and economics has shared the problem of how quantitative and qualitative information can be related to decision-making in organisations. While there is the thought that the study of value is extremely difficult, as it targets qualitative assessments of value, there is also the thought that value judgements in the public domain are more qualitative in nature.

In addition, the study of value in business administration must not only provide a comprehensive understanding of quantitative and qualitative information, but also clarify what quantitative and qualitative information consists of in the first place.

## 1.2 Logic models in local government performance management

### 1.2.1 Administrative reforms in Japanese local government over the past 30 years

In the late 1990s, many local governments in Japan embarked on administrative reforms (Ishihara, 2022). These reforms were due to the deteriorating financial situation of local governments, and the main objective of the reforms was to rebuild public finances. A book that was popular in Japan at the time was

(Osborne, 1993). Leading municipalities that led the reforms at the time included the Tokyo Metropolitan Government, Mie Prefecture, Sapporo City and Usuki City in Oita Prefecture (Ishihara, 2001). In these municipalities, aggressive public accounting reforms were initiated. And accrual accounting was introduced on a trial basis as a complement to cash-based accounting methods. Balance sheets and statements of administrative costs (income statements) prepared on an accruals basis revealed the enormous liabilities and inefficient administrative costs incurred by local governments.

As well as this introduction of accrual accounting, administrative reform in Japanese local government at the time can be characterised by the introduction of performance management. The opportunity for this was the introduction of administrative performance management (i.e. the evaluation of projects and affairs that are below the level of policy) in Mie Prefecture. In the late 1990s, administrative performance management in Japan, including in Mie Prefecture, was introduced by several prominent consultants who were influenced by Osborne's book (Osborne, 1993). It was there that the famous logic model of input→output→outcome was first introduced in Japanese local governments.

This logic model explained that no matter how large the budget and other inputs are, they are meaningless unless outputs equivalent to administrative services are produced. It was also explained that what is more important than the outputs are the outcomes, which show the level of satisfaction of the residents. The logic model's assertion that local government performance needs to be measured in terms of outputs and outcomes rather than inputs created quite a stir in local government administrative reform in Japan at the time. The storm of administrative reform, which could be described as revolutionary, spread throughout Japan, and almost all local governments in Japan proceeded with administrative reforms based on performance management.

However, since the late 2000s, many local governments have pointed out problems with the introduction of performance management, which could be called a boom. As a technical problem, it was pointed out that performance management places a heavy workload on local government staff, as it generates a huge amount of paperwork in the preparation of evaluation sheets. Problems were also pointed out, such as the fact that it is not clear who and how the huge amount of standardised sheets are used for decision-making, or that the same evaluation sheets are repeatedly prepared year after year. Ultimately, some finance departments voiced that the data on inputs, outputs and outcomes collated in the performance management sheets are difficult to compare with each other and cannot be used at all for prioritising between projects when drawing up the budget.

Efforts to improve performance management, which cannot be used effectively, have been promoted by Japanese local government officials and researchers since the late 2000s. The simplest idea is to merge performance management with accrual-based accounting, with the idea of precisely calculating the cost of production per unit of administrative service by linking more accurate cost information to inputs. However, the resulting calculations were not really useful as a reference material for budgeting, as they were based on the cost of lending out a single book in a library or the cost of a single use of a public swimming pool by a child. Given the difficulties in integrating accrual accounting and performance management, some researchers worked on the integration of Activity Based Costing (ABC) and performance management. There, the logic model was extended from input→process→output→outcome. Attention was then focused on activity as a component of process. This activity is the activity in Activity Based Costing (ABC). Here, the logic model is input→$\Sigma$ activity→output→outcome.

In the 2010s, some Japanese local governments and public service organisations began to link performance management and accrual accounting to management strategy. Attention was then focused on strategy maps and balanced scorecards (Kaplan, R. S., & Norton, D. P., 2004). In the Strategy Map and Balanced Scorecard framework, first, in the Growth and Learning Perspective, inputs other than financial capital, such as human, information and organisational capital, are subject to thought. In the Process Perspective, various activities are the subject of consideration; in the Financial Perspective, financial capital itself is considered. And in the Customer Perspective, customer value propositions for customers are presented. The evolution using the Strategy Map and the Balanced Scorecard suggests the possibility of a multifaceted consideration of "value", which could not be resolved by performance management or accrual accounting.

These improvements in administrative reform were only practised by a few reform-minded local authorities; by the late 2010s, very few Japanese local authorities were seriously engaged in administrative reform via the introduction of performance management and accrual-based accounting. Academically, research on value in local government was sprouting, but in local governments that actually provide public services, the mindset on value disappeared and the issue of municipal bonds to avoid deficit financing (in cash-based local government accounting, the accounts can be turned into surplus with revenue from debt) and uniform cuts to the budget were made. For both value research and local government administrative reform, the 2010s can be described as a "winter period" in the case of Japan.

### 1.2.2　Initiatives in Usuki City, Oita Prefecture

Even today, the accounting system of the central and local governments in Japan is cash-based accounting. Cash-based accounting enables the understanding of revenue and expenditure in conjunction with cash-based budgets. It is therefore very easy for government officials, legislators and residents without advanced accounting knowledge to grasp its contents. However, in pursuit of the advantage of ease of understanding, cash-based accounting has a number of fatal drawbacks. These shortcomings have become an obstacle to the fiscal consolidation of central and local governments in Japan, even though their serious negative effects are not fully understood, despite the fact that they are triggering a worsening of the financial situation of central and local governments.

One of the most notable shortcomings of the cash basis of accounting is the inability to precisely define the concepts of red in figure and black in figure. In corporate accounting, a company is "in the black" if its revenues exceed its expenditure and "in the red" if they fall below it. A "black in figure" implies profit, while a "red in figure" implies deficit. In central and local governments, however, which use the cash basis of accounting, a red in figure and a black in figure merely mean a shortfall or excess in income and expenditure.

Hence, red in figure and black in figure do not serve a signalling function for fiscal consolidation.

In 1998, the city of Usuki in Oita Prefecture introduced accrual accounting on a trial basis to address this problem. Usuki City's approach also had no small influence on the accrual accounting introduced by the Tokyo Metropolitan Government. The efforts of a small regional city with a population of 40,000 influenced the accounting reforms of the metropolis of Tokyo. The aim of Usuki City's efforts at the time was to ascertain the amount of borrowings and other liabilities, and to clarify the assets of Usuki City, which were the common property of its citizens. The net assets of the city were calculated by subtracting assets from liabilities, and it was thought that the increase or decrease in the net assets of the city was the creation of value, i.e. the property of the citizens by the city council.

The Mayor of Usuki at the time, Mr. Kunitoshi Goto, said that Usuki City Council, which was in charge of the citizens' property, needed to tell the citizens how much their property had increased over the annual year, and was one of the earliest local governments in Japan to introduce a balance sheet. The fundamental reason for this was the idea that the balance sheet was a method of explaining increases and decreases in the "value" of citizens' property.

The idea of value as a monetarily calculable economic value has been the most mainstream idea in economics and has been supported by many researchers. The approach taken by Usuki City to explain the increase in the value of its residents using a balance sheet is based on precisely this traditional understanding. However, Usuki City's approach did not stop there. The year after the preparation of the balance sheet, Usuki City prepared the "Citizen Service Formation Account". The essence of this report is a statement of costs by administrative purpose. In other words, it attempts here to explain how much expenditure (but calculated on an accruals basis) was made on educational, welfare, industrial, etc. objectives, and how much value was formed in accordance with each objective.

In accounting terms, the idea of "cost = value" is present in the service formation accounts of the Usuki City Council. Usuki City's approach is thus an attempt to explain 'value creation' using the amount of costs incurred as well as the increase or decrease in net assets. The idea that costs to the administration are actually in line with benefits to the residents has since been adopted by several progressive administrative reform municipalities in Japan, including Chiyoda Ward, Tokyo. This is a very important practical example of how the increase, decrease and generation of economic value has been integrated with the thinking of municipal public accounting. It is also recognised as a very prominent case study in Japanese public sector accounting research.

### 1.2.3 Performance measurement system in Mie Prefecture

Mie Prefecture implemented a high-profile administrative reform at the same time as Usuki City in Oita Prefecture. Mie Prefecture's population and budget rank it in the middle of Japan's 47 prefectures. Mr.Masayasu Kitagawa was the governor of Mie Prefecture for two terms of eight years from 1995. The administrative reform methods introduced by Mie Prefecture during Kitagawa's governorship were the introduction of accrual-based accounting and a performance measurement system. The performance measurement system, in particular, had a major impact on local governments throughout Japan. At the time, performance measurement adopted by local governments across Japan focused mainly on financial resources and expenditure (input). It was unclear what administrative services were provided by the expenditure, and there was little awareness of what changes were made to the residents and beneficiaries. In other words, performance measurement was only an analysis from the supply side and there was little awareness of the demand side of services.

The performance measurement system introduced by Mie Prefecture at this time required analysis not only of inputs but also of outputs and outcomes, and the idea of analysing outputs and outcomes was a dramatic culture shock not only to the Mie Prefectural Government but also to most local authorities throughout Japan. Outcomes in particular were explained in Japan by the concept of "resident satisfaction", and the idea that residents are the customers of the administration spread among local government officials throughout Japan. Mie Prefectural Government was inundated with administrative inspections from all over Japan and was recognised as the most reformed local government in Japan at the time.

The Mie Prefecture's method of performance management system has spread to municipalities throughout Japan. It is needless to explain that at the root of this is the idea of the logic model "resource $\rightarrow$ input $\rightarrow$ process ($\Sigma$ activities) $\rightarrow$ output $\rightarrow$ outcome". Many local authorities across Japan, regardless of size, have introduced the Mie Prefecture methodology. However, it was later discovered that there was a major pitfall here. That is, many local authorities that attempted to introduce the Mie method in a tokenistic way relied on consultants to set output and outcome indicators. The administrative services provided by local authorities must reflect the circumstances of each locality. Hence, the indicators set should have also reflected local characteristics.

Nevertheless, the consultancy provided indicators that did not reflect local circumstances in exchange for a large consultancy fee. Although the introduction of the tokenistic Mie method was a major source of revenue for the consultancy firms, only a few local authorities achieved the kind of culture shock, i.e. organisational culture reform, that was achieved in Mie Prefecture. In addition, in municipalities that were trying to introduce performance management systems on their own, a great many local government officials struggled with what indicators should be set. Although the Government and its training institutions, as well as private training organisations, provided numerous training courses on the concept of how to set indicators in performance management systems, their knowledge did not spread to local authorities across Japan.

The performance measurement system introduced by Mie Prefecture has since been introduced and operated by local authorities across Japan in various forms. However, while the system has had some positive effects in terms of raising staff awareness of outcomes and reforming the organisational culture, the situation remains very unsatisfactory in terms of whether the crucial performance measurement is being carried out accurately. Needless to say, one of the root causes of this is the logic model that captures the provision of administrative services in a linear fashion. This was in fact already recognised in Mie Prefecture at the end of the 20th century.

In Mie Prefecture, the evaluation of projects has been carried out by identifying the objectives of the projects subject to evaluation as the main objective and other secondary objectives. By identifying the outcomes and impacts associated with these secondary objectives, the shortcomings that linear logic models have are overcome.

In fact, despite the fact that the strength of the Mie method of performance measurement lies in the recognition of this secondary objective, few local authorities across Japan have realised this important content. In recognising what value is created by the administrative services provided by local governments, this concept of secondary objectives set by Mie Prefecture is very important in the formation of theories of public policy and public management. At the very least, the idea that value creation should be recognised in a multifaceted structure rather than a single structure has been elucidated in subsequent discussions of value in the public sector and can be positioned as a precedent leading to Osborne's Public Service Logic (Osborne 2020). Theoretical studies of value creation will therefore be required to clarify what the multifaceted structure is.

In other words, Mie Prefecture's administrative reform was the most typical introduction of NPM (New Public Management) in local government in Japan. However, even in Mie Prefecture, there was a need for a next logic that goes beyond NPM. In Japan, as in NPM advanced countries in Europe and the United States (Virtanen and Stenvall, 2014), the thinking of reform has overlooked the transition from NPM to co-production and co-creation of value.

### 1.2.4 Setouchi City Integrated Report

In the private sector, there is a form of non-financial reporting known as sustainability reporting, and research into this is quite extensive. And this research is not limited to large companies, but also includes small and medium-sized enterprises (Gholami *et al.*, 2022). Some local governments in Japan are working on methods to more adequately communicate the status of multifaceted value creation to their residents. Accountability from local governments to their residents does not mean that they only have to report on their financial situation. Rather, providing financial information alone does not unlock accountability, and local government leaders need to work on pursuing more precise accountability. In this regard, the Sustaibability Reporting approach, which attempts to hold municipalities accountable for their sustainability by appending non-financial information to financial information, has been accumulating results in the field of public sector accounting research.

However, clearly defining sustainability in financial and other reports issued by local governments and other administrations is a very difficult problem. Sustainability in public administration is an assumption to begin with, and there are logical contradictions in efforts to apply sustainability reporting, which is applied in private sector corporate accounting, to public administration bodies. Public administration organisations do not go bankrupt. They are also under the stipulation that they must always continue to exist, even if they go bankrupt financially.

Therefore, an alternative reporting format to sustainability reporting is necessary for the lifting of multifaceted accountability of local authorities. CIPFA and the World Bank have published a report on the application of the International Integrated Reporting Council's (IIRC) International Integrated Reporting Framework to administrative and public service delivery organisations such as local governments (CIPFA, 2016). Based on this CIPFA report and the IIRC's IIRF, Setouchi City, Okayama Prefecture, became the first local government in Japan to publish an integrated report for FY2022 in March 2023 (Setouchi City Council, 2023).

Setouchi City's Integrated Report attempts to explain value creation (or destruction) in terms of six capital increases or decreases. This thinking is based on the IIRC's IIRF, which does not provide separate specific examples or other examples of indicators for assessing the six capital increases and decreases (IIRC, 2014; CIPFA, 2016). Setouchi City has defined indicators for assessing capital increases and decreases as shown in **Table 1.1** outcomes following discussions within the city hall. In addition, the city has set 10-year value increase targets as Targets. Setouchi City states that 'Under our guiding principle, outlined in the motto "A City Where People and Nature Happily Coexist, Setouchi", our aim is to realise a city where anyone can feel at home and live a happy, contented life' and describes the value creation process (Setouchi City Council, 2023, 11).

The attempt to prepare an integrated report in Setouchi City was supported by the Ishihara Laboratory of Kwansei Gakuin University. Laboratory members Hiroki Sekishita, Associate Professor at Wakayama University, and Yozo Maruyama, Associate Professor at Hokuriku University, together with Professor Ishihara, attended study groups in Setouchi City and exchanged views numerous times with Setouchi City officials involved in the preparation. The series of work there can be positioned academically as similar to a participatory observation.

The methods of participatory observation include, of course, the issue of representativeness as a sample of the sample studied. However, the integrated

**Table 1.1** Six elements of value creation and target values

| | Outcomes (2021) | Targets (2030) |
|---|---|---|
| Financial Capital | Financial Capability Index (2021): 0.57<br>Real income/expenditure ratio (2021): 5.4%<br>Real debt-to-GDP ratio (2021): 8.6% | Percentage increase of citizens who think that the city's finances are improving: 50%<br>Percentage increase of citizens satisfied with the city's urban development efforts: 45%<br>Real debt expenditure ratio: $\leqq 13.0\%$ |
| Manufactured capital | Ordinary construction project spending (2021): 4,565 million yen<br>Fibre-optic network installation: 100% | Population coverage of sewage treatment: 80.1%<br>Road pavement rate: 84.9% |
| Intellectual capital | Public awareness-raising and promulgation of a correct understanding of leprosy<br>"*Kodomo Hiroba* ('Children's Plaza') Project" participants (2021): 2,894 | Preservation of Nagashima and transmission of memories<br>Percentage of citizens who feel the city is a safe place to have and raise children: 75% |
| Human capital | Population dynamics (2020 National Census): Reduction of 242 people<br>System for the deployment of private-sector human resources to revitalise local communities | Population: c. 33,000 people |
| Social capital | Beginning of citizen participation and collaboration proposal initiative<br>Creation of a memorandum of understanding on the location of Iris Ohyama Inc. | Number of applications for citizen activity support grants: 115<br>Percentage of citizens who feel that the city provides conducive conditions for business expansion: 40% |
| Natural capital | Promotion of renewable energy use in public facilities | Carbon neutral<br>Percentage of citizens who feel that the city has truly inherited its wonderful nature, scenery, traditions, history, and culture: 75.0% |

Source: Prepared by the author

report prepared in Setouchi City is the only sample of integrated report preparation in local government in Japan, and it is believed that there are not a few findings to be gained from it. The following are generally pointed out as advantages of participatory observation, for example

- It is easy to identify problems and to clarify the nature of problems.
- It is easier to draw an overall picture of the problem. It is possible to understand the subject's experience of the event in question retrospectively and to make sense of the subject's actions.
- It is possible to go back in time and capture the process of change of the subject.

What the members of the Ishihara Lab have identified from this research, which is similar to participatory observation, can be summarised as follows, focusing on the changing attitudes of Setouchi City officials with regard to their perception of value.

- The value created by the services provided to citizens can be perceived from different perspectives (Loci of value creation).
- Instead of seeing value as economic or social, they have become more aware of non-economic and personal value as well (existence of non-economic value).
- Value is not only created but also destroyed (value destruction).
- It was recognised that by making better use of capital outside the city hall, the assets of the city hall could be more effectively used in the creation of value (co-creation of value).

The above summary is not based on a strictly participatory observation method, but on the subjective impressions of the Ishihara Lab members who attended the workshop. However, the comments made by Setouchi City officials at the study group clearly converge in the direction described above. Therefore, these aggregated contents can be regarded as evidence of a certain academic significance in theoretical research on public policy and public management, when value is the subject of research.

## 1.3   New trends of value research in business administration

### 1.3.1   Professor Osborne's PSL Logic

In the area of Public Administration and Management (PAM) research, Professor Stephen Osborne of the University of Edinburgh has published groundbreaking research findings on value creation as Public Service Logic (PSL). The results of this research have been considered, analysed and demonstrated by a number of researchers and a number of research papers have been published (Capolupo *et al*., 2020). Some of them strengthen the theoretical framework of PSL (Jenhaug, 2021; Cui & Aulton 2023; Rossi *et al*., 2021; Mills *et al*., 2023; Liljeroos-Cork and Luhtala, 2024), while others critically analyse the research content of PSL (Engen *et al*., 2021; Jenhaug, 2021; Kinder and Stenvall, 2023).

However, it is undeniable that PSL has had a very significant impact on the field of PAM research. In this sense, the contribution of Professor Osborn's PSL theory to value research in management studies as well as PAM is remarkable. The characteristics of Professor Osborn's PSL can be summarised as follows.

- By expanding the traditional concept of value, such as the creation of customer value in commercial transactions or the added value in economic calculations, the four concepts of Value-in-Use, Value-in Production, Value-in Context and Value-in Exchange were clarified. By expanding the concept of value in this way, it became possible to discuss the creation of value in a more general sense, not limited to commercial transactions or economic calculations. In addition, the existence of such a multi-faceted concept of value has been organised into the concept of value dimensions (Osborne, 2021, chap.2).

- The specific content of value is organised into five concepts that are collectively referred to as 'value elements'. The five value elements are: satisfaction, outcome, lived experience, capacity creation (capacity development) and societal value. The matrix that combines value dimensions and value elements is referred to as the value creation matrix (Osborne, 2020, chap 4).

- The concept of "locus" of value creation is introduced in PSL. There is a view, like Grönroos's, that value is generated by the users of a service. However, while this view may be reasonable in the context of commercial transactions, it is not necessarily reasonable in the context of the provision of broader public services. In PSL, the locus of value creation is shown as the individual, society and the service system (Osborne, 2020, chap 4).

- In PSL, the process of co-creating value is identified in more detail, and the concepts of Co-design, Co-production, Co-experience, Co-construction, and Co-destruction are derived. Here, it is important to note that co-creating value is not only a process of creation, but also refers to the possibility of destroying something through collaboration (Osborne, 2020, chap 4).

- In PSL, the existence of a public service ecosystem is demonstrated. In this ecosystem, there is an interaction between value dimensions and value factors. Here, value factors refer to value elements, value spaces, and value creation processes. By making use of these value dimensions and factors within the ecosystem and conducting pre- and post-analysis, it is possible to smoothly formulate policies and evaluate them (Osborne, 2020, chap 5) .
- Value does not only arise as Value-in-Use (Grönroos, 2008), but also in various dimensions.

PSL has presented a new field for the study of value in business administration. Until now, research into value has been led by the logic of marketing and service management, but PSL has expanded the scope of this research to include PAM. Value is fundamentally related to the concept of effectiveness or benefit. The concepts of effectiveness and benefit have been combined with the concepts of expenditure and cost, and have been considered as cost-effectiveness or cost-benefit.

Therefore, it has been thought that value, like effectiveness and benefit, must also be compatible with objective financial effects or monetary evaluation. However, PSL has revealed that adhering to this way of thinking makes the study of value in business administration difficult. What is important in the study of value in business administration is to deepen the study of many values that are impossible to evaluate using objective numerical values, and to systematically structure the content of that study.

### 1.3.2 How to share an understanding of values

If we assume that value is not something that lends itself to objective measurement, then the question becomes how to share a common understanding of such value among a series of stakeholders. Financial accounting figures and various KPIs have provided a basis for common discussion, even if their setting and evaluation methods are problematic. However, if value is not of that nature, we need to recognise ways to develop that common understanding as an important part of value research in management studies.

Japanese local governments currently have one distinctive staff training theme. This is training in the acquisition of methods known as coaching or facilitation. Some local authorities invite external trainers to provide training not only through classroom lectures, but also with the aim of acquiring facilitation qualifications. Many local authorities also employ facilitation specialists as full-time municipal employees. Recently, it is not unusual to find situations where municipal employees who have acquired facilitation techniques and implemented facilitation to coordinate with residents and stakeholders work as volunteers.

Chapter 3 of this book provides a literature review of the relevance of design thinking to the study of value in management studies. Facilitation also has a close relationship with this design thinking. Visiting Associate Professor Takayuki Karube of Kyushu University described this to the author of this chapter as follows.

I see facilitation as "enabling" in relation to design thinking. Design is a series of processes consisting of purpose setting, planning and specification expression. Facilitation, which emphasises process, can also be seen as the act of creating design itself. For example, although the sense of effectiveness may vary depending on the definition of "design management" in individual organisations and sites, as well as the expectations and meanings attached to it, for example, the functions of design and facilitation are considered to fit well together as a means of advancing the following three processes. (1) idea generation (e.g. brainstorming), (2) dialogue between members (e.g. feedback) and (3) collaboration with diverse actors (e.g. coordination and integration of opinions through collaboration/visualisation).

In this context, the World Café is particularly effective as one of the methods to promote (1) and (2), as a way of diverging and sharing diverse viewpoints, building exchanges and relationships among members, and preparing the ground for deepening the theme. In addition, I am sorry that I have not asked for details, but many members of the Japan Facilitation Association are using facilitation to promote business planning and other activities based on "design thinking", so I have the impression that there are many needs in the field from that point of view. In particular, "visualising the process" using frameworks for organising thoughts and integrating ideas, and "creating questions" to deepen the theme seem to be points of interest.

Methods of sharing the understanding that makes for value also include the issue of disclosure methods triggered by non-financial reporting, as discussed in Chapters 4 and 5 of this publication. As social media has become an important medium for connecting individuals and society, in addition to face-to-face facilitation, there is a need to research methods to deepen stakeholders' understanding of value through the sharing of a variety of internet-mediated information. The use of generative AI is also likely to be one of the most important future research questions in the study of value in management studies.

### 1.3.3   General theory or contingency theory?

The research of value in management studies has only just begun to take off. To be precise, there are not many research papers that have examined the subject of value, as the discussion in the chapters of this book makes clear. Importantly, no structure has been formed to systematise such a series of researches. In order to form this theoretical structure, it is necessary to start the discussion from the definition of what value is in the first place. However, there is no shortage of such researches in the past. In this respect, a leading previous study exists in (Cui and Aulton, 2023).

In the end, it is difficult to define value in any more formulaic way than that it is something good. Where, then, should value research begin? This is where the idea of promoting value research as a contingency theory comes in. Of course, it is most desirable that a system of value research is formed as a general theory of management science. However, as this is seen as difficult, it will be necessary to promote value research in management studies by restricting conditions and content.

Business administration is often referred to as a practical science. Business administration provides some solutions to problems that arise in the management practice of various organisations. In the extreme, there are many practical problems that can be solved without, for example, forming a general theory of the definition of value. Even if the content of the value imagined by stakeholders differs from one another, it is possible to share understanding through facilitation and other methods and find some kind of landing point. And that landing point is the content of value that most of the stakeholders agree on. In most cases, the value content cannot be expressed in financial or other figures. But the problem is still solved nonetheless. This can be understood, for example, by taking the example of local government budgeting. Local government budget documents contain a huge number of projects and policies, their objectives, their foreseen effects, and the amount budgeted and financed. The statements on objectives and effects are all written, and it is difficult to compare them with the financial budget and funding amounts, no matter how sophisticated the mathematics or mathematical formulae are. Nevertheless, budgets are usually still approved. Budget proposals are often concluded by a unanimous or near-unanimous vote. In other words, the quantitative and qualitative content is fused together in the minds of the stakeholders to make some kind of decision. This understanding is essential to the basis of value research.

In the second part of the book, Part II, individual theory of value research is developed, with Japanese management organisations as the subject of study. The chapters are based on the following topics. In Chapter 5, universities (Akhter and Ishihara, 2018); in Chapter 6, prominent hot spring resorts; in Chapter 7, Usuki City, Oita Prefecture (local government), which is also mentioned in this chapter; in Chapter 8, shipbuilding in local cities; in Chapter 9, Japan's proud community comprehensive care (as one of the public service ecosystems); and in Chapter 10, cooperation between universities and local SMEs are the subject of research. Each chapter exemplifies the content of the logic and practical application of the value concept to solve the managerial challenges faced by the respective management actors. In this sense, Part II can be positioned as a collection of practices of value research in management studies applicable only in the country of Japan. There are also research results such as (Katsuda *et al.*, 2024) on Japanese healthcare management and PSL. Although it is not an international general theory, Part II is characterised by a collection of value research in contingency theory-based management studies at the national level in Japan.

## 1.4 Directions for value research in business administration

### 1.4.1 Integration with neighbouring sciences

In economics and economics-influenced accounting (accounting is at present a branch of business administration), the study of value has been seen as the most important research issue, the objective quantification of which is the most important. However, it is necessary to realise that this is the biggest mistake in business administration research.

For example, in accounting research, several accounting postulates are first applied in defining accounting information. One of these conventions is the monetary valuation convention. Under the accounting postulates of monetary valuation, economic events that cannot be valued in terms of financial figures are not subject to accounting valuation. For example, enterprises have human capital. The presence of competent employees who are familiar with the individual circumstances and business of the enterprise should undoubtedly increase economical value of the enterprise and be a source of excess revenue capacity. However, human capital is not recorded in the assets section of a company's balance sheet. Nor is that excess revenue capacity recorded on the balance sheet as an intangible asset. Thus, as long as there are monetary valuation postulates in accounting, it is impossible to comprehensively measure value within the scope of accounting.

When looking at accounting methodology from the perspective of value research, since the 20th century, accounting has emphasised the integration of financial and non-financial information. Problems that cannot be solved by accounting information that only conforms to monetary valuation postulates, such as environmental auditing and sustainability reporting, are being solved by integrating non-financial information. This perspective of fusion of neighbouring sciences is a particularly important idea in value research in management studies. Business administration has originally gained a reputation as a discipline that consolidates advanced practices recognised in practice. Today, although business administration has a research discipline as a pure academic discipline, it is undeniable that it has a "mishmash" element in its nature. If this is the case, then the study of value in business administration should further pursue the aspect of fusion with neighbouring sciences in its research design in the future.

### 1.4.2   Creating value through philanthropy

There are still many social problems that are difficult to solve by administrative services financed by taxes and other public funds, or by organisations providing public services such as hospitals (Katsuda *et al.*, 2024), schools and homes for the elderly. Intractable diseases and poverty, as well as global environmental degradation and discrimination, are social problems that cannot be easily solved.

Philanthropy is an initiative that allocates the property and capital of private organisations and people as financial resources to solve social issues such as the above (Jung & Harrow, 2015). It goes without saying that behind philanthropy there are thoughts of human love, compassion and dignity (Jung *et al.*, 2016). Philanthropy also has the philosophy of appropriating personal assets and property to realise these thoughts in a "spirit of altruism". Philanthropy does not require a return in the form of corporate revenues, and it exists as an ongoing, rather than a temporary, commitment. The fundamental difference between charity and philanthropy is this continuity. But who appropriates their wealth in this altruistic spirit, and when and how? It is precisely here that philanthropy research seems to lie at its core.

In fact, philanthropy research is also closely related to the study of value in management studies. The evaluation of value has often been perceived in terms of its impact in relation to the costs and sacrifices required to realise its visibility. If the costs and sacrifices are too big, the investment has been regarded as a low-impact realisation of value (even if the value is realised well). This denominator-numerator relationship has been the practice in value-related evaluation. However, value creation based on philanthropy is an investment where there are no costs or sacrifices to be made in return. Why do people and organisations practise philanthropy, i.e. social investment where the denominator is zero? This tremendous question is, in fact, a research question related to the existence of the UN Sustainable Development Goals. The private sector (not only large corporations but also small and medium-sized enterprises), not only in Japan but also in other countries around the world, is active in efforts to engage with the Sustainable Development Goals. At times, the results of these efforts have been made public in the disclosure of information by companies and others, using a large number of papers and other means. There are even studies that show that working towards the Sustainable Development Goals contributes to increasing the profits of companies and their ability to generate excess revenues (Gholami,A. *et al.*, 2022).

As companies become more active in relation to the Sustainable Development Goals, organisations and individuals will be asked what value they attach to philanthropy, which does not directly achieve its original objectives. Professor Osborn has proposed the concepts of societal value as an element of value, Value-in Production as a value dimension, and Co-construction as a process of value creation (Osborne, 2020). In order to relate philanthropy to a series of value studies, the challenge is to elaborate on the relationships between these components of value. If this is resolved, philanthropy research can be linked to value research in management studies as an adjoining science, allowing discussion within a more comprehensive framework.

### 1.4.3 Significance of value research in management studies

Business administration has a history of development as the logic for decision-making and performance measurement in companies. Therefore, value research in business administration has been developed exclusively on the basis of quantitative evaluation. There, quantitative evaluation has been the premise of value research, and there has been a history of seeking even arbitrary quantitative evaluations of things that can only be evaluated qualitatively. One example can be glimpsed in the application of KPIs lacking logic that has been applied in the Balanced Scorecard However, non-objective, qualitative assessments of traits and values are difficult to create a common understanding among stakeholders.

This results in a situation of Policy-Based Evidence Making rather than Evidence-Based Policy Making. From this point on, it is important to explain the content of such qualitative evaluations without quantifying them, rather than forcing them to seek methods for quantification. What is important in value research in management studies is to understand this quantitative value through quantitative evaluation and qualitative value through, for example, textual evaluation, and then to find a method that integrates the two to enable decision-making. It is an important future research question to examine how facilitation and the World Café method can be theoretically related to the sharing of qualitative value assessments or to the fusion of quantitative and qualitative assessments.

It is not important to form a smart framework as an academic discipline, but the original purpose of business administration is to accurately share the actual situation and find precise methods for future decision-making and current performance measurement. It is not only a matter of demonstrating "what is shared in the world of practice" on the basis of objective evidence through extensive questionnaires, interviews, etc., but it is also a matter of finding out what is being faced in the world of practice. It must also be the high road of the discipline of business administration to seek out the logic to formulate thoughts and common intentions to solve the difficulties faced in the world of practice. The research of value in business administration is precisely an attempt to form a path on this high road.

It is also clear from the cost-effectiveness or cost-benefit analysis that, even if the value corresponding to the benefit can be lightened, the subsequent analysis of the numerator-denominator does not allow for as objective an analysis as one might expect. Forced quantification of value is not as useful as it could be. This is also evident in studies on auditing and inspection. The study of PFI and PPP is also an important point of contention in PAM. However, with such a current perception of VFM, accurate PFI and PPP implementation is difficult; one of the reasons why PFI and PPP are not working well is the negative impact of the arbitrary calculation of VFM, which requires an objective assessment of value. This negative impact will forever be impossible to resolve if the assumption is made in management studies that value is simply to be quantitatively ascertained. The study of value must always be considered from both quantitative and qualitative perspectives.

The study in Chapter 2 focuses on the value created by family business. In Japan, family business is common not only in small and medium-sized enterprises

(SMEs) but also in large enterprises. What value does family business create for shareholders and stakeholders? In order to examine these issues, a theoretical framework for qualitative value assessment has to be formed, and in Public Administration and Management, Professor Osborne formed the PSL logic (Osborne, 2020). The same kind of research is required in other areas of management studies, for example in the area of the management of commercial enterprises in particular.

● References────────────────────

Akhter, T., Haider, M. B., & Ishihara, T. (2022). A comparison of integrated reporting practices in Japan and the UK. In *Corporate Narrative Reporting* (pp. 151-170). Routledge.

Akhter, T., & Ishihara, T. (2018). Assessing the gap between integrated reporting and current corporate reporting: A study in the UK. *International Review of Business*, (18), 137-157.

Capolupo, N., Piscopo, G., & Annarumma, C. (2020). Value co-creation and co-production in the interaction between citizens and public administration: A systematic literature review. *Kybernetes*, 49(2), 313-331.

Chartered Institute of Public Finance and Accountancy (CIPFA). (2016). *Integrated thinking and reporting: Focusing on value creation in the public sector*, 1-46. World Bank Group.

Cui, T., & Aulton, K. (2023). Conceptualizing the elements of value in public services: insights from practitioners. *Public Management Review*, 1-23.

Cui, T., & Osborne, S. P. (2023). Unpacking value destruction at the intersection between public and private value. *Public Administration*, 101(4), 1207-1226.

Gholami, A., Murray, P. A., & Sands, J. (2022). Environmental, social, governance & financial performance disclosure for large firms: is this different for SME firms ? . *Sustainability*, 14(10), 6019.

Grönroos, C. (2008). Service logic revisited: who creates value? And who co creates?. *European Business Review*, 20(4), 298-314.

International Integrated Reporting Council (IIRC)(2014). *International Integrated Reporting Framework*, 1-44.

Ishihara, T. (2022). Public sector reform and public management theory  cases of Japan. *Public Management Review*, 24(11), 1653-1662.

Ishihara, T. (2001). Accounting Revolution in Sapporo and Usuki City. *Government Auditing Review*, 8, 35-50. Board of Audit of Japan.

Engen, M., Fransson, M., Quist, J., & Skålén, P. (2021). Continuing the development of the public service logic: a study of value co-destruction in public services. *Public Management Review*, 23(6), 886-905.

Jenhaug, L. M. (2021). Suggestions for developing public service logic through a study of interactive value formation. *International Journal of Public Administration*, 44(9), 728-740.

Jung, T., Phillips, S. D., & Harrow, J. (Eds.). (2016). *The Routledge Companion to Philanthropy*.

Routledge.

Jung, T., & Harrow, J. (2015). New development: Philanthropy in networked governance—treading with care. *Public Money & Management*, 35(1), 47-52.

Katsuda, A., Naito, Y., & Ishihara, T. (2024). Value co-creation in the health-care ecosystem for sustained excellence: realization of patient-centered medicine through task shifting of nurses. *The TQM Journal*, 36(3), 832-846.

Kaplan, R. S., & Norton, D. P. (2004). *Strategy Maps: Converting Intangible Assets into Tangible Outcomes*. Harvard Business Review Press.

Kinder, T., & Stenvall, J. (2023). A critique of public service logic. *Public Management Review*, 1-23.

Liljeroos-Cork, J., & Luhtala, M. (2024). Value co-destruction through misintegration of resources within a public service ecosystem. *Public Management Review*, 1-24.

Mills, D., Cucciniello, M., Keast, R., Nabatchi, T., & Verleye, K. (2023). Evaluating and extending public service logic–introduction to the special issue. *Public Management Review*, 1-9.

Osborne, D. (1993). Reinventing government. *Public productivity & management Review*, 349-356.

Osborne, S. (2020). *Public service logic: Creating value for public service users, citizens, and society through public service delivery*. Routledge.

Rossi, P., & Tuurnas, S. (2021). Conflicts fostering understanding of value co-creation and service systems transformation in complex public service systems. *Public Management Review*, 23(2), 254-275.

Setouchi City Council (2023). *Setouchi City Integrated Report*, 1-48.

Virtanen, P., & Stenvall, J. (2014). The evolution of public services from co-production to co-creation and beyond: New Public Management's unfinished trajectory?. *International Journal of Leadership in Public Services*, 10(2), 91-107.

Chapter **2**

# How Do Family Firms Create Value for Shareholders?

Koji Kojima

**Bishnu Kumar Adhikary**

◆

**Abstract**

This paper sheds light on how family firms create value for their shareholders. In doing so, the paper extensively reviews the extant literature to understand value creation. Besides the financial measure, the paper explores non-financial aspects such as family relationships, decision-making dynamics within the company, and long-term vision to create shareholder value. Furthermore, the paper analyzes the coaction between these forces and their influence on creating shareholder value, offering a comprehensive perspective. The paper reveals that value creation is a broad concept and often a complex and critical process. The paper noted that the significance of family businesses in creating value for shareholders extends beyond just profit margins and growth numbers. It is deeply linked to socio-emotional feelings associated with the firms, family values, morality, ethics, and a strong desire to protect firm values for successive generations. The paper argued that family firms generate value for shareholders because they possess a unique mindset to ensure the firm's resilience. Also, they can adapt flexibly to changing business landscapes as they carefully design business portfolios. Each hallmark value bears positive implications for the family and the business, and family firms adopt diverse strategies to nurture and reinforce these values. Hence, family-owned firms can align with their intrinsic values to create value for shareholders, perceiving their business as a platform for increased community engagement and social contribution. The findings of the study are expected to have significant policy implications for family enterprises and the broader business community. However, the paper noted that value creation is not univocal across firms. Thus, it warrants more studies across countries and firms to accumulate experience.

**Keywords**

Family firms, Value creation, Financial and non-financial measures, Japan

## 2.1 Introduction

The question of how family-owned enterprises generate shareholder value has been a critical focus for researchers and industry practitioners in recent years. The latest report published by Mckinsey & Company in 2023 unveiled that family firms account for more than 70% of global GDP with an annual turnover of 60-70 trillion USD (McKinsey & Company, 2023). Further, McKinsey & Company (2023) report that family firms tend to show superior economic performance over non-family firms in the last couple of decades (**Figure 2.1**). Also, numerous empirical works claim that family firms outperform non-family firms because they hold long-term views in strategic decision-making, allocation of financial resources,

**Figure 2.1** Economic Performance of 600 Listed Family and 600 Listed Non-family Firms in the World

Average economic spread for family-owned businesses (FOBs) and non-FOBs,[1] %

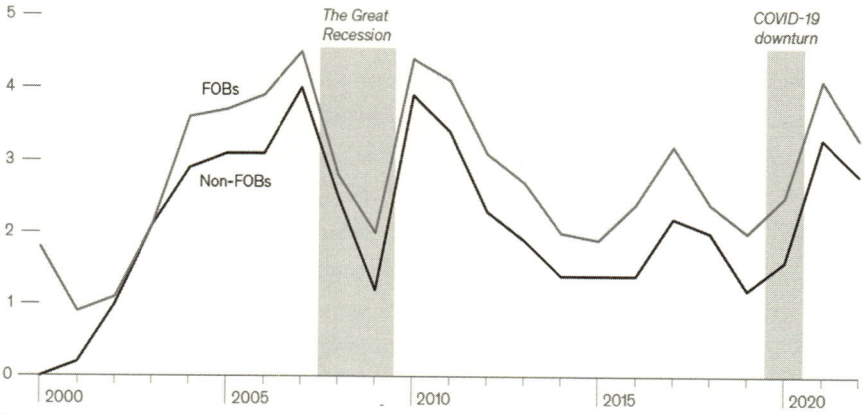

Source: Adapted from McKinsey & Company (2023).

[1] The performance of 600 publicly listed FOBs was analyzed and compared with that of 600 publicly listed companies that are not family owned. Another 600 primarily private FOBs around the world were also surveyed.

retaining talents, and developing a critical mindset of purpose beyond profits that builds social and relational capital, leading to improved financial performance (Miller & Le Breton-Miller, 2005; Pearson, Carr, & Shaw, 2008).

However, some studies highlighted several disadvantages of family firms, such as internal clashes among family members, poor governance system, and excessive concerns of risks while allocating financial resources as factors that reduce shareholders' value (Morck & Yeung, 2003; O'Boyle *et al.*, 2012; Cabrera-Suarez, Saa-Perez, &  Garcia-Almeida 2001; Lee & Rogoff 1996). Therefore, despite a wealth of metaphysical premises and empirical confirmation highlighting family-owned businesses' competitive strengths and weaknesses, an extensive overview of how these firms create value remains challenging.

Notably, the issue of how family firms generate shareholder value is complex and critical.  In today's diverse and competitive business environment, the significance of family businesses in creating value for shareholders extends beyond just profit margins and growth numbers. It is closely tied to a deep connection with family values, socio-emotional feelings associated with the firms, the capability to adapt flexibly to changing business landscapes, long-term strategic decisions, and a solid commitment to protecting firm values for successive generations. Thus, value creation is a broader concept and requires the accumulation of experience from family firms around the globe.

To this end, this paper aims to explore a deeper understanding of specific factors within family-owned businesses that contribute to shareholder value creation. The paper doesn't solely focus on financial measures. It explores nonfinancial aspects such as family relationships, decision-making dynamics within the company, and long-term vision to create shareholder value. Furthermore, the paper analyzes the coaction between these forces and their influence on creating shareholder value, offering a comprehensive perspective on the impact of family enterprises on shareholders and the broader business community.

## 2.2 Definition

### 2.2.1 What are Values?

Empirical observations show that while dictionary definitions serve their purpose, a more precise and scholarly clarification is indispensable to comprehensively depict the multifaceted concept of "Value." Meglino and Ravlin (1998, p.353) assert that scholarly exploration in this field has predominantly focused on categorizing "behavioral values" due to their alignment with values understood by academics and policymakers to explain an organization's cultural framework. However, they note that an organization's cultural principles and behavioral patterns are best evaluated by observing its members' tangible actions rather than relying solely on explicit statements or declarations. In this context, the widely accepted adage "Deeds, not words" emphasizes the importance of actions over verbal expressions. Furthermore, Meglino and Ravlin (1998, p.354) highlight an additional aspect of values in behavior. They suggest that within the context of behavior, the concept of desirability can be understood as the sense of "oughtness": values outline an individual's subjective convictions regarding how one "should" or "ought to" conduct themselves.

- Attitudes: These encapsulate how individuals engage with various entities such as events, individuals, or objects. Positive attitudes often reflect values. Examples include "optimism," "client-oriented focus," "dedication," "accountability," "empathetic concern," "pursuit of excellence," and "customer-centric orientation."

- Technical values or skills: These denote acquired proficiency or competence in performing a task or producing an outcome accurately and precisely. They involve mastery of specific actions or practices. Examples include "negotiation skills" and "effective communication."

- Moral or ethical values: As Scheler (1973) described, these are termed "virtues." They encompass ingrained tendencies to engage in morally upright behavior, representing acquired predispositions to act commendably. Illustrative examples include "integrity" and "benevolence."

As outlined in his work (1973, pp. 1913-1916), Scheler's taxonomy of values consists of five distinct categories: the values of the holy spirit, life, and the noble, pleasure, and utility. This classification is derived from an analysis of inherent attributes in these values, including their extent, durability, and depth. Scheler's categorization shares similarities with Aristotle's concept of "good" as described in his influential work, "Nicomachean Ethics."

Aristotle's perspective asserts that objects are considered "good" when they possess utility, bring about pleasure, or embody nobility, which represents intrinsic goodness or moral excellence. Individuals evaluate and conduct themselves based on perceiving these objects as inherently good, pleasurable, or useful. Aristotle establishes a hierarchy among these notions of "good," with noble good at the highest level, pleasurable good, and useful good. Consequently, noble or honest values hold utmost significance, pertaining not merely to a specific aspect of goodness like utility but to the essence of goodness itself, characterized by excellence and completeness. The term "integrity," when applied to personal conduct, precisely signifies this understanding—an individual of integrity acts in harmony with the most comprehensive form of goodness. This doesn't imply that "nobility" excludes "pleasure" or "utility." Instead, the former takes precedence over the latter two in human behavior, as they represent certain aspects of goodness for the individual, while "integrity" encompasses what is integral and beneficial for the person as a complete individual.

In his Nicomachean Ethics (Book VIII, p.1156), Aristotle utilizes the same classification to elaborate on friendship. In the realm of friendship, individuals engage in reciprocal exchanges of goods, forming the basis for Aristotle's inclusion of friendship in his discourse on virtues. Different types of friendships emerge based on utility, pleasure, or mutual good. The highest and noblest form of friendship arises when individuals are committed to each other's welfare. Remarkably, such friendships yield the greatest utility and pleasure as they prioritize each other's well-being. Relationships founded solely on pleasure or utility may seem rewarding initially but tend to be transient and fleeting.

Utility might be more important than pleasure when assessing a company's Mission Statement from a value-oriented perspective. While a company's primary aim is profitability, it doesn't represent the sole or ultimate objective. Current corporate social responsibility trends highlight the idea that companies, as human entities, should pursue goals beyond just financial gains, focusing on the common good. This underlines the essence behind creating Mission Statements for firms. Aristotle's viewpoint (Nicomachean Ethics, Book I, p.1096) supports that wealth alone cannot be the ultimate sought-after good; it serves as a means to an end. Although this notion aligns with family business leadership, its origin lies in Aristotle's philosophy. Consequently, a practical implication arises: Mission Statements typically encompass "useful" values, considering the necessity of generating value, but they should also include "noble" values. Conversely, Mission Statements that explicitly highlight "pleasurable" values, such as "Enjoying work" or "Creating an enjoyable workplace," are relatively less common.

### 2.2.2   What is Shareholder Value?

Shareholder value, also known as the maximization of shareholders' wealth or the shareholder value model, is a prevalent concept in the business empire. Shareholder value asserts that a company's success is primarily measured by its ability to increase the wealth of its stockholders or shareholders. The core principle of this concept revolves around prioritizing shareholders' interests, making optimizing overall share value the foremost objective for a business. Critics of this concept raise concerns about the potential negative impacts of excessively focusing on shareholder value on other stakeholders such as customers, suppliers, and the workforce. When a company's management effectively expands its sales revenues, net income, and free cash flow over time, it often increases its share value, thereby satisfying shareholders. The key factors determining a business's present and future success lie in the strategic decisions made by senior management and their capability to make wise investments and produce a resilient return on invested capital. If senior managers consistently create value in the long term, the company's share price is likely to rise, allowing it to provide significant cash dividends to its shareholders. Achieving this objective signifies that the company has fulfilled its primary mission of enhancing shareholder value.

The term "shareholder value" is widely used by different individuals, such as fund managers, shareholder activists, and company managers. However, there is often ambiguity surrounding its precise definition and usage. In an article printed in the Financial Times in January 2015 titled "Exactly what do we mean by shareholder value?" columnist Terry Smith expressed doubts about whether everyone who employs this term genuinely understands its intended significance (Smith, 2015). He argued that it is frequently misinterpreted. Smith defined value creation as a company's ability to generate returns surpassing the cost of capital used in their generation. Drawing a comparison between companies and individuals, he illustrated that if a person borrows money at a 10% annual cost and invests it at a 5% annual return, their wealth decreases. Conversely, investing at a 20% annual return leads to wealth growth. Similarly, companies consistently achieving returns higher than their cost of capital become more valuable, while those falling short become less valuable. According to Smith, a company nourishing capital return over its cost of capital facilitates the creation of value for shareholders. This implies that shareholders favor a company that retains a portion of its profits for reinvestment at these satisfactory rates of return rather than distributing all profits as dividends or using them for share buybacks.

## 2.3   Governance Structure: Creation of Shareholder's Value

### 2.3.1   A Model of Fit

While substantial empirical works have delved into investigating the influence of ownership on the objectives, resources, and governance structures of family firms (e.g., Kammerlander *et al*., 2015; Carney, 2005; Chrisman, *et al*., 2012; Habbershon, Williams, & MacMillan, 2003; Sirmon & Hitt, 2003), the current academic viewpoint on value creation in family-owned firms lacks cohesion. Previous studies tend to focus on isolated aspects of the value creation model in family enterprises, such as goals, resources, or governance, and their impact on firm performance (Kammerlander *et al*., 2015). However, the contingency-based view (Drazin & Van de Ven, 1985) suggests that researchers should avoid singular focus and instead consider the critical interplay or 'fit' between this definition of various elements, alongside aligning the specific firm with its external environment (Kammerlander *et al*., 2015). This holistic approach necessitates evaluating various levels—the environment, the proprietors, and the business (Kammerlander et al. 2015). This methodology aligns with the 'strategy as practice' paradigm (Jarzabkowski 2004; Whittington 1996), advocating for a more comprehensive assimilation of diverse institutional and administrative levels, deeper scrutiny of involved actors, and considering reinforcing mechanisms.

Researchers and practitioners need to analyze the harmony between the objectives, resources, and governance structures of family-owned enterprises to evaluate value creation within these entities accurately. In essence, even if a family firm has amassed distinct resources, its value generation might falter if these assets don't align with the firm's contextual demands. For example, the ineffective utilization of precious resources can stem from governance structures impeding efficient resource management. When discrepancies exist between the family's specific objectives, the output from the firm's resources, and the governance arrangements, the resultant "value" may not be perceived as "valuable" by the family proprietors (Kammerlander *et al.*, 2015). Achieving synchronization among these "value creation ingredients"— such as goals, resources, and governance—raises the question of which of the three elements should take precedence in initiating the alignment process (Kammerlander *et al.*, 2015). These are discussed below.

### 2.3.1.1  Prioritizing goals

Certain family-owned enterprises may prioritize goals in their strategic planning as a means to align the objectives of family principals with the firm's strategic actions. Advocates of this goal-centric approach often assume that those setting the goals, typically the family members at the helm of the corporate structure, own sufficient information about the prospects, threats, and viability of these objectives (Kammerlander *et al.*, 2015). This approach can prove advantageous for matured companies operating in relatively stable environments that pursue strategic goals resulting from a planning process (Brinckmann, Grichnik, & Kapsa, 2010). However, emphasizing causation exclusively neglects the risk of unavailable resources and poor governance structures. In such cases, strategic planning might remain a theoretical exercise. For instance, the ambitious goals set by family owners might not align with the available resources and existing governance mechanisms, such as incentives and control measures. In extreme cases, a goal-centered strategic approach may lead to disappointment for both the family (due to unattainable goals) and the company (due to the unrealistic nature of the goals from the outset).

Three typical categories of family-owned firms can be delineated regarding the nature and significance of family owners' objectives. The first category, "dreamers," primarily concentrates on nonfinancial goals, paying less emphasis on financial goals. However, the challenge of this type lies in the longstanding sustainability of such firms due to their disregard for financial achievements. For instance, to sustain a positive image and effectiveness, these family-led firms might endure adverse financial outcomes and overlook upcoming opportunities before revitalizing their business model (Kellermanns, Eddleston, & Zellweger 2012). Such companies may face significant competitive weaknesses that other players in the industry may face, and eventually, they may disappear from the competitive landscape (Kammerlander *et al.*, 2015).

The second category, "traders," comprises family members who prioritize financial goals exclusively. Such firms might miss out on valuable opportunities associated with family involvement, such as fostering employee loyalty (Miller & Le Breton-Miller, 2005), maintaining brand reputation (Krappe, Goutas, & von Schlippe, 2011), and streamlining innovation processes (Duran, Kammerlander, van Essen, & Zellweger, 2016). Consequently, these firms might be susceptible to the downsides of short-term thinking and managerial narrow-mindedness.

The third category, "professional owners," comprises family owners who simultaneously pursue financial and nonfinancial interests. While these objectives often conflict, theories on paradoxes (Smith & Lewis, 2011) guide managing these continuing conflicts between urgencies and leveraging synergies to the greatest extent. This perspective underscores that solely pursuing financial or nonfinancial goals can be detrimental, fostering disorder and unproductive division. Similarly, research on organizational ambidexterity (Kammerlander, Burger, Fust, & Fueglistaller, 2015) suggests that successful firms need to engage in both exploratory and exploitative activities. This view highlights that professional family business owners should aim for ambidexterity in their goals. The underlying idea behind this approach is that when firms try to reconcile all simultaneous contradictions and pursue logical consistency, they might hinder excellence by removing the creative tension generated by paradoxes (Zellweger, 2013). Ultimately, a balanced pursuit of both financial and nonfinancial goals can enable family owners to maximize their utility function (Kammerlander *et al.*, 2015).

### 2.3.1.2 Prioritizing Available Resources

On the other hand, certain family-owned enterprises may opt to prioritize their available resources and tailor their "fitting process" for that reason. These businesses adopt an effectuation-based approach, as articulated by scholars in entrepreneurship (Sarasvathy, 2001). This effectual method in strategic planning is implicitly supported in the families literature (Habbershon & Williams, 1999), which underscores the evaluation of families' productive and restraining aspects without directly considering the firm's ultimate strategic objectives. While this approach proves effective, especially in uncertain circumstances and during a firm's establishment, it carries the risk of being reactive rather than proactive. Overemphasizing available resources while neglecting strategic goals may lead family-owned businesses to overlook crucial opportunities to anticipate and actively shape their future business landscape, potentially sacrificing their competitive edge. Moreover, this approach might leave family owners with unfulfilled (financial or nonfinancial) objectives. Disassociating strategic decisions from the aspirations of the dominant family coalition risks significant criticism, particularly from within the family itself, as it neglects the anxieties, inspirations, and ambitions of the family members as crucial stakeholders (Kammerlander *et al.*, 2015).

### 2.3.1.3 Prioritizing Governance Structures

Circumstantial evidence suggests that certain family-owned businesses embark on their "fitting process" without considering specific goals or resources but prioritize the firm's existing governance structure. For instance, some family enterprises might perceive the current control, incentive, and monitoring systems as fixed elements and evaluate what can be accomplished within these governance restraints (Kammerlander *et al.*, 2015). This approach aims to ensure organizational stability, requires less managerial effort, and escapes disruptive changes within the organization (Kammerlander *et al.*, 2015). However, adhering to the "strategy follows structure" paradigm, as proposed by Burgelman (1983), restricts family firms from adapting to evolving environments and grabbing new opportunities. Solely focusing on "how the firm has traditionally operated" can lead to path dependency (Sydow, Schreyo¨gg, & Koch, 2009), ultimately resulting in organizational inertia.

Moreover, a significant challenge in establishing governance structures in family-owned firms is determining the appropriate level of governance within the organization. Excessive governance leads to bureaucracy, hinders entrepreneurial activities, and generates double agency costs (Carney, Gedajlovic, & Strike, 2014). These costs emerge when supervisors overseeing others begin acting as principals, having significant discretion to line up with subordinates and seek personal gains (Zellweger & Kammerlander, 2015). Conversely, insufficient governance reduces accountability and efficiency, potentially leading to excessive slack that renders a firm lethargic (Leonard Barton, 1992).

In addition to the established governance structures, informal governance facets also merit consideration. This is particularly relevant in family-owned enterprises, where not all decision-making processes are formalized in written form, and interpersonal interactions among family and non-family members might substitute documented contracts in organizational procedures (Kammerlander *et al.*, 2015; Mustakallio, Autio, & Zahra, 2002). These informal governance elements encompass group dynamics in decision-making, underlying conflicts among decision-makers (Kammerlander *et al.*, 2015; Eddleston & Kellermanns, 2007), and internal organizational communication. Although such informal governance practices are often effective, they present significant challenges as they are implicit, tacit, and difficult to assess, especially for "outsiders" like newly hired employees and managers. Furthermore, changing these informal decision-making practices might be problematic, causing suboptimal returns to shareholders.

In the governance domain in family-owned businesses, scholars frequently emphasize relational governance, which encompasses any social control form that potentially influences the behavior of members within an organization

(Kammerlander *et al.*, 2015; Mustakallio *et al.*, 2002; Suess, 2014). Relational governance compliments contractual governance, representing control exercised through formal mechanisms like boards. It involves aspects such as communication among family members within the company (Kammerlander *et al.*, 2015; Berent-Braun & Uhlaner, 2012). A significant challenge for family businesses is that the effectiveness of such relational governance apparatuses can heavily depend on specific circumstances within the family firm, including family structures or institutional context (Melin & Nordqvist, 2007).

Another noteworthy aspect of governance in many family-owned firms deserving greater scholarly attention is the existence of ceremonial governance elements. Ceremonial governance refers to governance components, such as advisory boards or decision-making committees, that exist formally but lack genuine authority or influence (Kammerlander *et al.*, 2015). For instance, in a detailed case study presented by Kammerlander and Ganter (2015, p.368), they portray a large German family business where the board's primary role is to endorse predetermined decisions of the (family) CEO, which are crafted through private discussions before board meetings. Ceremonial governance is not merely a historical relic but serves a crucial purpose by providing legitimacy within the organization and to external stakeholders. Thus, academics and policymakers in the hunt to assess family firm governance mechanisms must prudently differentiate between functional and ceremonial elements despite their underlying intentions.

## 2.4   Ways for Family Firms to Create Shareholder Value

### 2.4.1   Long-term perspective

The first approach to creating value for shareholders in a family business is adopting a long-term perspective. This refers to focusing on sustainable growth and long-term profitability instead of solely concentrating on short-term gains. Here are some key points to analyze regarding this first approach:

- Focus on sustainable growth: Family-owned enterprises with a forward-looking approach prioritize establishing an organization capable of enduring across generations. Rather than concentrating solely on immediate profits, they emphasize constructing a robust foundation, developing high-quality products and services, and nurturing enduring relationships with customers, partners, and employees.

- Investment in research and development: Family businesses with a long-term perspective often prioritize investing in research and development as a fundamental aspect. They recognize that ongoing innovation and enhancement are critical for maintaining competitiveness and generating shareholder value. Through R&D investments, they can create novel products, explore new markets, and attain sustainable competitive advantages.
- Cultivation of enduring relationships: The long-term focus of family businesses is evident in their dedication to establishing and nurturing lasting connections with customers, partners, and employees. They acknowledge that these relationships can generate enduring and consistent value for the enterprise. By fostering trust and cultivating solid relationships with stakeholders, family businesses can create a dependable and stable environment, thereby earning support and trust from shareholders.
- Strategic alignment: A long-term outlook necessitates family businesses to possess a well-defined strategic direction and a visionary perspective. They don't just concentrate on short-term yearly plans but also consider objectives and developmental strategies for the future. Maintaining a long-term strategy enables family businesses to focus on endeavors and investments that yield sustainable value, such as venturing into new markets, investing in innovative technologies, or expanding their operations.
- Resilience to market fluctuations: Embracing a long-term mindset enables family enterprises to navigate short-term market fluctuations and identify enduring opportunities. Instead of reacting impulsively to minor market shifts, they adhere to their long-term goals and strategies while adjusting execution methods to adapt to market dynamics. This approach fosters stability and patience during the development process, contributing to value creation for shareholders.

Consider a family-owned manufacturing firm specializing in renewable energy equipment, like solar panels, which adopts a forward-thinking approach in its operations. Emphasizing sustainable development, they allocate resources to research and development to enhance product quality and explore innovative technologies. Cultivating enduring partnerships with clients, suppliers, and staff is of paramount importance. A well-defined strategic roadmap steers their objectives for global expansion, product diversification, and market presence. By adhering to its long-range vision and adeptly managing market fluctuations, the enterprise generates enduring value for its shareholders.

### 2.4.2  Strong governance:

Robust governance plays a pivotal role in enhancing shareholder value within a family enterprise. It encompasses establishing efficient decision-making mechanisms and clear frameworks that foster accountability and equity and safeguard the shareholders' concerns. Here are several fundamental components of sound governance within a family business:

- Well-defined governance framework: A family enterprise with robust governance establishes a transparent governance framework outlining the specific roles and responsibilities of family members, shareholders, and management. This framework prevents conflicts of interest and ensures that decision-making aligns with the company's and shareholders' best interests.

- Independent board of directors: Strong governance within a family business often entails the inclusion of independent directors within its board. These directors contribute diverse perspectives, expertise, and impartiality to decision-making processes. They serve as a check on the influence of family members, guaranteeing decisions are made in the company's and shareholders' best interest.

- Transparent and efficient communication: Effective governance emphasizes transparent and efficient communication among family members, shareholders, and management. Consistent and transparent communication fosters trust and alignment among stakeholders, ensuring everyone remains well-informed about the company's performance, strategies, and decisions.

- Conflict resolution mechanisms: In family-run enterprises, conflicts might arise due to differing opinions, goals, or personal dynamics. Strong governance involves implementing effective conflict resolution mechanisms to address and resolve conflicts fairly and constructively. This can involve establishing family councils, mediation processes, or utilizing impartial third-party advisors.

- Succession planning: Strong governance in a family business includes robust succession planning. This entails identifying and grooming the upcoming generation of leaders within the family to assume key business roles. Succession planning ensures a seamless leadership transition, minimizing disruptions that could affect the company's value and performance.

Implementing robust governance practices empowers family enterprises to improve transparency, accountability, and decision-making processes, thereby delivering value to shareholders. It aids in mitigating conflicts of interest, fostering effective communication, involving impartial viewpoints, resolving disputes, and facilitating a seamless leadership transition. Ultimately, strong governance contributes to the enduring sustainability and triumph of family businesses, serving the interests of their shareholders.

An illustration of effective governance in a family-owned corporation that generates shareholder value can be observed in the BMW Group. A prominent global automotive company, BMW boasts a resilient family governance structure. While the Quandt family holds controlling rights and holds significant sway in the board of directors, they've established an autonomous and professional governance framework to ensure equity and value generation for shareholders. BMW's board includes members devoid of familial ties to the Quandt family. This ensures that pivotal decisions concerning business strategy, investments, and leadership are based on the company's and its shareholders' collective interests rather than family relations or personal motives.

Transparency and communication are paramount for BMW. They furnish comprehensive financial reports and business strategies to shareholders, conducting regular shareholder meetings to encourage discussions and feedback on significant matters. This fosters transparency, reliability, and trust, fostering shareholder confidence and support. Furthermore, BMW has meticulously planned the succession of top-level leadership roles. They've identified and trained potential successors within the company, guaranteeing a seamless transition in pivotal positions. This guarantees continuity and steadiness in corporate governance while fostering lasting value for shareholders. Through robust governance, BMW has established a flourishing family-owned enterprise, consistently surpassing shareholder expectations while ensuring stability and sustainable progress in the competitive automotive industry.

### 2.4.3   Focus on core competencies.

Creating value for shareholders in a family-owned enterprise can be achieved by focusing on its fundamental strengths, commonly known as core competencies. These competencies represent the distinctive abilities, resources, and knowledge that distinguish a company from its competitors, forming the bedrock of its competitive edge. When a family business identifies and harnesses these core competencies, it can efficiently allocate resources and make strategic decisions that maximize shareholder value. Several crucial considerations in this regard include:

- Identifying Core Strengths: The company must comprehensively evaluate its capabilities, strengths, and specialized knowledge. This involves analyzing its unique family heritage, industry expertise, intellectual property, customer relationships, and operational efficiencies. The company can concentrate on areas where it holds a competitive advantage by pinpointing these core competencies.

- Strategic Resource Distribution: After identifying the core competencies, the company should strategically distribute resources, such as funding, talent, and technology, to bolster and support these strengths. This requires aligning investments and initiatives with the areas where the company can generate the most value. By prioritizing resource allocation based on core competencies, the company can optimize its performance and yield higher returns for shareholders.

- Cultivating and Expanding Core Strengths: To sustain and enhance shareholder value, the company must consistently nurture and expand its core competencies. This involves investing in research and development, fostering innovation, providing employee training and development opportunities, and forming strategic partnerships that reinforce and broaden its competitive advantages. By continually evolving and adapting its core competencies to meet evolving market needs, the company can outpace competitors and generate enduring value for shareholders.

- A family-owned enterprise can effectively leverage its distinct strengths and advantages to generate shareholder value by concentrating on its core competencies. This strategy enables the company to stand out in the marketplace, enhance profitability, and maintain its competitive edge over time. Nevertheless, it's essential for the company to periodically reassess and evaluate its core competencies to ensure their continued relevance and alignment with market trends and shareholder preferences.

An example illustrates how a family-owned company, IKEA, creates shareholder value by focusing on core competencies in its successful furniture and retail business. IKEA has prioritized its core competency in innovative product design. The company has cultivated a recognizable design style centered on simplicity, functionality, and value for its customers. By consistently delivering inventive and appealing furniture offerings, IKEA attracts and retains a substantial customer base, driving substantial sales and revenue growth, thus delivering shareholder value.

Additionally, IKEA demonstrates proficiency in supply chain management and operational efficiency. The company has established a global network that covers procurement, warehouse management, and product distribution. Through streamlining processes and reducing expenses, IKEA gains a competitive edge in terms of pricing and consistent product availability. This bolsters profitability and earnings, ultimately contributing to shareholder value creation.

Another aspect of IKEA's success lies in its direct interaction with customers. The company has invested in a widespread network of retail stores worldwide, offering customers hands-on experiences and personalized assistance from sales staff. Additionally, IKEA has introduced convenient online shopping options and efficient delivery services. By providing a seamless and customer-centric shopping journey, IKEA fosters customer loyalty, drives sales, and augments revenue, thus generating shareholder value. Through its focus on core competencies like distinctive product design, supply chain management, and customer engagement, IKEA has amplified shareholder value through increased sales, profitability, and sustained competitive positioning in the furniture and retail sector.

Another real-life example showcasing the creation of shareholder value in a family-owned enterprise by leveraging core competencies is Mars, Incorporated. Mars operates globally in confectionery, pet care, and food sectors and has effectively harnessed its core strengths to benefit shareholders. A primary core competency for Mars is its robust research and development (R&D) capabilities. The company invests substantially in scientific research and innovation to create improved and innovative products. For instance, Mars hosts a dedicated research center focusing on extensive R&D efforts to craft high-quality and innovative confectionery and pet care products. Introducing new and appealing products continually to the market helps Mars garner a devoted customer base, foster revenue growth, and generate shareholder value.

Another critical area of expertise for Mars lies in its adeptness in supply chain management and operational efficiency. The company has implemented a strong, globally integrated supply chain network to streamline sourcing, production, and distribution processes. This leads to cost efficiencies, improved product availability, and punctual customer deliveries. By upholding operational excellence, Mars maximizes profitability and augments shareholder value. Additionally, Mars demonstrates proficiency in brand management and marketing strategies. They have established well-known and reputable brands such as M&M's, Snickers, Pedigree, and Whiskas. Through effective marketing initiatives, product distinction, and strategic brand positioning, Mars has established a formidable market presence and cultivated brand loyalty. This culminates in expanded market share, customer preference, and enhanced shareholder value. By concentrating on core competencies like R&D, supply chain management, and brand management, Mars has effectively generated value for shareholders by sustaining revenue growth, optimizing costs, and securing industry leadership positions.

### 2.4.4 Value-based culture

Creating value for shareholders within a family-owned enterprise can be achieved by nurturing a culture rooted in values. A value-based culture denotes a shared set of beliefs, principles, and conduct that guides the company's decisions and actions. Embracing such a culture can drive sustained growth and generate shareholder value for the long term. Here are key considerations:

- Establishing Clear Mission, Vision, and Values: Defining a clear mission and vision aligned with shareholder interests provides purpose and direction. Core values, reflecting integrity, transparency, and customer-centricity, mold the company's culture and decision-making.
- Ethical Business Practices: Upholding high ethical standards and responsible practices is vital. Transparency, fair treatment of stakeholders, and compliance foster trust enhancing the company's reputation and bolstering shareholder confidence.
- Employee Engagement and Growth: Investing in employees through engagement, empowerment, and development is critical. Providing growth opportunities, creating a supportive workplace, and recognizing contributions drive innovation, productivity, and customer satisfaction - ultimately benefiting shareholders.
- Customer-Focused Approach: Prioritizing customer needs, delivering exceptional products or services, and cultivating enduring relationships drives shareholder value. Exceeding customer expectations boosts loyalty, market share, and profitability.
- Long-Term Focus: Encouraging a long-term outlook over short-term gains is essential. By leveraging their advantage, family-owned enterprises can concentrate on sustainable growth, strategic investments, and innovation, balancing immediate profits with long-term value for shareholders. A family-owned enterprise can generate shareholder value by nurturing a culture founded on values that underscore a clear mission, ethical conduct, employee engagement, customer focus, and a long-term approach. This culture shapes decision-making processes and behaviors across the organization, steering sustainable growth and financial success.

An example of this value-based approach in creating shareholder value within a family-owned company is Johnson & Johnson (J&J), a prominent player in the pharmaceutical, healthcare, and medical devices sectors. J&J has effectively built shareholder value through its commitment to a value-driven culture. They have identified core values like ethics, innovation, and customer-centricity, aiming for profitability and improving individuals' health and well-being. Ethical considerations underpin every aspect of their operations, from research and development procedures to advertising strategies. J&J has fostered an environment fostering creativity and empowerment among its employees. They prioritize employee development, encouraging novel ideas and innovative solutions. This approach facilitates the introduction of new products and services, addresses customer needs, and ensures competitiveness and industry growth. Central to J&J's value-driven culture is their dedication to customers and society. They prioritize delivering high-quality, safe, and effective products while actively engaging in social and community initiatives and supporting community healthcare programs and educational endeavors. This commitment fosters trust among customers and society, strengthens positive relationships, and drives sales revenue and profitability, thereby creating value for shareholders. Through instilling a value-based culture rooted in ethics, innovation, and commitment to customers and society, Johnson & Johnson has effectively enhanced shareholder value by achieving sales growth, boosting profitability, and maintaining a competitive edge in the pharmaceutical and healthcare industry.

### 2.4.5 Succession planning

Succession planning is pivotal in generating shareholder value within a family-owned enterprise. It involves identifying and developing competent successors and ensuring a smooth transfer of leadership and managerial duties. Here is an in-depth analysis of how effective succession planning can create value for shareholders in a family-owned business:

- Continuity and Stability: Succession planning fosters continuity and stability within the organization. The family business can secure a seamless leadership transition between generations by identifying and nurturing potential successors early in the process. This stability instills confidence among shareholders by reducing disruptions and uncertainties commonly associated with leadership changes.
- Leadership Development: Succession planning provides avenues for leadership growth and talent management. It offers family members and key executives the chance to acquire essential skills, knowledge, and experience needed for elevated roles and increased responsibilities. Investing in

leadership development guarantees a robust pool of competent leaders capable of driving growth, making strategic decisions, and delivering long-term value to shareholders.

- Strategic Vision and Direction: Effective succession planning empowers the family business to maintain a strategic vision and direction. As potential successors are groomed and readied for leadership roles, they can align their objectives and strategies with the company's long-term vision. This alignment ensures consistent prioritization of shareholder interests and growth objectives, contributing to sustained value creation.
- Professionalization and Expertise: Succession planning often incorporates the introduction of external talent and specialized skills. This infusion enhances the company's capabilities and competitiveness by integrating fresh viewpoints, specialized knowledge, and industry-leading practices. By merging the family's legacy and values with external expertise, the company gains improved readiness to navigate market complexities, capitalize on opportunities, and yield shareholder value.
- Shareholder Engagement and Confidence: A well-executed succession plan nurtures shareholder engagement and bolsters confidence. Engaging shareholders actively in succession planning allows for addressing their concerns, meeting expectations, and securing their endorsement. When shareholders witness a transparent and well-structured plan in action, their confidence in the company's future strengthens, leading to increased trust and support.
- Risk Mitigation: Succession planning serves as a risk mitigation strategy against unexpected leadership changes or gaps. Identifying potential successors and providing them with proper training and development curtails disruptions and uncertainties arising from sudden leadership vacuums. This risk mitigation strategy fortifies the company's stability and adaptability, ultimately benefiting shareholders.

One real-life illustration of creating shareholder value in a family-owned enterprise through a values-driven ethos is The Hershey Company. Renowned in the confectionery industry, The Hershey Company has successfully enhanced shareholder value by embracing a values-based culture centered on its mission of "bringing goodness to the world." The company's value-centric culture prioritizes integrity, innovation, and stakeholder commitment. Hershey emphasizes ethical practices, transparency, and responsible conduct, establishing credibility and trust with shareholders. Their culture extends to employees, focusing on their well-being, growth, and engagement, fostering an environment that encourages innovative contributions, driving productivity, and ultimately adding value for shareholders.

Furthermore, Hershey prioritizes product quality, safety, and customer satisfaction, earning them a loyal customer base and market share. Their consistent delivery above customer expectations drives revenue growth and profitability, directly benefiting shareholders. Additionally, Hershey's values are reflected in its commitment to community-centric initiatives, like education support and sustainable sourcing programs. These efforts strengthen brand reputation and build positive relationships with customers, shareholders, and the broader community. The Hershey Company has enhanced shareholder value through its values-based culture by promoting sustainable growth, establishing a robust brand, and maintaining consistent financial performance. By aligning its actions with core values, Hershey's has laid a strong foundation for long-term success and shareholder value generation.

In conclusion, effective succession planning within a family-owned company ensures seamless transitions, promotes leadership development, aligns strategies, professionalizes operations, engages shareholders, and mitigates risks. These aspects collectively contribute to long-term value creation for shareholders by facilitating stable leadership changes, fostering growth, and sustaining shareholder trust and backing. Through proactive readiness for leadership transitions, the family firm positions itself for long-term prosperity, fostering enduring value for its shareholders.

### 2.4.6 Flexibility and adaptability

Flexibility and adaptability greatly enhance shareholder value within a family-owned company. Let's delve into how these characteristics contribute to shareholder value:

- Market Responsiveness: The family-owned business can adapt to market shifts due to its flexibility and adaptability. Observing market trends and consumer preferences allows the organization to swiftly adjust strategies, products, and operations to meet evolving needs. This agility enables the business to capitalize on new opportunities, surpass competitors, and augment shareholder value.

- Innovation and Growth: The business's culture of innovation is fostered by its flexibility and agility. The company stimulates continual improvement and seizes growth prospects by encouraging innovative thinking among employees, exploring new concepts, and embracing change. Diversifying offerings, entering new markets, and expanding the customer base contribute to shareholder value through innovation.
- Risk Management: Flexibility and adaptability are pivotal in mitigating risks and reinforcing resilience. Embracing change and adaptability in unforeseen circumstances enable the family-owned company to navigate challenges and minimize disruptions. This risk management capability assures shareholders that their investments are safeguarded and ensures the company's long-term stability and value creation.
- Operational Efficiency: Flexibility and adaptability empower the family-owned company to optimize operations and enhance efficiency. Embracing new technologies, adopting lean practices, and constantly evaluating and adjusting processes drive productivity and reduce costs. Improved operational efficiency translates into better financial performance, increased profitability, and higher shareholder returns.
- Customer-Centric Approach: Flexibility and adaptability enable the company to address evolving customer requirements and preferences. Factors such as continuous market surveys to understand market trends and customer feedback help build customer loyalty and design appropriate offerings to drive revenue growth. Satisfied and loyal customers boost long-term shareholder value by increasing sales, market share, and brand reputation.
- Succession Planning and Transition: Flexibility and adaptability are crucial during leadership transitions in a family-owned company. A flexible approach to succession planning ensures a smooth handover of leadership and management responsibilities. This includes considering external candidates,

embracing new viewpoints, and adjusting the management structure when necessary. A successful leadership transition instills shareholder confidence and preserves the company's value proposition. In summary, flexibility and adaptability are essential for creating value for shareholders in a family-owned company. They enable the company to respond to market changes, foster innovation, manage risks, improve operational efficiency, meet customer expectations, and facilitate smooth leadership transitions. By embracing these attributes, the family-owned company can enhance its competitiveness, profitability, and long-term success, ultimately benefiting shareholders.

In this case, LEGO Group, an actual example of a family-owned enterprise, effectively employed flexibility and adaptability to enhance shareholder value. Encountering challenges in the late 1990s due to digital entertainment competition, LEGO Group demonstrated flexibility by recentering its efforts on its core product: brick-based construction sets. This strategic decision enabled the company to capitalize on the enduring appeal of its iconic bricks and regain its competitive edge. Moreover, LEGO Group showcased adaptability by embracing digital trends and integrating them into its product lineup and marketing strategies. Understanding the significance of merging physical play with digital experiences, the company introduced LEGO Mindstorms programmable robotics kits and developed LEGO Digital Designer, virtual building software. By adapting to the digital landscape, LEGO Group broadened its consumer base, fueling revenue growth and ultimately benefiting its shareholders.

Collaboration and partnerships played a pivotal role in LEGO Group's success. The company tapped into its established fan bases by strategically aligning with popular entertainment franchises like Star Wars, Marvel, and Harry Potter. This flexibility in collaborating and adjusting its products to incorporate licensed themes resulted in increased sales, elevated brand visibility, and amplified shareholder value. In addition to product-related adjustments, LEGO Group exhibited flexibility and adaptability in its supply chain management. Recognizing inefficiencies in its production processes, the company implemented a restructuring plan that involved outsourcing production to lower-cost countries while upholding rigorous quality standards. This adaptability streamlined operations, trimmed costs, and enhanced profitability, ultimately generating value for shareholders.

Overall, LEGO Group's ability to remain flexible and adaptable in its product portfolio, digital integration, partnerships, and supply chain management enabled the family-owned company to navigate changing market dynamics adeptly. LEGO Group revitalized its business through these strategies, achieved significant growth, and ultimately created shareholder value.

### 2.4.7 Use of 4+5 Value Creation Approach

According to McKinsey & Company (2023), family firms hold a unique mindset against non-family firms to create value for shareholders. They report that family firms have four purpose-oriented unique mindsets and five complementary actions that help them achieve long-term success. The four purpose-oriented mindsets are purpose beyond profits, long-term perspective, cautious financial stance, and

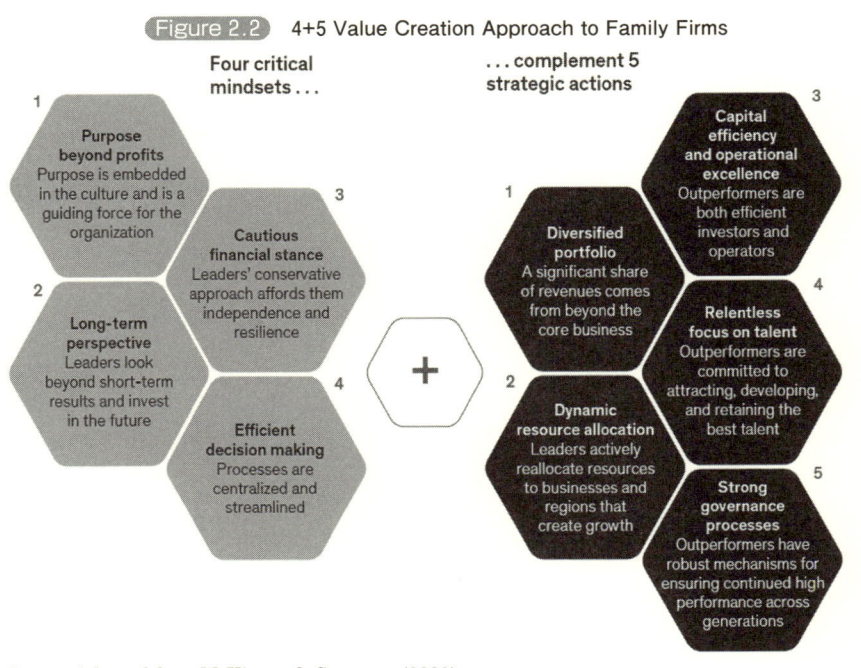

**Figure 2.2** 4+5 Value Creation Approach to Family Firms

Source: Adapted from McKinsey & Company (2023).

efficient decision-making. The five complementary actions are a diversified portfolio, dynamic resource allocation, capital efficiency, operational excellence, relentless focus on talents, and a robust governance process. These are illustrated in **Figure 2.2**.

## 2.5 Principles of creating value for shareholders

### 2.5.1 Do not manage earnings or provide earnings guidance

Firms that fail to squeeze the initial shareholder value principle will likely struggle with adhering to subsequent principles. Regrettably, this eliminates most corporations as virtually all publicly traded companies engage in the game of meeting earnings expectations. A series of surveys conducted during the 2000s by the National Investor Relations Institute revealed that 66% of 654 companies surveyed regularly offer profit guidance to analysts on Wall Street (NIRI, 2001, 2003, 2005, & 2006). Another survey conducted by Duke University's John Graham, Campbell R. Harvey, and Shivaram Rajgopal in 2005 on 401 financial executives uncovered that firms manipulate earnings using methods beyond mere accounting tactics. They revealed that 80% of respondents reduce investment in value-creating areas like research and development, advertising, maintenance, and recruitment to meet earnings targets (Graham, Harvey & Rajgopal, 2005). Additionally, over half of these executives postpone a new project even if it destroys potential value.

The drawbacks of solely focusing on earnings are manifold. Firstly, the bottom line presented by accountants doesn't accurately represent either a firm's value or its value fluctuation over the reporting period. Secondly, organizations compromise their value by either investing below the cost of capital (leading to overinvestment) or neglecting investment in opportunities that create value (resulting in underinvestment) to enhance short-term earnings. Thirdly, the practice of offering favorable earnings through decisions that erode value or by pushing accounting boundaries eventually catches up with companies. Furthermore, firms that are unable to meet investor expectations often significantly reduce, if not entirely erase, a considerable portion of their market value. Prominent examples of this phenomenon are Enron, WorldCom, Tyco, Satyam Computers, and　American International Group (AIG).

### 2.5.2　Make strategic decisions that maximize expected value, even at the expense of lowering near-term earnings

Firms that manipulate earnings almost inevitably violate this second central principle. Many firms are likely to assess and compare strategic decisions based on their anticipated impact on reported earnings, not on evaluating these decisions against the anticipated incremental value of future cash flows. Anticipated value refers to the average value across a range of plausible scenarios, calculated by multiplying the value added for each scenario by the probability of that scenario occurring and summing up the results. A comprehensive strategic analysis conducted by a company's operational units should yield informed answers to three key questions:

(1) How do different strategies influence value?

(2) Which strategy tends to generate the highest value?

(3) For a chosen strategy, how sensitive is it to the firm value when there is a change in competitive dynamics, assumptions about technology life cycles, the institutional environment, and other relevant factors?

At the corporate level, executives must also tackle three critical questions:

(1) Do any operational segments possess enough potential to create value that justifies additional capital investment?

(2) Which units have narrow potential and are deemed for restructuring or divestment?

(3) What combination of investments in operational units tends to generate the highest overall value?

### 2.5.3　Carry only assets that maximize value

The third principle elevates the concept of value creation by influencing the selection of the business model that conscientious, value-focused firms will embrace. This principle consists of two components:

(1) Companies focused on value routinely assess if purchasers are willing to pay a substantial premium beyond the estimated cash flow value for the

company's business segments, brands, properties, and other separable assets. This assessment poses a sensitive situation for businesses performing favorably compared to forecasts or competitors yet holding higher value under different ownership. Nonetheless, neglecting to capitalize on these opportunities can significantly undermine shareholder value.

(2) Businesses have the opportunity to decrease the capital they utilize and enhance value through two approaches: emphasizing high-value activities, such as research and development, operational intelligence, design, and customer interaction, where they possess a comparative advantage, and subcontracting low-value tasks, for example, manufacturing, to external parties capable of performing these tasks at a lower cost reliably. A famous example in this case is Apple Computer, which designed its iPod in Cupertino, California, and manufactured it in Taiwan. Similarly, hotel chains like Hilton Hospitality and Marriott International operate hotels without owning them. Another example is Dell, known for its direct-to-customer, customized personal computer assembly business model, which minimizes the capital needed for investment in sales force, distribution, inventory, and manufacturing facilities.

### 2.5.4 Return cash to shareholders if no credible value-creating opportunities exist

Even firms that base their strategic decision-making on robust ideologies for creating value can make errors in decisions regarding cash allocation. The significance of abiding by the fourth principle has never been more crucial. Companies conscious of value, holding substantial excess cash with limited opportunities for creating value, opt to return the funds to shareholders through dividends and share repurchases. This offers shareholders the opportunity for potentially better returns elsewhere and diminishes the risk that management might misuse surplus cash on investments that diminish value – incredibly misguided, inflated acquisitions.

In the context of family-owned or controlled businesses, the strategy regarding cash allocation and investment choices might differ from publicly traded corporations. Family-run enterprises often emphasize a long-term outlook, prioritizing sustainability, preserving the family's legacy, and ensuring continuity rather than focusing solely on immediate returns or payouts to shareholders. Nevertheless, fundamental principles of effective financial management, such as evaluating surplus cash, seeking value-generating investments, and avoiding potential pitfalls in fund allocation, remain universally applicable.

Certain family-owned companies opt to distribute surplus cash to family shareholders through dividends or alternative methods. This choice may be more prevalent if limited investment opportunities align with the family's long-term objectives or if family members rely on dividends as a primary source of income. However, this approach might not be uniform across all family firms, as some may prefer to reinvest profits into the business to foster expansion innovation or to uphold control and autonomy. Ultimately, the specific strategy regarding cash distribution and investment decisions in family-run businesses can significantly vary based on the family's objectives, principles, and vision for the company's future.

### 2.5.5   Reward CEOs and other senior executives for delivering superior long-term returns

Firms require effective incentive schemes at all levels to optimize the potential for exceptional returns. Let's commence with senior executives. In the realm of family-owned or controlled enterprises, the methodology for executive compensation and incentive structures could diverge from publicly traded corporations. Family businesses often possess distinctive dynamics and considerations when remunerating senior executives. Within certain family-owned companies, compensation frameworks for senior executives might more closely mirror the family's principles and long-term goals rather than focusing exclusively on stock options or immediate financial gains. Such firms may prioritize stability, perpetuity, and upholding the family legacy over instant financial incentives. In lieu of traditional stock options or in addition to them, family-run businesses might implement alternative compensation methods such as profit-sharing models, performance-based bonuses, or enduring incentives that align with the family's values and the company's sustained viability. The decision-making process concerning executive compensation in family-owned firms could be more adaptable and tailored, taking into account the family's involvement, the distinct culture of the company, and its specific objectives.

Nevertheless, it's vital to recognize that family businesses exhibit a wide spectrum of approaches to executive compensation and incentives, and there's no universally applicable strategy. The compensation framework within a family firm can be shaped by various factors, including the family's preferences, the company's financial circumstances, industry norms, and governance practices within the organization.

### 2.5.6 Reward operating-unit executives for adding superior multiyear value

Companies commonly implement yearly and longer-term (often three-year) incentive schemes, rewarding operational executives for surpassing financial metrics like sales and operating profit and occasionally achieving nonfinancial goals. However, a significant issue arises when bonuses are linked to the budgeting process because such practices encourage managers to underestimate potential performance. Moreover, the traditional accounting metrics, when used semi-annually or quarterly, in particular, do not consistently correlate with the long-term cash flows responsible for generating shareholder value. Companies should devise measures such as Shareholder Value Added (SVA) to establish effective incentives for operational units. SVA involves applying standard discounting methods to predict operating cash flows driven by sales growth and operating margins, then deducting the investments made during the period. As SVA relies entirely on cash flows, it avoids accounting distortions, providing a distinct advantage over conventional measures.

To ensure this metric captures long-term performance accurately, companies should extend the evaluation period to, for instance, a rolling three-year cycle. This approach can also preserve a portion of incentive payouts to mitigate potential future underperformance. Also, this strategy eliminates the need for separate plans by integrating long-term incentive plans into one. Instead of establishing budget-based thresholds for incentive compensation, companies can establish criteria for notable year-to-year performance enhancement, benchmarking against peers, and even performance expectations inferred from the share price.

### 2.5.7  Reward middle managers and frontline employees for delivering superior performance on the critical value drivers they influence directly

Family businesses often value sustainability and focus on long-term success, similar to the objective of enhancing Shareholder Value Added (SVA). Utilizing specific leading indicators of value (e.g., new product launch time, product quality, employee loyalty, customer retention, timely setting up of new stores or manufacturing facilities) can align well with the ethos of family firms that prioritize the continuous enhancement of the company's worth.

Furthermore, concentrating on some leading indicators can be particularly relevant for family businesses to capture long- term value-creation potential. These firms often emphasize a more streamlined and personalized approach to decision-making and operational strategies, allowing them to focus more attentively on a few critical performance metrics. However, adopting these strategies might vary based on each family-owned firm's unique characteristics, goals, and culture. Some family businesses may have distinct priorities or specific focus areas that influence their choice of leading indicators. Hence, while this approach generally aligns well with the principles of many family-owned enterprises, it's essential to tailor these strategies to fit each family firm's characteristics and objectives.

### 2.5.8  Require the alignment of senior executives' interests with shareholders' interests

In general, stock options do not effectively align shareholders' interests with senior executives' long-term interests because executives frequently sell vested options. The option to sell shares early incentivizes them to concentrate on short-term earnings instead of prioritizing long-term value to increase the current stock price. Numerous firms implement stock ownership guidelines for senior management to enhance alignment between these interests. These guidelines typically specify a minimum ownership threshold expressed as a multiple of the base salary, which is then translated into a specified number of shares. As an example, eBay's guidelines mandate the CEOs to hold stock equivalent to five times their annual base salary, while other executives can hold stock amounting to three times their salary. Additionally, top managers are obligated to retain a portion of shares obtained from exercising stock options until they accumulate the required number of shares specified by the guidelines.

However, in many instances, stock ownership plans do not subject executives to the same degree of risk as shareholders. One reason behind this is that certain companies exonerate stock purchase loans in cases where shares perform poorly, arguing that such an arrangement no longer incentivizes top management. Companies engaging in these practices, akin to those modifying option prices, risk institutionalizing a compensation system that undermines the essence and goals of the incentive compensation program. Additionally, outright grants of restricted stock, essentially options set at an exercise price of $0, often count as shares toward meeting minimum ownership requirements. These stock grants encourage key executives to remain with the company until the restrictions expire, typically within three or four years, allowing them to convert their shares into cash. Consequently, these grants motivate CEOs and top managers to prioritize maintaining existing value, play it safe, and avoid termination. As a result, restricted stock plans are frequently criticized and referred to as "pay for presence" rather than rewarding actual performance.

Many companies offer performance shares to counter the critique that restricted stock plans are overly generous. These performance shares mandate the executive's continued employment and require the company to achieve predetermined performance benchmarks linked to metrics like EPS growth, revenue targets, or return-on-capital-employed thresholds. However, while performance shares do necessitate some level of performance, they often fail to promote the right kind of performance for generating long-term value because these metrics typically lack a close linkage to actual value creation.

Companies aiming to align the interests of executives and shareholders better must strike a balance between requiring senior executives to maintain meaningful and ongoing ownership stakes and the limitations this imposes on their ability to access liquidity and diversification. Without equity-based incentives, executives might become excessively risk-averse to evade failure and potential dismissal. Conversely, owning excessive equity may lead them to avoid risks to safeguard the value of their largely undiversified portfolios. Extending the duration before executives can sell shares obtained through option exercises and not considering restricted stock grants as shares toward meeting minimum ownership requirements would undoubtedly assist in aligning the risks faced by executives and shareholders.

### 2.5.9  Provide investors with value-relevant information.

The ultimate principle revolves around investor communications, particularly a company's financial reports. Enhanced disclosure not only counteracts the fixation on short-term earnings but also diminishes investor uncertainty, potentially reducing the cost of capital and bolstering the share price. One suggested approach, as outlined in my article "The Economics of Short-Term Performance Obsession," published in the May-June 2005 issue of the Financial Analysts Journal, is creating a corporate performance statement. This statement, illustrated in the exhibit "The Corporate Performance Statement" as a template, aims to achieve the following:

- Segregate cash flows and accruals, establishing a historical reference for estimating a company's cash flow prospects and enabling analysts to assess the reasonableness of accrual estimates.
- Categorize accruals with extended cash-conversion cycles into varying levels of uncertainty - low, medium, and high.
- Present a range and the most probable estimate for each accrual rather than traditional single- point estimates that disregard potential outcome variability.
- Omit arbitrary accruals not pertinent to value, such as depreciation and amortization.
- Outline assumptions and risks for each line item while showcasing key performance indicators influencing the company's value.

Could such detailed disclosure incur excessive costs? In reality, executives in well-run companies already utilize similar information within a corporate performance statement. The absence of such data may prompt shareholders to question whether management comprehensively understands the business and if the board adequately fulfills its oversight role. Given the current stringent environment regarding accounting practices, companies focused on value creation have an unprecedented opportunity to generate value by simply enhancing the structure and substance of corporate reports.

## 2.6 Conclusion

In this paper, we aimed to reveal how family firms create value for shareholders. We explored value in a broader context and asserted that value creation is a complex and critical process. We noted that the significance of family businesses in creating value for shareholders extends beyond just profit margins and growth numbers. It is deeply linked to socio-emotional feelings associated with the firms, family values, morality, ethics, and a strong desire to protect firm values for successive generations. We argued that family firms generate value for shareholders because they possess a unique mindset to ensure the resilience of the firm. Also, they can adapt flexibly to changing business landscapes as they carefully design business portfolios.

We clarified that family firms place a greater emphasis on people-centric values, prioritize collectivity over individuality, focus on keeping talents in the business, efficiently allocate business portfolios, and uphold a long-term outlook alongside a strong sense of stewardship and responsibility toward the future of the family and the community in which they operate. Each of these hallmark values bears positive implications for both the family and the business, and diverse strategies exist to nurture and reinforce these values. Hence, family-owned firms can align with their intrinsic values to create value for shareholders, perceiving their business as a platform for increased community engagement, personal fulfillment, and social contribution.

However, we must note that value creation is not univocal across firms. It embraces the founder's and the founding family members' business philosophy, firm age, culture, society, and long-term vision for protecting firm value for successive generations. For example, small and new firms may concentrate on preserving profits for reinvestment and shoring up their governance mechanisms to create value for shareholders. Owners of vulnerable firms may focus on designing optimum business portfolios, maintaining harmony with investment partners, and enhancing investments in R&D and new businesses to generate value for shareholders. By contrast, an established firm should focus on expanding business to new areas and markets, build a strong R&D sector, allocate capital judiciously to ensure resilience, and a proper succession plan. Apart from these, sound governance mechanisms, long-term vision, a solid commitment to preserving firm value, and ethical practices are of paramount importance in creating long-term value for shareholders.

## ● References

Aristotle (1934). *The Nicomachean Ethics (Book I&VIII)*. English Translation by H. Rackham, Harvard University Press, Cambridge, Massachusetts, London, England.

Berent-Braun, M. M., & Uhlaner, L. M. (2012). Family governance practices and teambuilding: Paradox of the enterprising family. *Small Business Economics*, 38(1), 103-119.

Brinckmann, J., Grichnik, D., & Kapsa, D. (2010). Should entrepreneurs plan or just storm the castle? A meta-analysis on contextual factors impacting the business planning–performance relationship in small firms. *Journal of Business Venturing*, 25(1), 24-40.

Burgelman, R. A. (1983). A model of the interaction of strategic behavior, corporate context, and the concept of strategy. *Academy of Management Review*, 8(1), 61-70.

Cabrera-Suarez, K., Saa-Perez, P., & Garcia-Almeida, D. (2001). The succession process from a resource- and knowledge-based view of the family firm. *Family Business Review*, 14(1), 37-48.

Carney, M. (2005). Corporate governance and competitive advantage in family-controlled firms. *Entrepreneurship Theory and Practice*, 29(3), 249-265.

Carney, M., Gedajlovic, E., & Strike, V. M. (2014). Dead money: Inheritance law and the longevity of family firms. *Entrepreneurship Theory and Practice*, 38(6), 1261-1283.

Chrisman, J. J., Chua, J. H., Pearson, A. W., & Barnett, T. (2012). Family involvement, family influence, and family-centered non-economic goals in small firms. *Entrepreneurship Theory and Practice*, 36(2), 267-293.

Drazin, R., & Van de Ven, A. H. (1985). Alternative forms of fit in contingency theory. *Administrative Science Quarterly*, 30(4), 514-539.

Duran, P., Kammerlander, N., van Essen, M., & Zellweger, T. (2016). Doing more with less: Innovation input and innovation output in family firms. *Academy of Management Journal*, 59(4), 1224-1264.

Eddleston, KA, & Kellermanns, F.W. (2007). Destructive and productive family relationships: A stewardship theory perspective. *Journal of Business Venturing*, 22(4), 545-565.

Graham, J.R., Harvey, C.R., & Rajgopal, S. (2005) The economic implications of corporate financial reporting. *Journal of Accounting and Economics*, 40(1-3), 3-73.

Habbershon, T. G., & Williams, M. L. (1999). A resource-based framework for assessing the strategic advantages of family firms. *Family Business Review*, 12(1), 1-25.

Habbershon, T. G., Williams, M. L., & MacMillan, I. C. (2003). A unified systems theory of family firm performance. *Journal of Business Venturing*, 18(4), 451-465.

Jarzabkowski, P. (2004). Strategy as practice: Recursiveness, adaptation, and practices in use. *Organization Studies*, 25(4), 529-560.

Kammerlander, N., & Ganter, M. (2015). An attention-based view of family firm adaptation to discontinuous technological change: Exploring the role of family CEOs' noneconomic goals. *Journal of Product Innovation Management*, 32(3), 361-383.

Kammerlander, N., Burger, D., Fust, A., & Fueglistaller, U. (2015). Exploration and exploitation in established small and medium-sized enterprises: The effect of CEOs' regulatory focus. *Journal of Business Venturing*, 30(4), 582-602.

Kellermanns, F. W., Eddleston, K. A., & Zellweger, T. M. (2012). Extending the socioemotional wealth perspective: A look at the dark side. *Entrepreneurship Theory and Practice*, 36(6), 1175-1182.

Krappe, A., Goutas, L., & von Schlippe, A. (2011). The "family business brand": An enquiry into the construction of the image of family businesses. *Journal of Family Business Management*, 1(1), 37-46.

Lee, M. S., & Rogoff, E. G. (1996). Research note: Comparison of small businesses with family participation versus small businesses without family participation: An investigation of differences in goals, attitudes, and family/business conflict. *Family Business Review*, 9(4), 423-437.

Leonard-Barton, D. (1992). Core capabilities and core rigidities: A paradox in managing new product development. *Strategic Management Journal*, 13(Summer), 111-125.

McKinsey &Company (2023). The secrets of outperforming family-owned business: How they create value and how they become one. Retrieved from https://www.mckinsey.com/industries/private-capital/our-insights/the-secrets-of-outperforming-family-owned-businesses-how-they-create-value-and-how-you-can-become-one. (Date of access: May 23, 2024)

Meglino, B.M., and Ravlin, E.C. (1998). Individual values in organizations: Concepts. Controversies, and research, *Journal of Management*, 24(3), pp. 351-389.

Melin, L., & Nordqvist, M. (2007). The reflexive dynamics of institutionalization: The case of the family business. *Strategic Organization*, 5(3), 321-333.

Miller, D., & Le Breton-Miller, I. (2005). *Managing for the long run*. Boston, MA: Harvard Business School Press.

Morck, R., & Yeung, B. (2003). Agency problems in large family business groups. *Entrepreneurship Theory and Practice*, 27(4), 367-382.

Mustakallio, M., Autio, E., & Zahra, S. A. (2002). Relational and contractual governance in family firms: Effects on strategic decision making. *Family Business Review*, 15(3), 205-222.

NIRI. (2001. 2003. 2005. & 2006). *Survey Results on Earnings Guidance Practices*.

O'Boyle, E. H., Jr., Pollack, J. M., & Rutherford, M. W. (2012). Exploring the relation between family involvement and firms' financial performance: A meta-analysis of main and moderator effects. *Journal of Business Venturing*, 27(1), 1-18.

Pearson, A. W., Carr, J. C., & Shaw, J. C. (2008). Toward a theory of familiness: A social capital perspective. *Entrepreneurship Theory and Practice*, 32(6), 949-969.

Sarasvathy, S. D. (2001). Causation and effectuation: Toward a theoretical shift from economic inevitability to entrepreneurial contingency. *Academy of Management Review*, 26(2), 243-263.

Scheler, M. (1973), *Formalism in ethics and non-formal ethics of values: A new attempt toward the foundation of an ethical personalism*, Evanston, IL Northwestern University Press (Original German edition. "Der Formalismus in der Ethik und die materiale Wertethik" pp 1913-1916).

Sirmon, D. G., & Hitt, M. A. (2003). Managing resources: Linking unique resources, management, and wealth creation in family firms. *Entrepreneurship Theory and Practice*, 27(4), 339-358.

Smith, T. (2015) What exactly do we mean by "Shareholder Value"? *Financial Times*, January 10. (URL: https://www.ft.com/content/463abec2-9721-11e4-845a-00144feabdc0)

Smith, W. K., & Lewis, M. W. (2011). Toward a theory of paradox: A dynamic equilibrium model of organizing. *Academy of Management Review*, 36(2), 381-403.

Suess, J. (2014). Family governance – Literature review and the development of a conceptual model. *Journal of Family Business Strategy*, 5(2), 138-155.

Sydow, J., Schreyogg, G., & Koch, J. (2009) Organizational path dependence: Opening the black box. *Academy of Management Review*, 34(4), 689-709.

Whittington, R. (1996). Strategy as practice. *Long Range Planning*, 29(5), 731-735.

Zellweger, T. (2013). Toward a paradox perspective of family firms: The moderating role of collective mindfulness of controlling families. In L. Melin, M. Nordqvist, & P. Sharma (Eds.), *The SAGE handbook of family business* (648-655). Thousand Oaks, CA: SAGE Publications.

Zellweger, T., & Kammerlander, N. (2015). Family, wealth, and governance: An agency account. *Entrepreneurship Theory and Practice*, 39(6), 1281-1303.

Chapter **3**

# Values of Design Thinking in Business Education: A Systematic Review

Satoshi Sugahara

Claudio Dell'Era

Ochilov Bobur Bakhtiyor

**Abstract**

This study conducted a comprehensive systematic literature review to explore current knowledge and conceptualizations of design thinking in business education. Additionally, we aimed to identify the various forms of value created through the application of design thinking. Our publication search retrieved documents addressing design thinking within the context of higher education in business. After thorough screening and eligibility checks, a total of 63 documents were included in the analysis. We found that number of the research articles regarding design thinking in the business education has been increasing in recent across the world. It is acknowledged that different research strategies offer unique methodologies, allowing researchers to gain a comprehensive understanding of the phenomenon from multiple perspectives. Moreover, our keyword in context analysis have revealed that the literature recognizes the value created by design thinking not only for students, the direct consumers of education, but also for other stakeholders involved in the learning process, such as educators, entities or institutions, and even communities. This is because effective design thinking is strongly associated with a constructivist environment, wherein students learn more through interaction with peers, such as participating in group discussions and constructive dialogue, thereby enabling the development of novel, shared knowledge. This characteristic of constructivism extends to other stakeholders and brings benefits to each key player. In conclusion, this study successfully defined the value of design thinking for business and management education as predominantly highlighted in the literature.

**Keywords**

Design Thinking, Business Education, Systematic Review

## 3.1 Introduction

There is an increasing trend of teaching design thinking in higher education, particularly to the business and management disciplines. Design thinking (DT) is defined as the theoretical framework and its methodology that incorporates the cognitive processes employed by skilled designers as well as their methods, techniques, and sensibilities for solving problems (Glen *et al*. 2014). Initially, the concept of DT gained attention within the industry for enhancing and sustaining customer experiences (Kolko 2015), and subsequently extending interest in the educational field to explore its implications (Pande and Bharathi 2020; Scheer *et al*. 2012). As the primary consumers of education, students or learners expect to deliver greater value from their learning by participating in or collaborating on design thinking classes (Tarabasz, *et al*. 2018). Consequently, enormous studies have emphasized the value of design thinking for business and management education (e.g. Cankurtaran & Beverland 2020; Pande & Bharathi 2020). However, none of these studies clearly defined what it is.

Literature demonstrates substantial evidence that applying design thinking concepts and methods in the business education enhances students' perceptions of acquiring soft and generic skills necessary for survival in the 21st century (Glen *et al*. 2014; Gomoll *et al*. 2018; Kuo *et al*. 2021; Owen 2007). Furthermore, when businesses and other institutions collaborate with schools to organize design thinking courses, both students and these entities gain benefits from the courses. Lusch and Vargo (2014) argue that the customer is always a co-creator of value, of which principle applies is to collaborate between universities and other external institutions. This could be another form of value derived from teaching and learning design thinking. Despite amplified arguments regarding value of design thinking in the literature, these research do not consistently and systematically address this research gap.

In the existing literature, several prior studies have provided comprehensive overview of research on design thinking (Bhandari 2022; Micheli *et al*. 2019; Yu *et al*. 2023). For example, Bhandari (2022) conduct a systematic literature review, bibliometric analysis and content analysis of design thinking to investigate the research pattern of the past decade and the potential research direction for the future. The authors collected their sampled articles from the Scopus database (https://www.scopus.com/home.uri) using various keywords such as design, thinking and design thinking, identified a total of 1,000 articles based on certain attributes. In conclusion, they identified sixteen existing research diversification in design thinking. Similarly, Micheli *et al*. (2019) implemented a systematic literature review to address the current lack of clarity relating design thinking, aiming to illustrate current knowledge and conceptualizations of design thinking, identify its principal attributes, highlight relevant issues and tensions in the literature and advocate for future studies to advance theory and practice. However, the scope of these studies were far limited to perspectives outside business education.

In the domain of business education, we also found a few studies have conducted comprehensive literature reviews (Graciano *et al*. 2023; Valenciano *et al*. 2019; Wu *et al*. 2023). Wu *et al*. (2023) for instance utilized a bibliometric analysis and content analysis method to address how specific research topics in social innovation in higher education have evolved. Their sampled publications have been collected during the study period from 1996 to July 2021. By conducting this investigation, this study found that design thinking was one of the themes that frequently emerged in the evolution of social innovation. However this study did not address issues specifically focusing on design thinking, but covered issues in general from the research domain of the social innovation. Other studies of Graciano *et al*. (2023) and Valenciano *et al*. (2019) also conducted systematic reviews to explore themes among literature based on their research interests. Although the scopes of their studies remained within domains of the business education, they did not address issue of design thinking.

Given aforementioned lack of clarity about value of design thinking in business education at the tertiary level, the present research aims to address this gap.

Utilizing comprehensive systematic literature review, we attempt to shed light on current knowledge and conceptualizations of design thinking in business education. In addition we seek to identify various forms of value created through the application of design thinking.

The remainder of this study is organized as follows. Followed by the introduction and discussion of related literature in this section 1, section 2 outlines the research methods. Section 3 presents the results of our data analyses. Finally section 4 offers the conclusions and limitations of our study.

## 3.2 Research Methodology

In this study, a systematic review analysis was conducted based on the following methodological sequence: 1) Data Collection and 2) Data Analysis, which included descriptive analysis and text analysis . The publication search undertaken for this study retrieved documents addressing design thinking within the context of higher education in business. Following screening and eligibility checks, a total of 63 documents were included in the analysis. The methodology and findings are detailed below.

### 3.2.1 Data Collection

The systematic review of the design thinking literature commenced by identifying commonalities in descriptive elements of the terms and patterns of its use, following the methodology outlined by Micheli *et al.* (2019). A systematic review necessitates the meticulous search and selection of pertinent literature on a given subject. In the data collection phase, we employed a multi-step approach to identify and select sources discussing "design thinking in business education." This phase adhered to the guidelines set forth by Micheli *et al.* (2019) and Graciano *et al.* (2023). The initial step involved searching three databases— Science Direct, Business Source Premier, and ProQuest—using the search string "Design thinking" AND "Education" in the title or abstract of peer-reviewed scholarly journals published within the past ten years, from January 2013 to July 2023 (conducted on July 23, 2023). This search yielded a total of 6,356 articles. Subsequently, we refined our selection by focusing on articles related to business, technologies, and social sciences. Each database's specific filtering function was utilized for this purpose, resulting in a subset of 618 documents (79 from Science Direct, 47 from Business Source Premier, and 259 from ProQuest). A thorough review of titles and abstracts, conducted by a group of authors, led to the exclusion of numerous articles not pertinent to the topic of business education, such as those focusing on art, architectural, and humanities education. Additionally, articles duplicated across databases and those written in non-English languages were discarded. Subsequently, each document was fully reviewed to confirm its relevance to our research objectives. For instance, while some documents addressed related topics in business education, they primarily discussed issues related to STEM education in primary and secondary schools. To maintain focus on university-level education, such articles were excluded. Similarly, articles focusing on business education implemented in practical settings within companies were omitted from the sample. However, documents articulating cases for collaboration with companies were included, provided they constituted formal courses within tertiary curricula. Following this rigorous filtering process, 54 records were discarded, leaving 63 documents eligible for text and content analysis (See **Figure 3.1**).

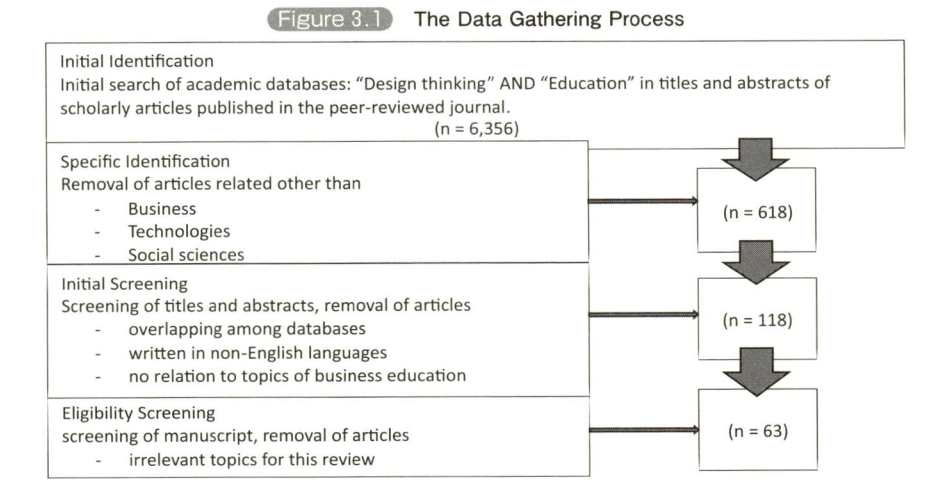

**Figure 3.1**   The Data Gathering Process

### 3.2.2 Date Analysis

Data analysis was conducted on the 63 resulting documents described above. Initially, descriptive analysis was conducted, followed by text analysis and Keyword in context analysis (KWIC) to identify values created by adopting design thinking in higher education setting. To facilitate the text analysis and keyword in context analysis, Voyant Tools (https://voyant-tools.org), an open-source online platform designed for the analysis of digitally recorded texts, was applied. Voyant Tools allows researchers to extract linguistic and statistical information from texts of various sizes, types, and languages. The platform also offers visual representations such as grids, graphs, and animations to aid in the interpretation of the analyzed data (Alhudithi 2021). Voyant Tools has been previously employed for quantitative text analysis in various peer-reviewed articles (Carracedo *et al.* 2021; Dwivedula & Singh 2021; Gabor *et al.* 2019; Gregory *et al.* 2022), demonstrating its suitability for analyzing qualitative data in a quantitative manner.

## 3.3 Analysis Results and Findings

### 3.3.1 Descriptive Analysis

Firstly, we conducted descriptive analyses. **Figure 3.2** shows numbers of publications addressed design thinking topics of business education at university for each year. According to this analysis result, the documents retained through our filtering process have been constantly published at a rate of nearly 10 articles annually since 2018. This increasing trend in publications on design thinking has been observed in previous studies. Micheli *et al.* (2019) implemented systematic review on design thinking using data from 1990 to 2017, and discovered cumulative numbers of sampled publications in this research domain has been increasing. Thus, our research confirmed the continuity of this upward trend. Similarly, Yu *et al.* (2023) also conducted a systematic literature review within the research area of design cognition. They reported a trend indicating the publication of more than 5 articles annually from 2018 to 2022. Although this prior study did

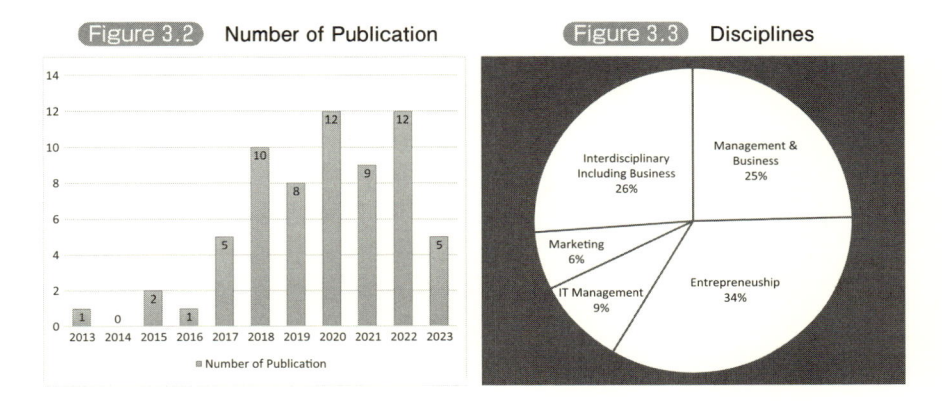

Figure 3.2 Number of Publication

Figure 3.3 Disciplines

not covered documents dealing with the design thinking topics in business education, it is observed that the number of research studies on design thinking substantially increased from around 2017.

The list of the specific disciplines discussed in each article regarding design thinking was illustrated by **Figure 3.3**. According to this analysis, we found that entrepreneurship is the most prominent discipline, followed by interdisciplinary studies including business and management, and business in general, with 22 (34.92%), 17 (26.98%) and 16 (25.40%) documents of all samples, respectively. This result is alligns with Valenciano *et al*. (2019), who suggested that entrepreneurship is thought as a subject that is currently being receiving considerable interest and depth in tertiary education program, and it is also regarded as the discipline of a great deal of scientific research published in the scholarly journals.

Among all documents, their majority research have adopted case studies as their research strategy (63.57%), followed by descriptive and normative analysis (19.05%) as the second, and survey (14.29%) as the third (see **Figure 3.4**). In terms of categories of data, there are more articles using qualitative data (63.49%), whereases quantitative data are also used to analyze by substantial number of articles (36.51%) (See **Figure 3.5**). It is noteworthy that 9 articles have adopted mixed methods using both qualitative data and quantitative data simultaneously. This trend contrasts with Micheli *et al*. (2019), who conducted a systematic literature review of scholarly documents on design thinking from 1990

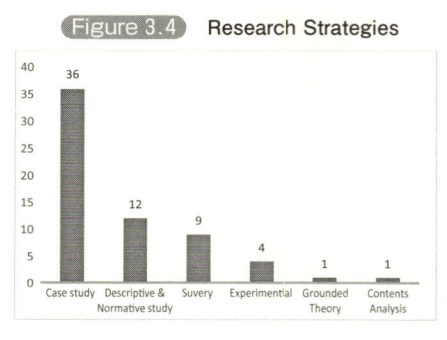

Figure 3.4 Research Strategies

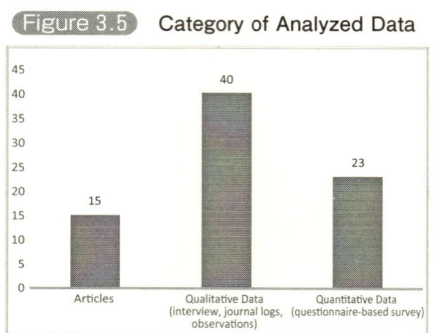

Figure 3.5 Category of Analyzed Data

to 2017. Their study revealed that normative studies were more common than empirical ones, with very few quantitative studies during their research period. However, our latest findings indicate a shift in research strategies, with case studies emerging as the dominant approach among authors. Over the past decade, there has been an increase in the adoption of various methodologies, including empirical and exploratory studies, often incorporating quantitative analysis.

**Figure 3.6** illustrated overview of geographical information for origin of researchers based on first author's affiliation. This analysis was previously implemented by Graciano *et al.* (2023) and Yu *et al.* (2023). Table 1 reveals that the top country of origin with the highest number of sampled publications were

Figure 3.6 Author's Geographical Region of Origin

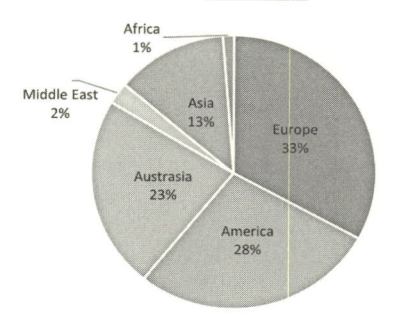

| Country | Number of Publications |
|---|---|
| USA | 13 |
| Australia | 7 |
| Brazil | 6 |
| Canada, Thailand, Germany, Italy, UK, Finland | 3 |
| Singapore, Taiwan, India, Poland, Norway, Portugal, Spain | 2 |
| India, China, Indonesia, Saudi Arabia, Dubai, South Africa, Netherlands, Romania, Russia, Belgium, Ukrain, Denmark | 1 |

the USA, Australia and Brazil, with 13, 7, and 6 of articles, respectively. We found that both Australia and Brazil were prominently contributing to the literature on design thinking in business education over the past decade. Overall, this research domain has been widely covered across geographical regions and countries, indicating significance and relevance.

## 3.3.2   Text Analysis

### 3.3.2.1   Overview of the Data

Before the primary analysis of our sampled 63 publications using Voyant Tools, some pre-processing steps were preliminary performed to improve the accuracy of the analysis (Alhudithi 2021)[1]. Irrelevant data were removed from the corpuses, and a list of stop words was manually created and filtered out. Additionally, stemming was applied to group related terms under their common root.

The analysis revealed that all 63 publications consisted of a total of 405,027 words, with 19,006 unique word forms. The longest document had a length of 15,472 words, while the shortest document had a length of 2,091 words. The average words per sentence were 43.0 for the highest value and 19.8 for the lowest value. The ten most frequent words were; "design (n = 5,681)", "thinking (n = 4,203)", "students (n = 3,398)", "learning (n = 1,986)", "process (n = 1,745)", "problem (n = 1,662)", "education (n = 1,287)", "innovation (n = 1,274)" "business (n = 1,080)" and "research (n = 984)".

### 3.3.2.2   Cyrrus Cloud Analysis

**Figure 3.7** shows the result of Cyrrus cloud analysis, which is a word cloud creation tool. In this result, the most frequent occurring words in the corpus are placed centrally, and large in size when compared to the less frequently occurring words. Words clouds should be interpreted with great caution, because the result do not reflect collocations, co-occurrences or possible meaning variations (Hetenyi *et al.* 2019). To triangulate this weakness of Cyrrus cloud analysis, we also applied a scatter plot analysis in the subsection bellow.

**Figure 3.7** Results of Cyrrus Cloud Analysis

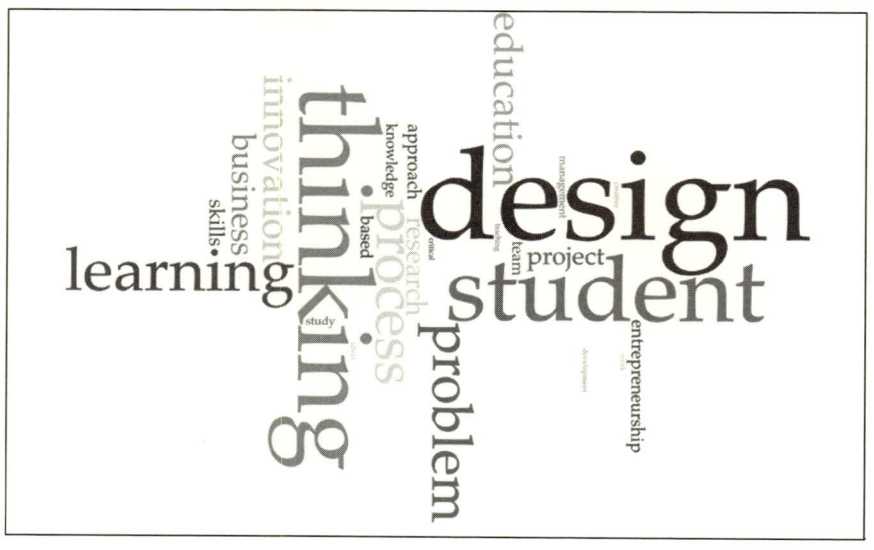

### 3.3.2.3   Principle Component Analysis

The scatter plot analysis is the most sophisticated method among the text analysis tools of Voyant tools. This tool includes Principle Component Analysis, Correspondence Analysis, Document Similarity Check and t-distributed Stochastic Neighbourhood Embedding (t-SNE) analysis. All four cluster plotting analyses use algorithms that create a 2 or 3 dimensional representation of the data in a multidimensional space (Hetenyi *et al.* 2019). Among these four different types of analyses, we implemented t-SNE analysis[2] to generate the two-dimensional model with five clusters. This allowed us to generate a scatter plot that identifies the closest words of each terms with considering collocations and co-occurrences. This t-SNE is often applied to high dimensional data sets such as qualitative textual data (Helenyi *et al.* 2019). In our analysis, the top 30 most frequently occurring terms were organized in five clusters. The term frequency-inverse document frequency (t-dif) weighing method was employed to perform the analysis. This method determines how important a word is to the corpus (Dwivedula and Singh, 2021). This also depends on the frequency of occurrence of that word in the entire corpus. In this study, the level of perplexity was set as 50.

Higher perplexity is more suitable for more dense data that is the case of this study. The scatter plot were obtained after 5,000 iterations. The colors of the words represent the cluster to which they belong to. The size of the points is relative to the frequency of the words.

As seen in **Figure 3.8**, our analysis revealed five distinct clusters. The most clearly detectable cluster focuses on "design thinking" as a learning tool for students. This finding is consistent with our search criteria, which targeted scholarly publications using keywords "design thinking" and "education". Thus it is reasonable that majority of the publications in our sample primarily discuss the application of design thinking in business education setting. This is in line with the the recent research trend, as evidenced by studies such as that of Dantas di Figueiredo (2021), which highlight the growing popularity of design thinking in

**Figure 3.8**   t-SNE Generated Clusters

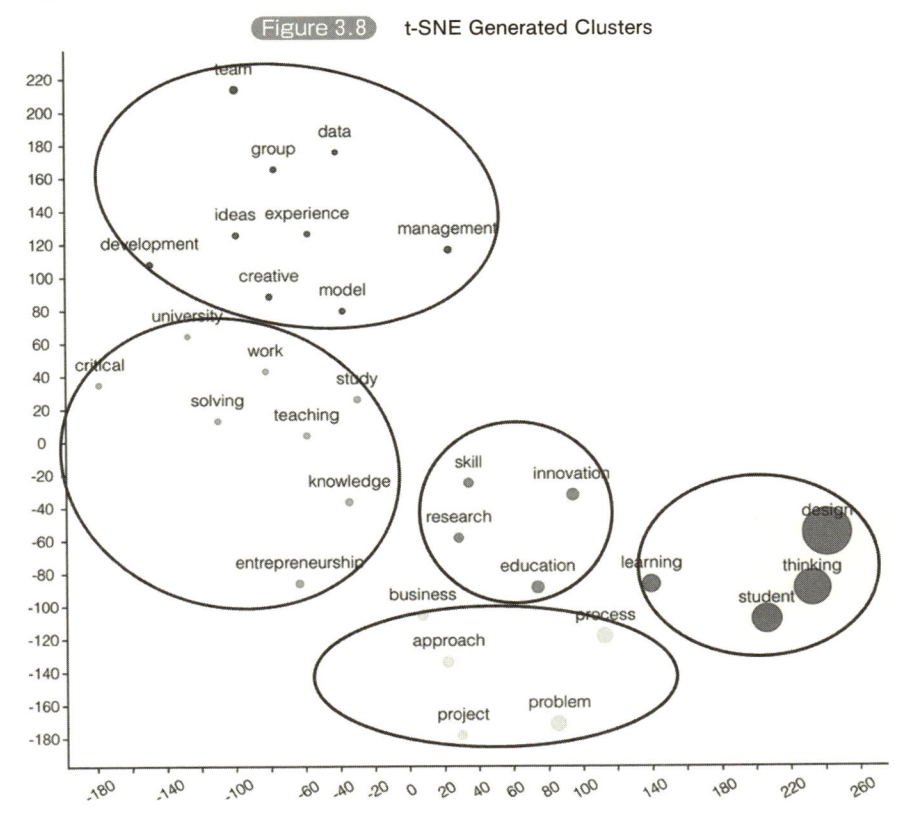

higher business education.

There were also several distinct clusters to explain design thinking as a learning toolkit. The second cluster represented a learning process known as a project-based learning (PBL), which provides students an approach to face and solve real-world business challenges. Meanwhile, the third cluster characterized design thinking as an innovative education method aimed at fostering a wider range of skills. Prior literature contended that PBLs integrating design thinking disciplines empower students to work on "wicked" problems of real businesses that also increase in students' positive experiences (Ewin *et al.* 2017: Kłeczek *et al.* 2020; Konkel 2023). Moreover, researchers has posited that design thinking serves as an innovative educational approach for developing exploratory skills necessary for navigating messy and ill-structured business issues (Glen *et al.* 2014), as well as analogical and metaphorical reasoning skills (Choi & Kim 2017), and convergent and divergent thinking skills (Kimbell, 2011).

Furthermore, the remaining clusters served to represent various characteristics of design thinking as a learning toolkit. The fourth cluster highlighted design thinking's role in imparting critical knowledge of entrepreneurship and facilitating problem-solving in entrepreneurial contexts. Along with this result, we found existing literature which posits that design thinking is relevant to entrepreneurship education due to its forward-looking and pragmatic approach. Design thinking equips students with the tools and methods necessary to identify and capitalize on new opportunities in an uncertain future (Neck & Greene 2011; Nielsen & Stovang 2015; Sarooghi *et al.* 2019), making it a suitable component for achieving this educational objective. As for the fifth cluster, our analysis result revealed a feature of the team-based learning which allows learners to develop creative ideas and experiences of management. This is supported by Blank & Dorf (2012), Fiore *et al.* (2019) and Zarzosa (2022), who assert that team learning is integral to start-up education as it fosters interactions among individuals from diverse disciplinary backgrounds, enhancing the overall learning experience.

### 3.3.2.4 Keyword in Context Analysis

We also conducted a Keyword in Context (KWIC) analysis to investigate the context of the usage of the word "value" in our sampled documents. This is also one of the analysis tools incorporated in the Voyant tools platform. Initially we examined 15 words to the left and right of the keyword "value", as we thought this to be the minimum range necessary to establish the context of use of the word in question. Subsequently, we manually reviewed the output from the KWIC tool of

**Table 3.1**   Value of Design Thinking

| Value (number of publication) | Category | Example of Publication |
|---|---|---|
| for students (learners) (n = 48) | • Obtain wicked-problem solving skill | Coco *et al.* (2020); Ericson (2022); Fiore *et al.* (2019); Garbuio *et al.* (2018); Kainzbauer & Lowe (2018); Matthee and Turpin (2019); Tarabasz *et al.* (2018) |
| | • Obtain creative thinking skill | Kuo *et al.* (2021) |
| | • Obtain collaborative & teamwork skill | Arnab *et al.* (2019); Ericson (2022); Fiore *et al.* (2019); Guaman-Quintanilla *et al.* (2022); Hennessey & Mueller (2020); Lai & Chen, (2021); Tarabasz *et al.* (2018); Witherspoon (2022); Zarzosa (2022) |
| | • Increase learning engagement | Ericson (2022); Whewell *et al.* (2022) |
| | • Increase learning motivation | Biffi *et al.* (2017); Kuo *et al.* (2021); Whewell *et al.* (2022) |
| | • Increase entrepreneurial intention | Fiore *et al.* (2019) |
| | • Increase sentiment value | Biffi *et al.* (2017); Sheppard (2020) |
| | • Increase empathy | Jussila *et al.* (2020); Schiele & Chen (2018) |
| | • Increase social skills | Gerbaudo *et al.* (2021); Kim & Strimel (2019) |
| | • Negative effect | Coco *et al.*(2020); Elsbach & Stigliani (2018); Kim & Strimel (2020); Kurtmollaiev *et al.* (2018) |
| for educators and administrators (n = 15) | • Effective educational material | Eloranta *et al.* (2021); Hennessey & Mueller 2020; Woraphiphat & Roopsuwankun (2023) |
| | • Challenges & Suggestions to improve | Bongiovanni & Balgabekova (2017); Kłeczek *et al.* (2020); Zarzosa (2022) |
| for businesses (n = 8) | | Biffi (2017); Chongwatpol (2020); Dijksterhuis & Silvius, (2017); Jussila *et al.* (2020); Lai & Chen (2021); Lake *et al.* (2022) |
| for community (n = 6) | | Aranha *et al.* (2018); Biffi *et al.* (2017); Cumming & Yur-Austin (2022); Lake *et al.* (2022) |

Note: Six publications of our sample did not explicitly mention the value of design thinking within the context of business educational.

the Voyant tools, and established the context of the word "value" of design thinking. Based on this analysis, we constructed a table classifying the sources of value into 4 main categories "for students (learners)", "for educators", "for businesses", and "for community" (See **Table 3.1**).

### 3.3.2.4.1 Value for students

According to this analysis result, the majority of 48 publications from our sample voided value of design thinking from perspectives of students (learners). Many researchers contended that design thinking program in the business education contributes to the development of valuable skills among learners, enhancing their entrepreneurship and employability. These skills include complex/wicked-problem solving skills (Coco, *et al.* 2020; Ericson 2022; Fiore *et al.* 2019; Garbuio *et al.* 2018; Kainzbauer & Lowe 2018; Matthee & Turpin 2019; Tarabasz *et al.* 2018), creative thinking skill (Kuo *et al.* 2021), collaborative and teamwork skill (Arnab *et al.* 2019; Ericson 2022; Fiore *et al.* 2019; Guaman-Quintanilla *et al.* 2022; Hennessey & Mueller 2020;Lai & Chen 2021; Tarabasz *et al.* 2018; Witherspoon 2022; Zarzosa 2022), as well as non-cognitive characteristics such as learning engagement (Ericson 2022; Whewell *et al.* 2022), learning motivation (Biffi *et al.* 2017; Kuo *et al.* 2021; Whewell *et al.* 2022) and entrepreneurial intention (Fiore *et al.* 2019). Furthermore, other publications have noted that business education programs incorporating design thinking are effective to improve emotional aspect such as sentiment value (Biffi *et al.* 2017; Sheppard 2020), empathy (Jussila *et al.* 2020; Schiele & Chen 2018) and social elements (Gerbaudo *et al.* 2021; Kim & Strimel 2020). Accordingly, acquisition of new skills and attitude through adoption of design thinking in the business education context is widely recognized as valuable for learners in the literature.

In contrast to the positive value of teaching design thinking, several studies have highlighted negative effects (value) of design thinking (Coco *et al.* 2020; Elsbach & Stigliani 2018; Kim & Strimel 2020; Kurtmollaiev *et al.* 2018). For example, Coco *et al.* (2020) has argued cultural clashes may arise when learners, who are accustomed to managerial and analytical skills typically taught in business education, encounter the concept and methodologies of design thinking, which emphasize emotional aspects. This clash between the rational and theoretical skills ingrained in students through traditional business education and the more experiential and emotionally-driven approach of design thinking can continusouly lead to tensions during the learning process. However, Coco *et al.* (2020) also intended that learner's struggles from this cultural clash serve as the the main mechanisms through which the experiential learning takes places and, thereby, triggering the main value of the design thinking approach.

### 3.3.2.4.2   Value for educators and administrators

Educators, instructors and educational managers (administrators) can take advantages from applying design thinking methodologies in the sense that they can create more engaging and effective courses tailored to the needs and interests of their students. Some studies of our sample supported this (Bongiovanni & Balgabekova 2021; Eloranta *et al.* 2021; Hennessey & Mueller 2020; Woraphiphat & Roopsuwankun 2023). For example, Hennessey and Mueller (2020) conducted research using a focus group of educators, and found that educators perceived that design thinking process as the effective way in which students could solve problems using a combination of previously acquired skills, knowledge and current learning outcomes. It is clearly articulated that applying design thinking as the educational materials give educators to manage their teachings more effectively. Other studies on the other hands reported suggestions or remind challenges for educators in order to achieve better education outcomes by utilizing design thinking. Kłeczek *et al.* (2020) for instance provided several managerial implications that may help higher education managers in developing innovative didactic projects in the future such as selection of wicked problems, considerations of frequencies, size and students' teams. Similarly Bongiovanni & Balgabekova (2021) demonstrated that the need to increase training opportunities for academics willing to adopt design thinking in their interactions with students.

### 3.3.2.4.3   Value for businesses

Based on our analysis, several publications have highlighted the value of design thinking for businesses (Biffi *et al.* 2017; Chongwatpol 2020; Dijksterhuis & Silvius 2017; Jussila *et al.* 2020; Lai & Chen 2021; Lake *et al.* 2022). In these studies, the value for businesses has primarily been described as the benefits for companies involving in the programs co-organized by educational institutions. For example, Lai & Chen (2021) conducted an entrepreneurship workshop incorporating design thinking across three universities and companies, and found that collaboration in co-creation through design thinking enabled both students and businesses to provide varied experiences and insights, facilitating the creation of mutually preferred outcomes jointly among all participants. Similarly, Biffi *et al.* (2017) investigated the effects of a similar entrepreneurship education program involving various stakeholders. This study revealed that businesses and their representatives emphasized the value of developing ideas through actual collaborations with universities, leading greater openness to collaborations beyond organizational boundaries. This is in line with Jussila *et al.* (2020) that acknowledged the value for businesses in their interactions with other stakeholders, fostering trust to facilitate rich social and information exchanges, and encouraging more valuable knowledge sharing. Although this value arises from collaborations involving various stakeholder throughout education programs, it is evident that successful outcomes of the collaborations would emerge from reflecting design thinking components such as empathizing and brainstorming phases.

### 3.3.2.4.4 Value for communities

A few publications have discussed the valuable impact of design thinking for community (Aranha *et al.* 2018; Biffi *et al.* 2017; Cummings & Yur-Austin 2022; Lake *et al.* 2022). For example, Cummings & Yur-Austin (2022) investigated the impact of MBA program incorporating design thinking components within their PBL approach to assess whether or not their program enables students to deliver meaningful outcomes to the businesses and community. Through an outreach project for university students and the community, they explored the possibility of collaboration and identified ways to facilitate economic development in the city. The authors concluded that the project promoted transformational power for turning students' academic experiences into creative forces in generating positive and impactful outcomes for various stakeholders. Similarly, Biffi *et al.* (2017) conducted a case study of the post-graduate entrepreneurship education program called ProSIT, where local enterprises provided students with projects to create innovative solutions to their problems. Following the program, the researchers implemented interviews with stakeholders, including local municipalities, and found that they recognized multiple achievements such as the development of functional competencies for the region, valuable employment opportunities, chances for effective collaborations among local actors, and support in the creation and development of entrepreneurial ventures.

## 3.4   Conclusion

This study implemented a comprehensive systematic literature review for the literature addressing value of design thinking in business education. The filtering process of the systematic literature review finally left 63 documents to adopt for text and content analyses using Voyant tools. The results indicate several findings and implications.

First, we found that number of the research articles regarding design thinking in the business education has been increasing in recent across the world. The result also demonstrated that research strategies adopted for design thinking research in this domain varies than before. Particularly, studies using empirical research methodologies including both qualitative and quantitative approaches have been increased. It is acknowledged that different research strategies offer unique methodologies, allowing researchers to gain a comprehensive understanding of the phenomenon from multiple perspectives. Also using multiple research strategies enables researchers to triangulate findings across different methodologies. This suggests that esearch in design thinking for business education has reached a mature stage and added further value in the literature.

Secondly, it was found that design thinking is widely recognized in the literature as an innovative educational approach for facilitating learning in the realms of business and entrepreneurship. Through our analysis, we identified five distinct clusters, namely "design thinking for students' learning," "problem-based learning (PBL)," "innovative educational tools," "entrepreneurship education facilitation," and "team-based learning." These clusters were delineated utilizing t-SNE analysis, which helped us carried out thematic analysis by providing an intuitive way to explore the distribution of topics within the corpus. Hence, the primary themes prevalent in the literature within this domain revolve around advocating for the value of design thinking as educational material.

In light of this disucssion, prior studies have pointed out unequal frequencies in utilizing design thinking practices, indicating that protoyping and experimentation are used less frequently than other components of design thinking in the classroom setting (McLaughlin *et al.* 2022; Lake *et al.* 2021). Our sampled articles also reported this deviation. Many of them focused on and articulated applications of limited practices within the contenxt of business education (e.g. Kainzbauer & Lowe 2018; Lynch *et al.* 2021; Liao *et al.* 2022; Whewell *et al.* 2022; Ericson, 2022; Law *et al.* 2021; Wasyluk & Kucner 2021). To enhance value of design thinking as the education tool, educators and administrator need to be ensure coverage of all components of design thinking practice throughout the teaching semester or project duration.

Thirdly, our keyword in context analysis have revealed that the literature recognizes the value created by design thinking not only for students, the direct consumers of education, but also for other stakeholders involved in the learning process, such as educators, entities or institutions, and even communities. This is because effective design thinking is strongly associated with a constructivist environment, wherein students learn more through interaction with peers, such as participating in group discussions and constructive dialogue, thereby enabling the development of novel, shared knowledge (Duffy & Kirkley 2004; Velu 2023; Woraphiphat & Roopsuwankun 2023). This characteristic of constructivism extends to other stakeholders and brings benefits to each key player. Furthermore, as previous studies suggested, successful collaboration among stakeholders is enhanced by design thinking practices such as empathizing and brainstorming (Jussila *et al.* 2020). These innovative tactics contribute to fostering the value of design thinking in business education.

Although this study successfully defined the value of design thinking for business and management education that basically prevailed in the literature, it is important to acknowledge the limitations of our discussion and further research possibilities.

The first limitation of this study pertains to the lack of investigation into non-English written publications. Our data filtering process only considered academic articles written in English, potentially overlooking important discussions occurring in non-English language countries. Cultural and linguistic differences can significantly influence communication styles among individuals. As design thinking is based on a human-oriented approach, these cultural and linguistic aspects may lead to variations in the application and perception of design thinking. Additionally, different cultures may prioritize or de-emphasize certain features of design thinking, resulting in a distinct set of values among stakeholders. Further research is warranted to explore the relationship between culture and the value of design thinking among associated people. This would involve investigating how cultural factors influence the adoption, implementation, and outcomes of design thinking practices in diverse contexts. By considering a broader range of cultural perspectives and language contexts, future studies can provide a more comprehensive understanding of the cultural nuances inherent in the utilization of design thinking principles.

Second, we observe a skewed proportion in research coverage, with the majority of studies addressing the value of design thinking for students and educators, while fewer studies focus on its implications for businesses and communities. Furthermore, there remains a notable lack of empirical research directly measuring the value or benefits of design thinking for these institutions. While some literature suggests that one of the values for businesses lies in facilitating valuable social and information exchanges or knowledge sharing among various educational stakeholders, this has not been objectively measured. To address this gap, future research should employ mixed methods utilizing both quantitative and qualitative approaches. This would allow for a more comprehensive understanding of the impact of design thinking on businesses, communities, and other stakeholders involved in the educational process. By combining quantitative data analysis with qualitative insights, researchers can provide a more robust assessment of the tangible benefits derived from implementing design thinking practices in various contexts.

## Notes

1 According to Rasid *et al.* (2017), the preprocessing of the dataset involves removing errors and inconsistencies. Firstly, all words should be converted to lowercase, and punctuation marks, num-

bers, whitespace, and symbols need to be eliminated from the corpora. Secondly, stemming and the removal of stop words are necessary. Stemming refers to reducing inflected or derived words to their word stem. Stop words, which are deemed unimportant and lacking contextual value, should be excluded. To automatically check for inflected and derived words, Voyant Tools was utilized, and any necessary adjustments were made using word processing software such as Microsoft Word's word replacement function. The stop word list provided by Christopher M. Church's website, "Textual Analysis with Voyant Tools" (http://www.christophermchurch.com), was employed for removing stop words.

2  According to Cao and Wang (2017), t-SNE is defined as the analysis tool that "tries to preserve local neighbourhood structure from high dimensional space in lowdimensional space by converting pairwise distances to pairwise joint distributions, and optimize low dimensional embeddings to match the high and low dimensional joint distributions".

## ● References

Alhudithi, E. (2021). *Review of Voyant Tools: See through your text. Language Learning and Technology*, 25(3), 43-50. Retrieved from https://scholarspace.manoa.hawaii.edu/server/api/core/bitstreams/05516ef7-dd9e-4461-a1c7-14eb895d740e/content

Aranha, E. A., Santos, P. H., & Garcia, N. A. P. (2018). EDLE: an integrated tool to foster entrepreneurial skills development in engineering education. *Educational Technology Research and Development*, 6, 1571-1599.

Arnab, S., Clarke, S., & Morini, L. (2019). Co-Creativity through Play and Game Design Thinking. *The Electronic Journal of e-Learning,* 17(3), 184-198.

Bhandari, A. (2022). Design Thinking: from Bibliometric Analysis to Content Analysis, Current Research Trends, and Future Research Direction. *Journal of the Knowledge Economy*, 14, 3097-3152.

Biffi, A., Bissola, R., & Imperatori, B. (2017). Chasing innovation: a pilot case study of a rhizomatic design thinking education program. *Education + Training*, 59(9), 957-977.

Blank, S., & Dorf, B. (2012). *The Startup Owner's Manual: The Step-by-Step Guide for Building a Great Company*. Pescadero: K and S. Ranch Publishers.

Bongiovanni, I., & Balgabekova, D. (2021). Ask me if I am Engaged: A Design-led Approach to Collect Student Feedback on their University Experience. *Design and Technology Education: An International Journal*, 26(1), 89-117.

Cankurtaran, P., & Beverland, M. B. (2020). Using design thinking to respond to crises: B2B lessons from the 2020 COVID-19 pandemic. *Industrial Marketing Management*, 88, 255-260. https://doi.org/10.1016/j.indmarman.2020.05.030

Cao, Y., & Wang, L. (2017). *Automatic selection of t-SNE perplexity*. arXiv:1709.03229. https://doi.org/10.48550/arXiv.1708.03229

Carracedo, P., Puertas, R., & Marti, L. (2021). Research lines on the impact of the COVID-19 pandemic on business: A text mining analysis. *Journal of Business Research,* 132, 586-593. https://doi.org/10.1016/j.jbusres.2020.11.043

Choi, H. H., & Kim, M. J. (2017). The effects of analogical and metaphorical reasoning on design thinking. *Thinking Skills and Creativity*, 23, 29-41.

Chongwatpol, J. (2020). Operationalizing Design Thinking in Business Intelligence and Analytics Projects. Decision Sciences. *Journal of Innovative Education*, 18(3), 409-434.

Coco, N., Calcagno, M., & Lusiani, M. (2020). Struggles as triggers in a design-thinking journey. *Creative Innovation Management,* 29(S1), 103-115.

Cummings, C., & Yur-Austin, J. (2022). Design thinking and community impact: A case study of project-based learning in an MBA capstone course. *Journal of Education for Business*, 97(2), 126-132.

Dantas de Figueiredo, M. (2021). Design is cool, but... A critical appraisal of design thinking in management education. *The International Journal of Management Education*, 19(1), https://doi.org/10.1016/j.ijme.2020.100429.

Dijksterhuis, E., & Silvius, G. (2017). The Design Thinking Approach to Projects. *The Journal of Modern Project Management*, 1(3), 33-41.

Duffy, T. M., & Kirkley, J. R. (2004). *Learner-centered theory and practice in distance education.* Lawrence Erlbaum Associates.

Dwivedula, R., & Singh, P. (2021). A qualitative approach to understand Generation Z work motivation. *European Journal of Behavioral Sciences*, 4(2), 1-17. https://doi.org/10.33422/ejbs.v4i2.542

Elsbach, K. D., & Stigliani, I. (2018). Design Thinking and Organizational Culture: A Review and Framework for Future Research. *Journal of Management*, 44(6), 2274-2306.

Ericson, J. (2022). Mapping the Relationship Between Critical Thinking and Design Thinking. *Journal of the Knowledge Economy*, 13, 406-429.

Eloranta, E., Sirviö, T., Ruotsalainen, A., & Säätelä, S. (2021). Service Design Thinking in Higher Education in Finland. *The International Journal of Design Education*, 16(1), 81-89.

Ewin, N., Luck, J., Chugh, R., & Jarvis, J. (2017). Rethinking project management education: A humanistic approach based on design thinking. *Procedia Computer Science*, 121, 503-510.

Fiore, E., Sansone, G., & Paolucci, E. (2019). Entrepreneurship Education in a Multidisciplinary Environment: Evidence from an Entrepreneurship Programme Held in Turin. *Administrative Sciences*, 9, 1-28.

Gabor, H., Attila, L., & Magdolna, S. (2019). Quantitative analysis of qualitative data: Using Voyant Tools to investigate the sales-marketing interface. *Journal of Industrial Engineering and Management* (JIEM), 12(3), 393-404. https://doi.org/10.3926/jiem.2929

Garbuio, M., Lovallo, D., Dong, A., Lin, M., & Tschang, T. (2018). Demystifying the Genius of Entrepreneurship: How Design Cognition Can Help Create the Next Generation of Netrepreneurs. *Journal of Business Venturing Insights*, 17(1), 41-61.

Glen, R., Suciu, C., & Baughm, C. (2014). The need for design thinking in business schools. *The Academy of Management Learning and Education,* 13(4), 653-667.

Graciano, P., Lermen, F. H., Reichert, F. M., & Padula, A. D. (2023). The impact of risk-taking and creativity stimuli in education towards innovation: A systematic review and research agenda. *Thinking Skills and Creativity*, 47, 1-17. https://doi.org/10.1016/j.tsc.2022.101220

88

Gerbaudo, R., Gaspar, R., & Lins, R. G. (2021). Novel online video model for learning information technology based on micro learning and multimedia micro content. *Educational and Information Technologies*, 26, 5637-5665.

Gomoll, A., Tolar, E., Hmelo-Silver, C. E., & Šabanovic, S. (2018). Designing human-centered robots: The role of constructive failure. *Thinking Skills Creativity*, 30, 90-102.

Gregory, K., Geiger, L., & Salisbury, P. (2022). Voyant Tools and Descriptive Metadata: A Case Study in How Automation Can Compliment Expertise Knowledge. *Journal of Library Metadata*, 22(1-2), 1-16. https://doi.org/10.1080/19386389.2022.2030635 .

Guaman-Quintanilla, S., Everaert, P., Chiluiza, K., & Valcke, M. (2022). Fostering Teamwork through Design Thinking: Evidence from a Multi-Actor Perspective. *Education Sciences*, 12, 1-24.

Hennessey, E., & Mueller, J. (2020). Teaching and Learning Design Thinking (DT): How Do Educators See DT Fitting into the Classroom? *Canadian Journal of Education*, 43(2), 501-521.

Hetenyi, G., Lengyel, A., & Szilasi, M. (2019). Quantitative analysis of qualitative data: Using Voyant Tools to investigate the sales-marketing interface. *Journal of Industrial Engineering and Management*, 12(3), 393-404. https://doi.org/10.3926/jiem.2929

Jussila, J., Raitanen, J., Partanen, A., Tuomela, V., Siipola, V., & Kunnari, I. (2020). Rapid Product Development in University-Industry Collaboration: Case Study of a Smart Design Project. *Technology Innovation Management Review*, 10(3), 48-58.

Kainzbauer, A., & Lowe, S. (2018). Embodied realism by design in Thai management education. *The International Journal of Management Education*, 16, 281-291.

Kim, E., & Strimel, G. J. (2020). The Influence of Entrepreneurial Mindsets on Student Design Problem Framing. *IEEE Transactions on Education*, 63(2), 126-135.

Kimbell, L. (2011). Rethinking design thinking: Part 1. *Design and Culture,* 3(3), 285-306.

Kłeczek, R., Kajdas, M., & Wrona, S. (2020). Wicked problems and project-based learning: Value-in-use approach. *The International Journal of Management Education,* 18(1), https://doi.org/10.1016/j.ijme.2019.100324

Kolko, J. (2015). Design thinking comes of age. *Harvard Business Review*, 2-7.

Konkel, M. T. (2023). Learning Orientation and Creativity: Design Mindsets in the First-Year Experience. *The International Journal of Design Education*, 17(2), 45-64.

Kuo, H. C., Yang, T. R. C., Chen, J. S., Hou, T. W., & Ho, M. T. (2021). The Impact of Design Thinking PBL Robot Course on College Students' Learning Motivation and Creative Thinking. *IEEE Transactions on Education,* 65(2), 124-131.

Kurtmollaiev, S., Pedersen, P. E., Fjuk, A., & Kvale, N. (2018). Developing Managerial Dynamic Capabilities: A Quasi-experimental Field Study of the Effects of Design Thinking Training. *Academy of Management Learning & Education,* 17(2), 184-202.

Lai, W. Y., & Chen, M. F. (2021). Co-Creation through Design Thinking in an International Context. *The International Journal of Design Thinking*, 15(2), 299-319.

Lake, D., Motley, P. M., & Moner, W. (2022). Completing the CiCLE: long-term assessment of community-involved collaborative learning ecosystems for social innovation in higher education. *Social Enterprise Journal*, 18(1), 28-50.

Law, E., Putra, A., Koh, E., Zuea, T., & Tat, K. E. (2021). *Innovation, Design & Entrepreneurship in Engineering Education. Advances in Engineering Education*, Fall, 1-12. Retrieved from https://files.eric.ed.gov/fulltext/EJ1316313.pdf

Liao, H., Pan, C., & Zhang, Y. (2023). Collaborating on ESG consulting, reporting, and communicating education: Using partner maps for capability building design. Frontiers in Environmental Science, 11, 1-10.

Luka, I. (2021). Design thinking in pedagogy: Frameworks and uses. *European Journal of Education*, 54(4), 499-512.

Lusch, R., & Vargo, S. (2014). *Evolving to a new dominant logic for marketing. Service-Dominant Logic of Marketing*. Routledge.

Lynch, M., Kamovich, U., Longva, K. K., & Steinert, M. (2021). Combining technology and entrepreneurial education through design thinking: Students' reflections on the learning process. *Technological Forecasting & Social Change*, 164, 119689.

McLaughlin JE, Chen E, Lake D, Guo W, Skywark ER, Chernik A, et al. (2022). Design thinking teaching and learning in higher education: Experiences across four universities. *\*PLoS ONE*, 17\*(3), https://doi.org/10.1371/journal.pone.0265902

Matthee, M., & Turpin, M. (2019). Teaching Critical Thinking, Problem Solving, and Design Thinking: Preparing IS Students for the Future. *Journal of Information Systems Education*, 30(4), 242-252.

Micheli, P., Wilner S. J. S., Bhatti S. H., Mura M., & Beverland M. B. (2019). Doing Design Thinking: Conceptual Review, Synthesis, and Research Agenda. *Journal of Product Innovation Management*, 36(2), 124-148.

Neck, H. M., & Greene, P. G. (2011). Entrepreneurship education: known worlds and new frontiers. *Journal of Small Business Management,* 49(1), 55-70.

Nielsen, S. L., & Stovang, P. (2015). *DesUni: university entrepreneurship education through design thinking*, 57(8/9), 977-991.

Owen, C. (2007). Design Thinking: Notes on its nature and use. *Design Research Quarterly*, 2(1), 16-27.

Pande, M. and Bharathi, S. V. 2020. Theoretical foundations of design thinking – A constructivism learning approach to design thinking. *Thinking Skills and Creativity,* 36, 1-17.

Rasid, N., Nohuddin, P. N. E., Alias, H., & Hamzah, I. (2017). Using Data Mining Strategy in Qualitative Research. International Visual Informatics Conference, conference proceeding. DOI:10.1007/978-3-319-70010-6_10.

Sarooghi, H., Sunny, S., Hornsby, J., & Fernhaber, S. (2019). Design Thinking and Entrepreneurship Education: Where Are We, and What Are the Possibilities? *Journal of Small Business Management*, 57(S1), 78-93.

Scheer, A., Noweski, C., & Meinel, C. (2012). Transforming Constructivist Learning into Action: Design Thinking in Education. *Design and Technology Education*, 17(3), 8-19.

Schiele, K., & Chen, S. (2018). Design thinking and digital marketing skills in marketing education: A module on building mobile applications. *Marketing Education Review*, 28(3), 150-154.

Sheppard, M. J. (2020). A case study of a radical constructivist approach to teaching innovation.

*Journal of Education for Business*, 95(8), 559-566.

Tarabasz, A., Selakovic, M., & Abraham, C. (2018). The Classroom of the Future: Disrupting the Concept of Contemporary Business Education. *Entrepreneurial Business and Economic Review,* 6(4), 231-245.

Valenciano, J. P., Uribe-Toril, J., & Ruiz-Real, J. L. (2019). Entrepreneurship and education in the 21st century: Analysis and trends in research. *Journal of Entrepreneurship Education,* 22(4), 1-20.

Velu, S. R. (2023). Design Thinking Approach for Increasing Innovative Action in Universities: ICT's Mediating Effect. *Sustainability,* 24(15), 1-17. https://doi.org/10.3390/su15010024

Wasyluk, P., & Kucner, A. (2021). Customer-centricity in Designing: Application of Design Thinking Methodology in Creating Educational Solutions at the University of Warmia and Mazury in Olsztyn. *European Research Studies Journal,* 24(s3), 84-95. https://www.um.edu.mt/library/oar/handle/123456789/104837

Witherspoon, A. (2022). The role of team processes in innovation development to sustain learning organizations. *The Learning Organization,* 29(1), 21-37.

Whewell, E., Caldwell, H., Frydenberg, M., & Andone, D. (2022). Changemakers as digital makers: Connecting and co-creating. *Education and Information Technologies*, 27, 6691-6713.

Woraphiphat, I., & Roopsuwankun, P. (2023). The impact of online design thinking-based learning on entrepreneurial intention: the case of vocational college. *Entrepreneurship Education and Pedagogy*, 6(1), 1-18. https://doi.org/10.1186/s13731-023-00278-z

Wu, Y. J., Goh, M., & Mai, Y. (2023). Social innovation and higher education: evolution and future promise. *Humanities & Social Sciences Communications*, 10, 283.

Yu, R., Schubert, G., & Gu, N. (2023). Biometric Analysis in Design Cognition Studies: A Systematic Literature Review. *Buildings,* 13(3), 630-654. https://doi.org/10.3390/buildings13030630

Zarzosa, J. (2022). Integrating Transformative Consumer Research into the Marketing Curriculum: A Design Thinking Pedagogical Approach. *Marketing Education Review*, 32(1), 163-168.

Chapter **4**

# Sustainability Reporting, Assurance, and Firm Value

Mohammad Badrul Haider

◆

**Abstract**

Sustainability reporting has become a common practice among leading companies worldwide. To enhance the credibility and completeness of such reporting, an increasing number of companies have also adopted third-party assurance in their reports. The purpose of this chapter is to examine the relationship between assurance in sustainability reporting and firm value. The analysis is based on a sample of 3,783 Japanese companies taken from the Refinitiv Eikon database. Cross-sectional regression analysis using the 2023 sustainability reporting and assurance data is conducted to estimate the variable coefficients. The results indicate that sustainability assurance has a significant positive impact on firm value. These findings have several implications for companies and policymakers, including the fact that the market rewards companies that publish sustainability reports with assurance. This should encourage company management to adopt voluntary assurance services in the future. Regulators can also undertake measures to improve the quality of sustainability reporting, including encouraging the use of assurance services.

**Keywords**

Sustainability reporting, Assurance, Firm value, Japan

## 4.1　Introduction

The last decade has witnessed significant advancements in the sustainability reporting landscape (PricewaterhouseCoopers, 2023). In June 2023, the

International Sustainability Standards Board (ISSB) of the International Financial Reporting Standards (IFRS) Foundation published the first two Sustainability Disclosure Standards in response to investor demand for complete, comparable, and credible disclosure about the social and environmental risks and opportunities of companies (IFRS Foundation, n.d.). In 2021, the European Commission adopted new rules for the Corporate Sustainability Reporting Directive requiring all large companies and listed small and medium-sized enterprises to report their impact on people and the natural environment based on European Sustainability Reporting Standards (ESRS). To harmonize sustainability reporting practice, the European Financial Reporting Advisory Group further issued the ESRS in 2023. The applicability of the ESRS to the entire company value chain ensures that this regulation will have a broad global impact. Published in 2017, the recommendations of the Task Force on Climate-related Financial Disclosures (TCFD) have also significantly influenced climate-related disclosure requirements worldwide. By 2023, some 5,000 organizations across more than 100 countries had publicly supported the TCFD's recommendations (TCFD, 2023).

Nonetheless, while sustainability reporting has become standard practice among the world's largest companies (KPMG, 2022), some academic observers remain concerned about the credibility and completeness of such reporting (O'Dwyer & Owen, 2005). These reports are still considered to disclose a positive and qualitative description of company sustainability initiatives, rather than ensuring social and environmental accountability to stakeholders. Similar to financial audits, assurance in sustainability reporting is considered an important mechanism for enhancing the credibility and quality of sustainability reporting and overcoming the problem of greenwashing (Adams & Evans, 2014). From the company point of view, there has been a steady increase in the adoption of assurance in sustainability reporting. While the assurance adoption rate among G250 companies was only 30% in 2005, this had increased to 63% by 2022 (KPMG, 2022). Nevertheless, early sustainability assurance practices have faced significant criticism for inconsistencies and the apparent lack of rigor (O'Dwyer & Owen, 2005). Recognizing the heightened demand for sustainability disclosure among capital market participants, the International Auditing and Assurance

Standards Board (IAASB) acknowledged the urgency of enhancing the quality of sustainability assurance. Consequently, the IAASB published an exposure draft of a new overarching International Standard on Sustainability Assurance ("ISSA") 5,000, titled General Requirements for Sustainability Assurance. The proposed standard defines sustainability assurance as "…an engagement in which a practitioner aims to obtain sufficient appropriate evidence in order to express a conclusion designed to enhance the degree of confidence of the intended users about the sustainability information"(IAASB, 2023).

While a broad academic literature has investigated the corporate governance and financial determinants of sustainability assurance (Haider & Nishitani, 2022; Martínez-Ferrero & García-Sánchez, 2017), studies concerning the economic consequences of voluntary assurance practice remain limited (Maroun, 2020). Moreover, the available studies about the relationship between sustainability assurance and firm value provide mixed results (Friske *et al.*, 2023; Oware & Appiah, 2022; Thompson *et al.*, 2022). Based on publicly listed companies included in the Fortune 500, Cho *et al.* (2014) concluded that market participants do not value assurance in corporate social responsibility (CSR) reporting in the US, while several other studies have suggested a positive relationship between sustainability assurance and market value (Jeriji & Nasfi, 2023; Khaireddine *et al.*, 2024). In this context, prior research has recognized that the value relevance of sustainability reporting and assurance varies depending on the country and is shaped by the sociopolitical context within which companies function (Coram *et al.*, 2009; Cormier & Magnan, 2007). In an international study encompassing 31 countries, Dhaliwal *et al.* (2014) concluded that the capital market benefits of CSR disclosure are more significant in stakeholder-oriented countries than in less stakeholder-oriented countries. Several studies have thus called for additional work in different geographic regions to obtain a better understanding of the impact of assurance on firm value (Birkey *et al.*, 2016; Uyar *et al.*, 2023). Accordingly, this chapter aims to investigate the impact of sustainability reporting and assurance on firm value using data from Japanese companies.

The research context is significant for several reasons. Despite Japan being a leading country globally in publishing sustainability reports, historically, there has been some reluctance among Japanese companies to adopt assurance services

(Haider & Kokubu, 2015). However, in recent years, there has been a notable shift, with an increasing number of companies opting for third-party assurance in sustainability reporting (KPMG, 2022). In the early 2000s, only a quarter of the top 100 companies pursued assurance services (Haider & Kokubu, 2015; KPMG, 2008), but by 2022, this had surged to 75% (KPMG, 2022). Nonetheless, little is known about the value relevance of sustainability reporting and assurance in Japan. This is important because Japanese corporate governance diverges significantly from the so-called Anglo-American governance model. One reason for this is that it adheres to the principle of internalism, wherein corporate boards are primarily composed of representatives from banks, other financial institutions, and internally promoted managers (Buchanan, 2007). This lies in sharp contrast to the Anglo-American governance model, which emphasizes external monitoring by independent directors. In the last decade, the Japanese government has pursued several initiatives to improve the Japanese corporate governance system, including placing an emphasis on board independence, highlighting the active role of institutional investors, and enhancing the quality and quantity of sustainability disclosure (Ministry of Economy Trade and Industry, 2014; The Council of Experts on the Stewardship Code, 2020; Tokyo Stock Exchange, 2018, 2021). An amendment to the Corporate Governance Code in 2021 also required prime market-listed companies on the Tokyo Stock Exchange to disclose climate-related information based on the TCFD's recommendations.

Consequently, the publication of integrated reports by integrating financial and nonfinancial disclosures has also significantly increased in Japan. Whereas only 23 companies published some kind of integrated reports in 2010, this had increased to 884 companies by 2022 (KPMG AZSA, 2023). The government also supported integrated reporting by publishing the Guidance for Collaborative Value Creation in 2017 (Ministry of Economy Trade and Industry, 2017). In 2023, the Financial Services Agency amended the disclosure regulation, mandating companies to include a separate section on sustainability in their annual Securities Report. According to this amendment, listed companies are required to disclose the governance, strategies, risk management, metrics, and targets of sustainability performance in the Securities Report in an integrated manner. Similar to the ISSB of the IFRS Foundation, the Sustainability Standards Board of Japan (SSBJ) was formed in 2022 to develop local sustainability standards. The SSBJ has already published an exposure draft of its sustainability standards, which are expected to be finalized by April 2025. These standards have been developed with a plan to make sustainability reporting mandatory, potentially affecting more than 4,000 listed Japanese companies (Lawless *et al.*, 2023). Together, these regulatory initiatives are expected to enhance the importance of sustainability reporting and related assurance services. Unfortunately, little research exists on the impact of assurance in sustainability reporting on firm value.

To address this issue, this chapter utilizes cross-sectional data from the Refinitiv Eikon and Corporate Governance Evaluation System (CGES) databases to examine the relationship between assurance in sustainability reporting and firm value in Japan. The results, based on 3,783 observations, show that companies that publish sustainability reports with assurance have higher market values when value is measured in terms of Tobin's Q. The remainder of the chapter proceeds as follows. Section 4.2 reviews the relevant literature and formulates the research hypothesis. Section 4.3 explains the research methods. Section 4.4 discusses the research findings and analysis. Section 4.5 summarizes the chapter.

## 4.2   Literature Review and Hypothesis Development

In a review study, Richardson *et al.* (1999) developed a comprehensive model to examine the relationship between CSR, CSR disclosure, and capital markets. They identified three mechanisms required for the positive impact of CSR disclosure on the capital market: market process impacts, expected cash flow impacts, and capital market preference impacts. Regarding the market process impacts, several studies have argued that CSR information increases the liquidity of the capital market (Dhaliwal *et al.,* 2014) because CSR disclosure reduces the information asymmetry between managers and investors. This enhances the willingness of investors to trade and reduces the transaction costs related to market illiquidity (Dhaliwal *et al.*, 2011). In addition, CSR disclosure reduces uncertainty about future cash flows and encourages financial analysts to follow the firm (Bernardi & Stark, 2018).

For the second mechanism, Richardson *et al.* (1999) argued that CSR can have a positive impact on a firm's financial performance, including its expected cash flows, which are also directly reflected in the capital market. Researchers have identified several benefits of CSR, including increased sales, improved operating efficiencies, and reduced costs (Ambec & Lanoie, 2008). Porter and Kramer (2011) introduced the term "creating shared value" to demonstrate how CSR can enhance firm competitiveness, along with the economic and social conditions of the communities in which they operate. The first mechanism to create shared value is to reconceive products and markets by introducing products and services that address societal needs. This innovation in products and markets differentiates and repositions the company in the traditional market, thereby enhancing the firm financial performance. Porter and Kramer (2011) further demonstrated that investing in advanced technology not only ensures the environmental sustainability of firms, but also yields long-term financial benefits by optimizing resource utilization, enhancing process efficiency, and elevating overall quality standards (Porter & Van Der Linde, 1995). Finally, Porter and Kramer (2011) argued that a company can create shared value by investing in local cluster development, including local infrastructure, suppliers, markets, and related businesses.

Several studies have employed legitimacy theory to explain sustainability reporting practice (Cho & Patten, 2007; Deegan, 2002). These studies consider sustainability reporting as an important tool for legitimatizing firm performance in society. Related studies have also confirmed that CSR enhances firm reputation and brand value (Bebbington *et al.*, 2008). Patten and Zhao (2014) analyzed the CSR reporting of the top 100 US retail companies. They demonstrated that CSR-reporting companies have better environmental reputation scores, which help them increase sales and attract and retain talented employees. Several studies have also argued that companies engage in voluntary CSR and related disclosures as a proactive measure to mitigate potential government efforts to impose costly regulations (Ambec & Lanoie, 2008; Richardson *et al.*, 1999). CSR disclosures could then provide the market with information to assess the likelihood of forthcoming regulatory measures and their potential impact on future cash flows.

Finally, Richardson *et al*. (1999) argue that the capital market reacts positively to CSR disclosure because of investor preference effects. Although all shareholders value cash flows equally, only specific groups, such as long-term institutional and socially responsible investors, truly value CSR performance (Friedman & Heinle, 2016). Some studies have shown that socially responsible investments have increased significantly over the last two decades. For example, the number of signatories to the United Nations' Principles for Responsible Investment increased from only 63 in 2006 to an impressive 5,391 by 2023 (Peng *et al*., 2023). As of 30 March 2021, the total assets under management of these signatories amounted to a staggering 121.3 trillion US dollars. These investors clearly prefer to invest in companies that behave responsibly, even with a lower market rate of return.

Several studies have duly empirically tested the relationship between sustainability reporting and firm market value. However, the results are inconsistent with indications of positive, negative, and no relationship (Richardson & Welker, 2001). Dhaliwal *et al*. (2011) conducted a study analyzing 1,190 standalone CSR reports from 294 firms in the US between 1993 and 2007 as a means of better comprehending the capital market advantages associated with voluntary reporting. Their research revealed that the initiation of CSR reporting influences firm value by reducing the cost of equity capital, attracting institutional investors, enhancing analyst coverage, and mitigating forecast errors and dispersion.

In two international studies, Dhaliwal *et al*. (2012) and Dhaliwal *et al*. (2014) empirically demonstrated the beneficial influence of CSR disclosure on the capital market. Their findings indicated that CSR disclosure enhances analysts' forecast accuracy and reduces the cost of equity capital. Moreover, they provided additional evidence suggesting that this impact is particularly accentuated in stakeholder-oriented countries. In their study, Cormier and Magnan (2007) concluded that the relationship between voluntary environmental disclosure and stock market valuation is influenced by the regulatory and institutional context of companies in that while environmental reporting appeared highly valued by investors in Germany, it did not appear to have a significant impact on market valuation for French and Canadian firms.

Clarkson *et al.* (2013) employed data from five polluting industries in the US in 2003 and 2006 to examine the mechanism through which environmental disclosure enhances firm value. Their findings indicate that voluntary environmental disclosure, whether in the form of standalone reports or web disclosure, has significance for firm valuation, assisting investors in forecasting future expected cash flows and profitability. Notably, the analysis did not identify any relationship between environmental disclosure and the cost of equity capital. Observing a positive relationship between social and environmental disclosure and analyst following in the UK, Bernardi and Stark (2018) concluded that capital market participants find such disclosure value relevant in their decision-making. Later, aiming to delineate the moderating role of environmental, social, and governance (ESG) disclosure in the relationship between ESG performance and firm value, Fatemi *et al.* (2018) investigated publicly listed US companies from 2006 to 2011. Their findings indicated that increased ESG disclosure diminishes the negative impact of poor ESG performance on firm value. They suggested that this phenomenon could be attributed to either disclosures assisting firms in legitimatizing their CSR practices to investors or convincing investors of their genuine efforts to address ESG deficiencies.

In an international study of financial institutions from the top 20 countries in achieving sustainable development goals, Buallay (2019) reported mixed results. While ESG disclosure was seen to have a positive impact on market performance as measured using Tobin's Q, such disclosure was found to be negatively related to operational performance as measured by the return on assets (ROA), and by financial performance as measured by the return on equity. Velte (2017) examined listed companies in Germany from 2010 to 2014. Their findings indicated a positive correlation between ESG performance and firm performance when assessed using ROA, but no significant impact when using Tobin's Q. Zhou *et al.* (2022) conducted a comprehensive investigation utilizing data from 167 companies in China spanning the period from 2014 to 2018. Their findings underscored the significant impact of ESG performance on firm market value, primarily attributed to enhancements in operational capacity. However, they did not find any mediating effect of company profitability or growth capacity on the relationship between ESG and market value. Nakamura (2011) demonstrated that the impact of corporate environmental investment on firm performance varies according to the duration over which the relationship is assessed. Using a sample of 3,237 listed Japanese companies, a significant positive relationship was identified between environmental investment and firm performance, but only over the long term. It was concluded that stakeholders take time to evaluate the outcome of corporate environmental initiatives (CEIs).

Hassel *et al.* (2005) investigated listed companies in Sweden during 1998 and 2000 and estimated a negative correlation between environmental performance and firm value. Aligning with the cost-centered perspective, they posited that investment in environmental initiatives and subsequent improvements in environmental performance carry associated costs, consequently exerting a negative impact on both earnings and market valuation. Later, in a comprehensive international analysis of 6,631 companies from 74 countries in 2015 that utilized data from the Bloomberg ESG database, Xie *et al.* (2019) concluded that ESG disclosure has a complex rather than a simple linear relationship with firm efficiency. Their analysis revealed that ESG disclosure exhibits a positive correlation with corporate efficiency, particularly at moderate levels of disclosure, as opposed to high or low levels of disclosure. Jacobs *et al.* (2010) investigated the impact of environmental performance on shareholder value by analyzing stock market reactions to announcements relating to CEIs and environmental awards and certifications (EACs). Using an event study methodology of 780 CEI and EAC announcements collected from business wire services and daily newspapers in the US and Europe from 2004 to 2006, they showed that the share market is selective in responding to corporate environmental performance announcements.

While these studies consider the impact of sustainability reporting on firm value, several others have extended the literature by incorporating assurance into reporting practice. In general, assurance increases the credibility and quality of disclosed information, thereby reducing information asymmetry between firms and capital markets (Wallace, 1987). Indeed, the efficacy of environmental disclosure in diminishing information asymmetry is significantly enhanced by the inclusion of assurance provisions, which augment user confidence in the reported data (Casey & Grenier, 2015). Khaireddine *et al.* (2024) contributed to this literature by investigating the correlation between sustainability assurance quality and firm value in France, where a robust regulatory framework exists for sustainability reporting and assurance. Examining data from 2010 to 2020 across the 40 largest French companies, they revealed a significant positive impact of sustainability assurance quality on firm value. Additionally, they found that this relationship was strengthened by the adoption of ISO standards for measuring corporate environmental performance. On this basis, the analysis concluded that high-quality sustainability assurance not only enhances a firm's reputation, but also mitigates social and environmental risks, thereby fostering increased trust among stakeholders and influencing financial markets. Rivière-Giordano *et al.* (2018) conducted an experimental study of 108 financial analysts in France prior to 2012, when environmental assurance was still voluntary. They showed that investors react negatively to assurance statements with a limited (low) level of assurance. They then argued that rather than the mere presence of assurance, it is the level of assurance of environmental disclosure that most affects investor decision-making.

In their experimental analysis of 213 professional investors in Thailand, Pratoomsuwan and Chiaravutthi (2023) showed that assurance increases the credibility and usefulness of CSR information in various settings. Their findings indicated that investors are more inclined to invest when positive CSR is confirmed through third-party assurance, irrespective of whether the CSR is material or immaterial. More recently, Friske *et al.* (2023) used signaling theory to test the competing hypotheses of whether sustainability reporting provides positive or negative signals to the market. Based on a sample of 9,077 firm-year observations from 2011 to 2020, their analysis showed that there is an evolving relationship between sustainability reporting and firm value, in that while sustainability reporting is initially a costly signal, it eventually enhances firm value as companies learn how to communicate sustainability initiatives to stakeholders more effectively and investors learn how to evaluate reports properly. Moreover, the findings evidenced that the external assurance of sustainability reports not only bolsters the credibility of disclosed information, but also signifies organizational commitment to transparency, thereby influencing market valuation.

In 2018, Malaysia introduced a revised edition of sustainability reporting guidelines, including a detailed provision of assurance of such reports. Bakry *et al*. (2023) investigated the top 100 listed companies in Malaysia and showed that these regulatory initiatives had significantly improved the extent of CSR reporting. The analysis also revealed that elevated levels of CSR reporting, coupled with assurance provision, generated "CSR goodwill", leading to a subsequent increase in market value for firms. In an examination of Indian manufacturing companies from 2010 to 2019, Sreepriya *et al*. (2023) found a significant positive relationship between sustainability disclosure and firm value. They argued that sustainability reporting affects the capital market by enhancing organizational transparency and reputation and demonstrating a strong commitment to social and environmental performance.

Drawing on legitimacy and stakeholder theory, Thompson *et al*. (2022) investigated the significance of sustainability reporting, along with related assurance services and the involvement of various assurance providers, in South Africa. Their analysis, based on a sample of the top 100 companies listed on the Johannesburg Stock Exchange, revealed a positive correlation between sustainability reporting and firm value. Moreover, the analysis highlighted the pivotal role of assurance in bolstering the credibility of sustainability reporting, consequently amplifying firm value. However, the results did not unveil any discernible link between the type of assurance provider and firm value. Overall, the findings inferred that the disclosure of sustainability information not only enriches firm reputation in the eyes of stakeholders, but also translates into tangible enhancements in firm value. On this basis, the study called for international studies to understand better the value relevance of sustainability assurance from different sociopolitical and regulatory contexts. Grassmann *et al*. (2022) conducted an international study analyzing 176 assurance statements from the integrated reports of Forbes Global companies between 2013 and 2015. They found that the inclusion of an assurance statement in an integrated report significantly reduced information asymmetry. However, they did not find a significant impact of the quality of the assurance statement on the credibility of reported information. Examining the South African context, Caglio *et al*. (2020) further elucidated the economic advantages of assurance in integrated reporting, specifically in enhancing market value, bolstering stock liquidity, and diminishing analysts' forecast dispersion.

Fuhrmann *et al.* (2017) concluded from their examination of assurance statements in European countries that the presence of an assurance statement alone does not directly correlate with information asymmetry. Rather, they revealed that the quality of the assurance process plays a significant role in determining the credibility of sustainability reporting and the degree of information asymmetry. Gerwanski *et al.* (2022) conducted an experimental study of nonprofessional investors and delivered mixed results about the benefits of assurance in integrated reporting. Reflecting upon the principles of agency theory, certain investors perceive assurance as an important corporate governance mechanism to limit managerial opportunism, reduce information asymmetry, and bolster investor confidence. However, skepticism persists among certain investors regarding the tangible advantages of assurance in integrated reporting, including doubts about the intrinsic value of integrated reporting, inconsistencies, and deficiencies in the quality of sustainability assurance.

In another experimental study involving 104 professional investors, Reimsbach *et al.* (2018) demonstrated that the assurance of sustainability information has a positive impact on how professional investors evaluate a company's sustainability performance, resulting in increased significance attributed to this data in their investment decisions. In an international study encompassing a large sample of 58,105 firm-year observations spanning from 2004 to 2019, Elbardan *et al.* (2023) investigated the economic incentives of CSR reporting and its associated assurance practices. Utilizing Tobin's Q to measure firm value and the volatility of Tobin's Q to assess firm risk, the findings provided incremental evidence indicating a positive correlation between nonfinancial reporting and assurance with firm value, and a negative correlation with firm risk. Oware and Appiah (2022) studied Indian stock exchange-listed companies, analyzing 800 firm-year observations from 2010 to 2019. Their findings suggested that sustainability assurance does not bolster communication or transparency, and thus does not affect investor decision-making.

In another study, Jeriji and Nasfi (2023) investigated the mandatory sustainability assurance frameworks in France and South Africa, revealing a positive correlation between sustainability assurance and firm value. Their results highlighted several benefits of sustainability assurance, including the enhancement of firm legitimacy and reputation, the provision of additional information about firm risks, future performance, and strategies, and the enhancement of the credibility of sustainability reports.

Horn *et al*. (2018) conducted an examination of CSR reporting among the top 100 companies in South Africa using data sourced from KPMG surveys conducted in 2008, 2011, and 2013. Their analysis revealed no significant relationship between CSR disclosure and Tobin's Q, but did indicate a significant negative correlation between CSR assurance and Tobin's Q. Consequently, it was concluded that sustainability reporting and assurance fail to enhance firm value within the context of South Africa. In a 2024 study of 220 Indian companies from 2018 to 2020, Narula *et al*. (2024) reported a significant negative correlation between social and environmental disclosure and firm performance, as measured by ROA, the return on capital, and Tobin's Q. They argued that ESG disclosure increases firm cost burdens, putting them at a competitive disadvantage. On this basis, they concluded that the benefits of ESG disclosure have yet to be realized in India.

In their analysis, Landau *et al*. (2020) examined the top 50 companies listed in European countries from 2010 to 2016. Utilizing the Ohlson model, they found that integrated reporting has a significant negative impact on the market value of firms. It was thus concluded that the costs associated with producing integrated reports, along with proprietary costs linked to disclosing supplementary information, could result in a diminished market value for the companies involved. Weber (2018) argued that the CSR performance of companies is an important variable in determining the relationship between CSR disclosure and the cost of equity capital. Examining 878 CSR reports from the US, there was no difference identified between good and poor CSR performers regarding the impact of CSR reporting on the cost of equity capital. However, the analysis showed that only poor CSR performers can benefit from a lower cost of equity capital by issuing CSR reports with external assurance. It was thus concluded that companies with poor CSR performance have a greater motivation to publish CSR reports with external assurance to demonstrate a strong commitment to CSR, enhance credibility, and address concerns about greenwashing.

Instead of viewing CSR reporting solely as a signal to investors, Birkey *et al.* (2016) argued that assurance in standalone CSR reporting enhances the corporate environmental image. Based on a sample of the 351 greenest companies in the US during 2009 and 2010, and after controlling for several corporate financial and environmental performance variables, they demonstrated a positive association between assurance in CSR reporting and environmental reputation scores. However, they did not identify any impact of assurance providers (whether accounting or other firms) on corporate environmental reputation, implying that the presence of assurance is more important than the provider. Finally, they also called for additional studies from stakeholder-oriented countries to examine the impact of assurance on corporate environmental reputation in more detail.

This survey of the literature indicates that a wide range of studies has been conducted to examine the value relevance of sustainability reporting and accompanying assurance services. Although the findings are inclusive, an increasing number of more recent studies have identified a positive relationship between sustainability reporting, assurance, and firm value. Consistent with these findings, we hypothesize that sustainability reporting and assurance will positively impact the market value of a firm. The rationale behind this is that sustainability reporting and assurance reduce information asymmetry between management and investors by providing relevant information about the firm's social and environmental performance and reducing uncertainty about future performance. In turn, this enhances the liquidity of the firm's shares and reduces the firm's cost of capital (Richardson *et al.*, 1999). The publication of sustainability reports with third-party assurance also demonstrates a strong organizational commitment to accountability for social and environmental impacts, resulting in several economic benefits, such as increased sales, the attraction and retention of talented employees, enhanced reputation, and appeals to socially responsible investors. Accordingly, I formulate the following hypothesis to be tested:

$H_1$: There is a positive relationship between sustainability reporting, assurance, and firm value.

## 4.3 Research Method

### 4.3.1 Sample and Data

The sample used in this analysis is drawn from Japanese companies available in the Refinitiv Eikon database. As a cross-sectional model, we analyze the sustainability reporting and accompanying assurance statements of companies published in 2023, with the sample downloaded on March 12, 2024. The initial sample consisted of 4,226 firms. After excluding companies with missing data, the final sample comprises 3,783 companies. Variable data are collected from two sources, the Refinitiv Eikon database and the Nikkei NEEDS CGES, both of which are widely used in the sustainability reporting literature (Elbardan *et al.*, 2023; Haider & Nishitani, 2022).

### 4.3.2 Regression Model

To examine the relationship between sustainability reporting, assurance, and firm value, we employ the following regression model, which is consistent with the prior literature on sustainability reporting and firm value (Thompson *et al.*, 2022).

**Tobin's Q = $\beta_0$ + $\beta_1$ SR_Assurance + $\beta_2$ ROA + $\beta_3$ Leverage + $\beta_4$ Firm_Size + $\beta_5$ Brd_Size + $\beta_6$ Brd_Indep + $\beta_7$ Brd_Gender + $\varepsilon$**

Following several prior studies that have used Tobin's Q as a dependent variable in valuation models (Bakry *et al.*, 2023; Khaireddine *et al.*, 2024), I also specify Tobin's Q as a proxy for the market value of firms. Tobin's Q is calculated as the sum of market capitalization and total liabilities divided by total assets. Sustainability reporting and assurance (SR_Assurance) is the main variable of interest in this study and is measured as an ordinal variable. Companies that did not publish sustainability reports are coded as 0, companies that published sustainability reports without assurance are coded as 1, and companies that published sustainability reports with third-party assurance are coded as 2. Consistent with prior studies (Oware & Appiah, 2022; Thompson *et al.*, 2022), I also control for the influence of several variables to avoid any biases in the regression analysis. The control variables are: return on assets (ROA), total assets to total liabilities ratio (Leverage), firm size (Firm_Size), measured using the log of sales revenue, board size (Brd_Size), as proxied by the number of board of directors, board independence (Brd_Indep), being the ratio of outside directors to the total number of board directors, and board gender diversity (Brd_Gender), as measured by the number of female directors to the total number of board directors.

## 4.4 Findings and Analysis

**Table 4.1** provides descriptive statistics for the variables. The table shows that approximately 11% of the sample companies published sustainability reports in 2023, 5.8% of which had adopted assurance in their reports. The mean value of Tobin's Q is 1.531 with a maximum of 38.718 and a minimum of 0.353. The average ROA is 3.315%. The mean values of total assets to total liabilities (leverage) and log of sales are 2.859 and 10.481, respectively. On average, the boards of sampled companies consist of eight directors, with a minimum of three

**Table 4.1**  Descriptive Statistics

| Variable | Mean | Std. dev. | Min. | Max. |
|---|---|---|---|---|
| Tobin's Q | 1.531 | 1.655 | 0.353 | 38.718 |
| SR_Assurance | 0.168 | 0.505 | 0 | 2 |
| No SR | 0.890 | 0.313 | 0 | 1 |
| SR without assurance | 0.052 | 0.222 | 0 | 1 |
| SR with assurance | 0.058 | 0.234 | 0 | 1 |
| ROA | 3.315 | 10.976 | −151.146 | 266.651 |
| Leverage | 2.859 | 2.268 | 0.522 | 37.759 |
| Firm_Size | 10.481 | 0.838 | 5.724 | 13.570 |
| Brd_Size | 8.012 | 2.501 | 3 | 20 |
| Brd_Indep | 0.395 | 0.135 | 0 | 0.889 |
| Brd_Gender | 0.135 | 0.128 | 0 | 1 |

Notes: No SR denotes companies that did not publish sustainability reports. SR without assurance represents companies that published sustainability reports without assurance. SR with assurance represents companies that published sustainability reports with assurance. Total number of observations was 3,783.

### Table 4.2  Correlation Coefficients

| | Tobin's Q | SR_ Assurance | ROA | Lever- age | Firm_ Size | Brd_ Size | Brd_ Indep | Brd_ Gender |
|---|---|---|---|---|---|---|---|---|
| Tobin's Q | 1 | | | | | | | |
| SR_Assurance | −0.036 | 1 | | | | | | |
| ROA | −0.041 | 0.047 | 1 | | | | | |
| Leverage | 0.093 | −0.065 | 0.028 | 1 | | | | |
| Firm_Size | −0.243 | 0.594 | 0.213 | −0.247 | 1 | | | |
| Brd_Size | −0.139 | 0.290 | 0.084 | −0.115 | 0.520 | 1 | | |
| Brd_Indep | 0.120 | 0.168 | −0.003 | 0.009 | 0.178 | 0.044 | 1 | |
| Brd_Gender | 0.069 | 0.250 | 0.039 | −0.037 | 0.239 | −0.010 | 0.256 | 1 |

Notes: This table provides the correlation coefficients between the research variables. The largest correlation coefficient, 0.594, is between firm size and assurance in sustainability reporting. Consequently, multicollinearity is not a major concern in the research model.

### Table 4.3  Regression Results

| Tobin's Q | Coefficient | Std. err. | t-stat. |
|---|---|---|---|
| SR_Assurance | 0.467 | 0.064*** | 7.31 |
| ROA | 0.004 | 0.002* | 1.85 |
| Leverage | 0.007 | 0.012 | 0.58 |
| Firm_Size | −0.761 | 0.046*** | −16.65 |
| Brd_Size | 0.009 | 0.012 | 0.75 |
| Brd_Indp | 1.743 | 0.198*** | 8.82 |
| Brd_Gender | 1.140 | 0.214*** | 5.32 |
| _cons | 8.475 | 0.442*** | 19.17 |
| | | | |
| No. of Obs. | | 3,783 | |
| F(7, 3775) | | 66.30*** | |
| Adj. R squared | | 0.108 | |

***, **, and * denote significance at the 1%, 5%, and 10% levels, respectively.

and a maximum of 20. While the mean value of the ratio of outside to total directors is 39.5%, on average, 13.5% of the board members are female.

**Table 4.3** presents the results of the regression estimation. The regression model is significant, with a F-statistic of 66.30 ($p$-value < 0.000) and an adjusted $R^2$ of 10.8%. The estimated coefficients indicate that the variable of interest, SR_

Assurance, is positively related to Tobin's Q and significant at the 1% level. Accordingly, the estimate supports the research hypothesis. This implies that companies publishing sustainability reports with third-party assurance have higher market values. In other words, the regression analysis confirms the value relevance of sustainability reporting and assurance in Japan. This finding is in line with the increasing number of studies that have found a positive relationship between sustainability reporting assurance and firm value (Khaireddine *et al.*, 2024; Maher & Nasfi, 2023; Thompson *et al.*, 2022; Velte, 2021). Among the control variables, corporate characteristics such as ROA, board independence, and board gender diversity have a significant positive impact on firm value. Conversely, firm size as represented by the log of sales revenue has a negative impact on firm value.

The positive impact of sustainability reporting and assurance on firm value as found can be explained from several different perspectives. Sustainability reporting and associated assurance, which enhance the credibility of the reported information, reduce information asymmetry between managers and investors. This disclosure reduces uncertainties about future cash flows and encourages financial analysts to follow the firm (Dhaliwal *et al.*, 2011, 2012). These factors then increase investors' willingness to trade and positively affect market liquidity. Studies have shown that sustainability reporting and assurance provide incremental information about firms' future performance (Jeriji & Nasfi, 2023). This information could be related to the positive impact of investment in CSR projects, a reduced future regulatory burden, and enhanced company reputations, which further helps firms increase sales and attract and retain talented employees (Richardson *et al.*, 1999). All of these factors positively impact future expected cash flow and, consequently, market value. Finally, socially responsible investors, such as long-term institutional investors, prefer to invest in companies with a better CSR reputation, even with a lower rate of return.

## 4.5   Conclusion

Sustainability reporting has become common practice among the largest companies worldwide. An increasing number of companies also have adopted third-party assurance in such reporting to improve the credibility of such reporting. However, the strand of academic research examining the impact of sustainability reporting and assurance on firm value has provided inconclusive findings. This study aimed to explore the relationship between sustainability reporting assurance and firm value utilizing data from Japanese companies. The sample companies were collected from the Refinitiv Eikon database. Cross-sectional regression of 3,783 companies showed that sustainability reporting assurance has a significant positive impact on firm value as measured by Tobin's Q. This implies that firms publishing sustainability reporting with assurance have higher market values. In other words, sustainability reporting and assurance provide value relevant information to the market. This finding is in line with the increasing number of studies that have also demonstrated the value relevance of sustainability reporting and assurance practice.

There are several reasons for the positive relationship between sustainability assurance and firm value. First, sustainability reporting and assurance reduce information asymmetry between management and investors, and this enhances the liquidity of the company's shares. Nonfinancial reporting also enhances the reputation and legitimacy of companies, brings several economic benefits, such as increased revenues and reduced operational costs, and attracts socially responsible investors, thereby positively impacting the whole capital market. While prior studies have mostly examined the Western context, little remains known about the value relevance of sustainability reporting and assurance practice in Japan. This study contributes to the literature by providing evidence from Japan, which has a very different socioeconomic and regulatory context.

The present findings have several implications. Although the regulatory environment of sustainability reporting is changing rapidly, while sustainability reporting remains a voluntary practice, third-party assurance in sustainability reporting is also voluntary. The finding that sustainability reporting and assurance enhances firm value may encourage management to publish higher quality and more credible reports. The capital market benefits of sustainability reporting and assurance would also be important to policymakers and regulators. As noted earlier, the Japanese government has undertaken several initiatives to improve corporate governance practices, including sustainability and integrated reporting. The stewardship code also encourages institutional investors to consider the sustainability performance of companies in their investment decisions. Investors are responding positively to these policies as they value highly companies that publish sustainability reporting with assurance. My findings thus support the effectiveness of recent regulatory initiatives regarding sustainability reporting in Japan.

Of course, the findings should be interpreted after considering some limitations of the analysis. First, as a cross-sectional study, I could only consider the relationship between sustainability reporting and assurance practice in a single year. This could be extended by conducting a longitudinal analysis to provide a more comprehensive understanding of the relationship between sustainability reporting and firm value. Second, as a voluntary practice, assurance in sustainability reporting is provided by a variety of parties, including accounting firms, certification firms, consulting firms, nongovernmental organizations, and individual experts. As I did not distinguish between the assurance provided by different service providers, future studies could examine whether the market values assurance differently when provided by different service providers.

## ● References

Adams, C. A., & Evans, R. (2014). Accountability, Completeness, Credibility and the Audit Expectations Gap. *Journal of Corporate Citizenship*, 2004(14), 97-115. https://doi.org/10.9774/GLEAF.4700.2004.SU.00010

Ambec, S., & Lanoie, P. (2008). Does It Pay to Be Green? A Systematic Overview Executive Overview. *Academy of Management Perspectives*, 22(4), 45-62. https://doi.org/https://doi.org/10.5465/amp.2008.35590353

Bakry, A. E. A., Azhar, Z., & Kishan, K. (2023). The effects of amended sustainability reporting requirements on corporate social responsibility reporting and firm value: the moderating role of assurance. *Journal of Financial Reporting and Accounting, ahead-of-print*(ahead-of-print). https://doi.org/10.1108/JFRA-11-2022-0414/FULL/XML

Bebbington, J., Larrinaga, C., & Moneva, J. M. (2008). Corporate social reporting and reputation risk management. *Accounting, Auditing & Accountability Journal*, 21(3), 337–361. https://doi.org/10.1108/09513570810863932/FULL/PDF

Bernardi, C., & Stark, A. W. (2018). *On the value relevance of information on environmental and social activities and performance-Some evidence from the UK stock market.* https://doi.org/10.1016/j.jaccpubpol.2018.07.001

Birkey, R. N., Michelon, G., Patten, D. M., & Sankara, J. (2016). Does assurance on CSR reporting enhance environmental reputation? An examination in the U.S. context. *Accounting Forum*, 40, 143-152. https://doi.org/10.1016/j.accfor.2016.07.001

Buallay, A. (2019). Between cost and value: Investigating the effects of sustainability reporting on a firm's performance. *Journal of Applied Accounting Research*, 20(4), 481-496. https://doi.org/10.1108/JAAR-12-2017-0137/FULL/XML

Buchanan, J. (2007). Japanese corporate governance and the principle of "internalism." *Corporate Governance: An International Review*, 15(1), 27-35. https://doi.org/https://doi.org/10.1111/j.1467-8683.2007.00539.x

Caglio, A., Melloni, G., & Perego, P. (2020). Informational Content and Assurance of Textual Disclosures: Evidence on Integrated Reporting. *European Accounting Review*, 29(1), 55-83. https://doi.org/10.1080/09638180.2019.1677486

Casey, R. J., & Grenier, J. H. (2015). Understanding and Contributing to the Enigma of Corporate Social Responsibility (CSR) Assurance in the United States. *AUDITING: A Journal of Practice & Theory*, 34(1), 97-130. https://doi.org/10.2308/AJPT-50736

Cho, C. H., Michelon, G., Patten, D. M., & Roberts, R. W. (2014). CSR report assurance in the USA: An empirical investigation of determinants and effects. *Sustainability Accounting, Management and Policy Journal*, 5(2), 130-148. https://doi.org/10.1108/SAMPJ-01-2014-0003

Cho, C. H., & Patten, D. M. (2007). The role of environmental disclosures as tools of legitimacy: A research note. *Accounting, Organizations and Society*, 32(7-8), 639-647. https://doi.org/10.1016/J.AOS.2006.09.009

Clarkson, P. M., Fang, X., Li, Y., & Richardson, G. (2013). The relevance of environmental disclosures: Are such disclosures incrementally informative? *Journal of Accounting and Public Policy*, 32(5), 410-431. https://doi.org/10.1016/J.JACCPUBPOL.2013.06.008

Coram, P. J., Monroe, G. S., & Woodliff, D. R. (2009). The Value of Assurance on Voluntary Nonfinancial Disclosure: An Experimental Evaluation. *AUDITING: A Journal of Practice & Theory*, 28(1), 137-151. https://doi.org/10.2308/AUD.2009.28.1.137

Cormier, D., & Magnan, M. (2007). *The revisited contribution of environmental reporting to investors' valuation of a firm's earnings: An international perspective*. https://doi.org/10.1016/j.ecolecon.2006.07.030

Deegan, C. (2002). Introduction: The legitimising effect of social and environmental disclosures – a theoretical foundation. *Accounting, Auditing & Accountability Journal*, 15(3), 282-311. https://doi.org/10.1108/09513570210435852/FULL/XML

Dhaliwal, D. S., Li, O. Z., Tsang, A., & Yang, Y. G. (2011). Voluntary Nonfinancial Disclosure and the Cost of Equity Capital: The Initiation of Corporate Social Responsibility Reporting. *The Accounting Review*, 86(1), 59-100. https://doi.org/10.2308/ACCR.00000005

Dhaliwal, D. S., Li, O. Z., Tsang, A., & Yang, Y. G. (2014). Corporate social responsibility disclosure and the cost of equity capital: The roles of stakeholder orientation and financial transparency. *Journal of Accounting and Public Policy*, 33(4). https://doi.org/10.1016/j.jaccpubpol.2014.04.006

Dhaliwal, D. S., Radhakrishnan, S., Tsang, A., & Yang, Y. G. (2012). Nonfinancial Disclosure and Analyst Forecast Accuracy: International Evidence on Corporate Social Responsibility Disclosure. *The Accounting Review*, 87(3), 723-759. https://doi.org/10.2308/ACCR-10218

Elbardan, H., Uyar, A., Kuzey, C., & Karaman, A. S. (2023). CSR reporting, assurance, and firm value and risk: The moderating effects of CSR committees and executive compensation. *Journal of International Accounting, Auditing and Taxation*, 53, 100579. https://doi.org/10.1016/J.INTACCAUDTAX.2023.100579

Fatemi, A., Glaum, M., & Kaiser, S. (2018). ESG performance and firm value: The moderating role of disclosure. *Global Finance Journal*, 38, 45-64. https://doi.org/10.1016/J.GFJ.2017.03.001

Friedman, H. L., & Heinle, M. S. (2016). Taste, information, and asset prices: implications for the valuation of CSR. *Review of Accounting Studies*, 21(3), 740-767. https://doi.org/10.1007/S11142-016-9359-X/METRICS

Friske, W., Hoelscher, S. A., & Nikolov, A. N. (2023). The impact of voluntary sustainability reporting on firm value: Insights from signaling theory. *Journal of the Academy of Marketing Science*, 51(2), 372-392. https://doi.org/10.1007/S11747-022-00879-2/TABLES/4

Fuhrmann, S., Ott, C., Looks, E., & Guenther, T. W. (2017). The contents of assurance statements for sustainability reports and information asymmetry. *Accounting and Business Research*, 47(4), 369-400. https://doi.org/10.1080/00014788.2016.1263550

Gerwanski, J., Velte, P., & Mechtel, M. (2022). Do nonprofessional investors value the assurance of integrated reports? Exploratory evidence. *European Management Journal*, 40(1), 103-126. https://doi.org/10.1016/J.EMJ.2021.03.003

Grassmann, M., Fuhrmann, S., & Guenther, T. W. (2022). Assurance quality, disclosed connectivity of the capitals and information asymmetry – An interaction analysis for the case of integrated reporting. *Meditari Accountancy Research*, 30(3), 852-892. https://doi.org/10.1108/MEDAR-11-2020-1087/FULL/XML

Haider, M. B., & Kokubu, K. (2015). Assurance and third-party comment in sustainability reporting in Japan: A descriptive study. *International Journal of Environment and Sustainable Development*, 14(3), 207-230. https://doi.org/10.1504/IJESD.2015.070133

Haider, M. B., & Nishitani, K. (2022). Ownership structure, corporate governance, and assurance in sustainability reporting: evidence from Japan. *International Journal of Disclosure and Governance*, 19(4), 374-388. https://doi.org/10.1057/S41310-022-00149-1/METRICS

Hassel, L., Nilsson, H., & Nyquist, S. (2005). The value relevance of environmental performance. *European Accounting Review*, 14(1), 41-61. https://doi.org/10.1080/0963818042000279722

Horn, R., de Klerk, M., & de Villiers, C. (2018). The association between corporate social responsibility reporting and firm value for South African firms. *South African Journal of Economic and Management Sciences*, 21(1). https://doi.org/10.4102/SAJEMS.V21I1.2236

IAASB. (2023). *Proposed International Standard on Sustainability Assurance 5000 General Requirements for Sustainability Assurance Engagements and Proposed Conforming and Consequential Amendments to Other IAASB Standards*.

IFRS Foundation. (n.d.). *IFRS - General Sustainability-related Disclosures*. Retrieved July 3, 2024, from https://www.ifrs.org/projects/completed-projects/2023/general-sustainability-related-disclosures/#about

Jacobs, B. W., Singhal, V. R., & Subramanian, R. (2010). An empirical investigation of environmental performance and the market value of the firm. *Journal of Operations Management*, 28(5),

430-441. https://doi.org/10.1016/J.JOM.2010.01.001

Jeriji, M., & Nasfi, A. (2023). The value relevance of mandatory sustainability reporting assurance. *South African Journal of Accounting Research*, 37(2), 122-138. https://doi.org/10.1080/1029195 4.2022.2148887

Khaireddine, H., Lacombe, I., & Jarboui, A. (2024). The trilogy in sustainability of environmental performance, assurance quality and firm value. *Sustainability Accounting, Management and Policy Journal*, 15(2), 482-519. https://doi.org/10.1108/SAMPJ-07-2022-0352

KPMG. (2008). *KPMG International survey of corporate responsibility reporting 2008*.

KPMG. (2022). *Big Shifts, Small Steps-Survey of Sustainability Reporting 2022*. https://assets. kpmg.com/content/dam/kpmg/se/pdf/komm/2022/Global-Survey-of-Sustainability-Reporting-2022.pdf

KPMG AZSA. (2023). *Survey of Corporate Reports in Japan 2022*. https://assets.kpmg.com/content/ dam/kpmg/jp/pdf/2023/jp-en-sustainable-value-corporate-reporting-eng-1.pdf

Landau, A., Rochell, J., Klein, C., & Zwergel, B. (2020). Integrated reporting of environmental, social, and governance and financial data: Does the market value integrated reports? *Business Strategy and the Environment*, 29(4), 1750-1763. https://doi.org/10.1002/BSE.2467

Lawless, K., Ushijima, K., & Hara, K. (2023). *What's next for Japanese sustainability disclosure standards*. https://www.ey.com/en_jp/sustainability/whats-next-for-japanese-sustainability-disclosure-standards

Maher, J., & Nasfi, A. (2023). The value relevance of mandatory sustainability reporting assurance. *South African Journal of Accounting Research*, 37(2), 122-138. https://doi.org/10.1080/1029195 4.2022.2148887

Maroun, W. (2020). A Conceptual Model for Understanding Corporate Social Responsibility Assurance Practice. *Journal of Business Ethics*, 161, 187-209. https://doi.org/10.1007/s10551-018-3909-z

Martínez-Ferrero, J., & García-Sánchez, I. M. (2017). Sustainability assurance and assurance providers: Corporate governance determinants in stakeholder-oriented countries. *Journal of Management and Organization*, 23(5), 1-24. https://doi.org/https://doi.org/10.1017/jmo.2016.65

Ministry of Economy Trade and Industry. (2014). *Ito review of competitiveness and incentives for sustainable growth - Building favorable relationships between companies and investors* (Issue August). http://www.meti.go.jp/english/press/2014/pdf/0806_04b.pdf

Ministry of Economy Trade and Industry. (2017). *Guidance for integrated corporate disclosure and company-investor dialogue for collaborative value creation (Guidance for collaborative value creation)*. https://www.meti.go.jp/english/press/2017/pdf/0529_004b.pdf

Nakamura, E. (2011). Does Environmental Investment Really Contribute to Firm Performance? An Empirical Analysis Using Japanese Firms. *Eurasian Business Review*, 1(2), 91-111. https:// doi.org/10.14208/BF03353800/METRICS

Narula, R., Rao, P., Kumar, S., & Matta, R. (2024). ESG scores and firm performance- evidence from emerging market. *International Review of Economics & Finance*, 89, 1170-1184. https:// doi.org/10.1016/J.IREF.2023.08.024

O'Dwyer, B., & Owen, D. L. (2005). Assurance statement practice in environmental, social and sustainability reporting: a critical evaluation. *The British Accounting Review*, 37(2), 205-229. https://doi.org/10.1016/J.BAR.2005.01.005

Oware, K. M., & Appiah, K. (2022). CSR assurance practice and financial distress likelihood: evidence from India. *Meditari Accountancy Research*, 30(6), 1470-1492. https://doi.org/10.1108/MEDAR-10-2020-1055/FULL/XML

Patten, D. M., & Zhao, N. (2014). Standalone CSR reporting by U.S. retail companies. *Accounting Forum*, 38(2), 132-144. https://doi.org/10.1016/J.ACCFOR.2014.01.002

Peng, H., Zhang, Z., Goodell, J. W., & Li, M. (2023). Socially responsible investing: Is it for real or just for show? *International Review of Financial Analysis*, 86, 102553. https://doi.org/10.1016/J.IRFA.2023.102553

Porter, M. E., & Kramer, M. R. (2011). Creating Shared Value-How to reinvent capitalism—and unleash a wave of innovation and growth. *Harvard Business Review* . https://hbr.org/2011/01/the-big-idea-creating-shared-value

Porter, M. E., & Van Der Linde, C. (1995). Toward a New Conception of the Environment-Competitiveness Relationship. *Journal of Economic Perspectives*, 9(4), 97-118. https://doi.org/DOI: 10.1257/jep.9.4.97

Pratoomsuwan, T., & Chiaravutthi, Y. (2023). Willingness to invest and the assurance of corporate social responsibility reports. *Corporate Social Responsibility and Environmental Management*, 30(1), 192-208. https://doi.org/10.1002/CSR.2348

PricewaterhouseCoopers. (2023). *Sustainability Counts II-State of Sustainability Reporting in Asia Pacific*. https://www.pwc.com/gx/en/issues/esg/asia-pac-esg/sustainability-counts-2023.pdf

Reimsbach, D., Hahn, R., & Gürtürk, A. (2018). Integrated Reporting and Assurance of Sustainability Information: An Experimental Study on Professional Investors' Information Processing. *European Accounting Review*, 27(3), 559-581. https://doi.org/10.1080/09638180.2016.1273787

Richardson, A. J., & Welker, M. (2001). Social disclosure, financial disclosure and the cost of equity capital. *Accounting, Organizations and Society*, 26(7-8), 597-616. https://doi.org/10.1016/S0361-3682(01)00025-3

Richardson, A. J., Welker, M., & Hutchinson, I. R. (1999). Managing capital market reactions to corporate social responsibility. *International Journal of Management Reviews*, 1(1), 17-43. https://doi.org/https://doi.org/10.1111/1468-2370.00003

Rivière-Giordano, G., Giordano-Spring, S., & Cho, C. H. (2018). Does the level of assurance statement on environmental disclosure affect investor assessment?: An experimental study. *Sustainability Accounting, Management and Policy Journal*, 9(3), 336-360. https://doi.org/10.1108/SAMPJ-03-2018-0054/FULL/PDF

Sreepriya, J., Suprabha, K. R., & Prasad, K. (2023). Does GRI compliance moderate the impact of sustainability disclosure on firm value? *Society and Business Review*, 18(1), 152-174. https://doi.org/10.1108/SBR-06-2022-0172/FULL/XML

TCFD. (2023). *Task Force on Climate-related Financial Disclosures 2023 Status Report*. https://assets.bbhub.io/company/sites/60/2023/09/2023-Status-Report.pdf

The Council of Experts on the Stewardship Code. (2020). *Principles for Responsible Institutional Investors Japan's Stewardship Code -To promote sustainable growth of companies through in-*

*vestment and dialogue-The Council of Experts on the Stewardship Code (FY2019).*

Thompson, K. E., Ashimwe, O., Buertey, S., Chi Minh City, H., & Kim, S.-Y. (2022). The value relevance of sustainability reporting: does assurance and the type of assurer matter? *Sustainability Accounting, Management and Policy Journal*, 13(4), 858-877. https://doi.org/10.1108/ SAMPJ-08-2021-0329

Tokyo Stock Exchange. (2018). Japan's corporate governance code:Seeking sustainable corporate growth and increased corporate value over the mid- to long-term. In *Tokyo Stock Exchange*. https://www.jpx.co.jp/english/news/1020/b5b4pj000000jvxr-att/20180602_en.pdf

Tokyo Stock Exchange. (2021). *Japan's Corporate Governance Code Seeking Sustainable Corporate Growth and Increased Corporate Value over the Mid-to Long-Term*. https://www.jpx.co.jp/english/equities/listing/cg/tvdivq0000008jdy-att/20210611.pdf

Uyar, A., Elmassri, M., Kuzey, C., & Karaman, A. S. (2023). Does external assurance stimulate higher CSR performance in subsequent periods? The moderating effect of governance and firm visibility. *Corporate Governance (Bingley)*, 23(4), 677-704. https://doi.org/10.1108/CG-04-2022-0188/FULL/PDF

Velte, P. (2017). Does ESG performance have an impact on financial performance? Evidence from Germany. *Journal of Global Responsibility*, 8(2), 169-178. https://doi.org/10.1108/JGR-11-2016-0029/FULL/XML

Velte, P. (2021). Determinants and consequences of corporate social responsibility assurance: a systematic review of archival research. *Society and Business Review*, 16(1), 1-25. https://doi.org/10.1108/SBR-05-2020-0077/FULL/XML

Wallace, W. A. (1987). The economic role of the audit in free and regulated markets: A review. *Research in Accounting Regulation*, 1, 7-34.

Weber, J. L. (2018). Corporate social responsibility disclosure level, external assurance and cost of equity capital. *Journal of Financial Reporting and Accounting*, 16(4), 694-724. https://doi.org/10.1108/JFRA-12-2017-0112/FULL/XML

Xie, J., Nozawa, W., Yagi, M., Fujii, H., & Managi, S. (2019). Do environmental, social, and governance activities improve corporate financial performance? *Business Strategy and the Environment*, 28(2), 286-300. https://doi.org/10.1002/BSE.2224

Zhou, G., Liu, L., & Luo, S. (2022). Sustainable development, ESG performance and company market value: Mediating effect of financial performance. *Business Strategy and the Environment*, 31(7), 3371-3387. https://doi.org/10.1002/BSE.3089

# Part 2

◆

# Japanese Perspectives

Chapter **5**

# Integrated Reporting in Japanese Universities: How are Pioneers Telling their Value Creation Stories?

Taslima Akhter

◆

**Abstract**

This paper examines integrated reporting practice of six Japanese universities by evaluating and comparing their 2022 integrated reports against the IIRC's (International Integrated Reporting Council) framework. A content analysis method is used here. Data is collected through a disclosure checklist to examine the quality of integrated reports of six universities in Japan for the year 2022. Only these universities published an integrated reports in English for the year. The study exhibits that although these universities have started disclosing information on their value creation process, the practice is still in its infancy. Their reporting system still lacks an integrated, balanced approach to disclose information on eight content elements of the IIRC framework and thereby affecting the overall IR disclosure quality. The sampled reports include better disclosure on certain elements such as Organizational overview and external environment, Business model, and Performance. In contrast, a generic or minimal disclosure is found in areas namely, Governance, Risks and opportunities, and Materiality.

**Keywords**

Integrated reporting, Higher education institutions (HEI), IIRC framework, Japan

## 5.1 Introduction

Integrated reporting (IR) is the latest advancement in the long history of corporate reporting, originating in an attempt to overcome the limitations of traditional financial reporting. Although beginning in private sector organizations, the applicability of this reporting framework is being examined in different organizational settings, including in higher education institutions (HEIs) or universities. HEIs are a fundamental part of sustainable value creation within society, as they play a critical role in creating intellectually sound citizens (Mohammed *et al.*, 2023). Universities and HEIs around the world are giving increasing priority to the challenges of sustainability, influenced by a variety of drivers including international and national policy, students' awareness, and societal pressures (Adams *et al.*, 2018). The British Universities Finance Directors Group (BUFDG) further clarified HEIs' role in education, research, innovation and creating sustainable value for their stakeholders. In their report, they opined that the diversity and complexity of university activities hinder the communication of its value creation story effectively to its stakeholders (BUFDG, 2016).

Despite all the developments in sustainability reporting over the last few decades, universities' reporting systems are still backward-looking, and compliance-related with some "feel good" information. They are not focusing on multi-stakeholders-oriented reporting and communicating their value creation story by linking with various categories of capital (Adams, 2018). IR could help universities to tell their stories in an effective and insightful way (BUFDG, 2016) and can be considered as an effective tool for reporting sustainability strategies (Mohammed *et al.*, 2023). This reporting practice has the potential to significantly improve corporate reporting by presenting a complete overview of the corporate value creation process. It can help to improve communication by consolidating information on both intellectual capital and nonintellectual capital into a single document, offering a holistic perspective (IIRC, 2021). An integrated report should explain the organization's value creation process and exhibit integrated thinking "in practice and in a sustainable manner" (The Institute of Directors in South Africa, 2016).

Extant literature reveals that the current IR practice in different HEIs lacks connectivity, integrated thinking, and effective communication of value creation. Universities have tended to be poor at communicating the value they create and its process, or "telling the stories that matter in a memorable way to the people who need to hear them" (BUFDG, 2016, p. 2). Another criticism of universities' reporting systems is that rather than developing "integrated thinking," university structures and strategies continue to reflect functional and discipline structures and a separation of the academic from operational activities (Adams, 2018). Evidence suggests that integrated thinking has the potential to enhance strategic initiatives and foster improved cross-functional communication (Barth *et al.*, 2017; Dumay & Dai, 2017). This study has also assumed that if integrated thinking is present in an organization such as universities, it should impact the level of disclosure in the annual report (Adams, 2018). Integrated thinking remains a concept that lacks clear definition and comprehension among both scholars and professionals (Busco *et al.*, 2020; Feng *et al.*, 2017). The ambitious objectives of IR have left managers dealing with confusion regarding its effective implementation and even the fundamental comprehension of its essence, and then incorporating these principles into everyday contexts of operations (Feng *et al.*, 2017; Jensen & Berg, 2012). Despite unclear guidance, organizations are trying to initiate the IR process, and integrated thinking could be the eventual outcome of the process. Integrated thinking could be related to the six categories of capital, their interrelationships, and respond to the material needs of the stakeholders where the business model could be the central idea of the IR process (Arul *et al.*, 2020).

Although IR practice in universities is receiving some attention from academia recently, the existing research is still very limited. Several studies have focused on the disclosure level of IR content elements for HEIs. Hassan *et al.* (2019) examined the disclosure level in the annual reports of universities in the UK, while some other studies investigated the practice of IR in other parts of Europe (Aras *et al.*, 2022; Brusca *et al.*, 2018; Iacuzzi *et al.*, 2020; Mauro *et al.*, 2020). In a recent study, Sun *et al.* (2023) conducted a comparison between a few South African and Japanese universities, whereas in a similar study, Arul *et al.* (2020) compared the disclosures related to integrated thinking provided in integrated reports in two different institutional settings, namely, South Africa and Japan. Using text mining technique, Nakagawa *et al.* (2020) analyze the differences between "good" and "not good" integrated reports based on a sample of 372 companies' reports from FY 2017 to FY 2019. Using similar methodology, Miura *et al*. (2021) evaluates whether the integrated report of some Japanese universities represents the characteristics of the university. Japanese experience in sustainability education is a neglected research topic in international academic journals, except for a few case studies (Nomura & Abe, 2010).

Based on the above conditions, the main objective of this study is to examine the extent and quality of selected Japanese universities' integrated reports. To pursue this objective, integrated reports of six universities for the year 2022 are taken into consideration as these reports are also available in English. These universities are Chiba University of Commerce, Hiroshima University, Tohoku University, Hokkaido University, Tsukuba University, and Okayama University. The contents of these reports are examined against the eight content elements of the IR framework provided by the IIRC (International Integrated Reporting Council). The present study is a response to the call for research on IR adoption in HEIs or universities as there is limited research in this sector and the available studies have mostly been carried out in countries other than Japan (Adams, 2018; Melloni *et al*., 2017; Veltri & Silvestri, 2015). Existing literature finds that the content element segment of the IR framework is the most relevant and widely used basis for assessing the level of IR adoption within an organization (Hassan *et al*., 2019). These content elements are substantially influenced by the eight guiding principles of the same framework. Using content elements of the IR framework is an effective way of assessing this (Arul *et al*., 2020; Hassan *et al*., 2019). Therefore, this study has used content analysis and all content elements of the IR framework to investigate the level of disclosure in Japanese universities to get a comprehensive understanding and further enrich this kind of research (BUFDG, 2016; Melloni *et al*., 2017; Rowbottom & Locke, 2016). To the best of the author's knowledge, this study is one of the few that examines IR practice in the HEI sector in Japan. This paper will continue as follows: the next section will provide a literature review on IR in HEIs. This will be followed by an explanation of methodology in section three. The paper then discusses the findings before the final section concludes the study.

## 5.2 Literature Review

Although there is a number of studies investigating IR practices of firms, studies on HEIs are scarce (Brusca *et al.*, 2018; Hassan *et al.*, 2019). Moreover, there are only a few studies regarding Japanese HEIs' reporting practice (Miura *et al.*, 2021). Using text mining technique, Miura *et al.* (2021) evaluated whether the integrated reports' characteristics represent well the characteristics of the universities and found some positive relationships, especially those related to social contribution, and that the integrated reports can be a useful resource for university evaluation. In a pioneering study, Veltri & Silvestri (2015) compared a South African public university integrated report with the contents and guidelines of the IIRC framework. By employing a case study approach, the study found that the report lacked some core guidelines, such as connectivity and outlook orientation, and had poor disclosure of the contents of the framework. In a similar study, Brusca *et al.* (2018) examined the IR of a Spanish university (University of Cadiz, UCA) against the IIRC framework, and critically analyzed what, why, who, and how the new models of reporting have been implemented. Based on a case study using semi structured interviews, the study showed that the UCA report mainly focused on social and sustainability values, lacked integrated thinking, and connectivity between capitals that create value. The key driver has been stakeholders' interests, represented by the university's social council, and aiming at increasing competitiveness of the university.

Hassan *et al.* (2019) found a significant increase in the number of IR content elements, which is positively associated with some HEI-specific characteristics and adoption of IR framework. To extend those findings, Adhikariparajuli *et al.* (2020) examine the level of disclosure on content elements of IR in Scotland's, Northern Ireland's, and Wales' HEIs or universities. The paper assumes integrated thinking as an internal process or an effective mechanism to improve accountability toward stakeholders. Using signaling theory, it also explained an increasing trend of disclosure and positive relationship of that with HEI-specific characteristics, such as the establishment year of HEI, adoption of IR framework, and governing board size (Adhikariparajuli *et al.*, 2020).

By conducting a case study of an Italian university, Iacuzzi *et al.* (2020) confirmed that IR can be considered more as an incremental than a revolutionary transformation of existing approaches and arrangements. IR requires the incorporation of integrated thinking in the organization, along with a focus on materiality and stakeholder engagement to cocreate value for society at large. Using content analysis of social or sustainability reports by several Italian public universities, Mauro *et al.* (2020) tried to detect which of the key elements of IR had been incorporated in the reports. Their findings show that some of those elements are included, but in a disintegrated manner. The study demonstrates that elements such as the organizational overview, external environment, and business models and stakeholders, are discussed more than governance and the analysis of risks and opportunities. Aras *et al.* (2022) investigated the extent to which the integrated annual report of a public university, namely, Yildiz Technical University (YTU), follows the IIRC framework in terms of content elements and guiding principles. The study reveals strong connections between various sections of content elements and disclosure of nonfinancial information to a satisfactory level. It also reveals the aim of the university to draw attention of its stakeholders to material sustainability issues by using an integrated approach.

Mohammed *et al.* (2023) analyzed the extent of the disclosure level of IR content elements in Malaysian Public Universities' (MPU) annual reports over the period 2016–2018. Their findings revealed an increasing trend in the disclosure level of IR content elements in MPUs' annual reports. Research universities exhibited a significant positive relationship with the disclosure level of IR content elements, whereas university size and report conciseness are insignificant variables. According to the study, public sector organizations could foster their accountability and social value creation by implementing the IR framework in their reporting. Institutions that understand better the needs of the stakeholders are more likely to increase the shareholder value (Aras *et al.*, 2022).

Sun *et al.* (2023) examined IR practices of two Japanese universities and three South African universities by analyzing their 2019 integrated reports. Using multiple case study research method and institutional theory to explain the differences between IR of these universities, the study reveals that IR is in its infancy at the sample universities. Universities lack a comprehensive approach to integrate financial and non-financial information. "Especially for Japanese universities, they should use the integrated report to tell their organisational 'story', rather than simply to display a large amount of financial information and non-financial information" (p. 594).

Existing studies, in general, demonstrate an increasing trend of IR-related disclosure in the reports. As an evolving area of knowledge, case study and content analysis are two widely used methods for research. Apart from extent and quality of disclosure, the effects of institutional features of IR and the level of integration through integrated thinking-related disclosures are the two most explored areas. However, the present study will limit its focus on the extent and quality of disclosure of the sample universities considering the IR practice is new to Japanese universities.

## 5.3 Methodology

As an exploratory and emerging area of research, a qualitative approach is more appropriate to the study of IR in HEIs. In addition, choosing a small sample of universities could facilitate an in-depth analysis (Stubbs & Higgins, 2014; Sun *et al.*, 2023; Veltri & Silvestri, 2015). Content analysis is conducted to examine the quality of integrated reports of six universities in Japan. Only these integrated reports are available in English for the year 2022.

Content analysis is commonly used in examining disclosure quality of annual reports (Ahmed Haji & Anifowose, 2017) prepared by profit-oriented and nonprofit organizations (Garanina & Dumay, 2017). Previous research has frequently used this methodology to examine the disclosure practice of HEIs. In this line, the present study also used this methodology for understanding the practice in Japan. In content analysis, data are obtained through a process of observation and analysis of the content or text to make valid inferences from text to the context of their use (Krippendorff, 2004). Written documents such as reports are very suitable for applying this technique. Based on the question "what to know" and what are the sources of information, researchers develop a coding system and collect the data to analyze. This technique has been widely used in analyzing information in written official documents, intellectual capital disclosure, and sustainability disclosure (Mauro *et al.*, 2020). A well-specified coding instrument in terms of specific categories and decision rules could facilitate the reliability of content analysis (Guthrie & Abeysekera, 2006). In this study, a disclosure checklist is developed as the coding instrument to assess the extent of disclosure in university reports against the IR framework. Information was searched and classified into predefined categories based on this checklist (see **Table 5.1**).

To generate the disclosure index, this study followed the IR framework provided by the IIRC (2013) and took guidance from extant literature. The IIRC framework requires an integrated report to include eight content elements which are: organizational overview and external environment, governance, business model, risk and opportunities, strategy and resource allocation, performance, outlook, and basis of preparation and presentation (IIRC, 2013). In the checklist, a total of 40 items are included under eight content elements and only content elements are focused. Based on extant literature (Adhikariparajuli *et al.*, 2020; Hassan *et al.*, 2019), a weighted scoring system for the disclosure items is used with values ranging from 0 to 3, where 0 = absence of disclosure, 1 = narrative or limited disclosure, 2 = narrative disclosure with limited quantitative information, and 3 = both narrative and quantitative disclosure with trends and linkages with other elements. The sample consists of annual reports of six Japanese universities for the year 2022. A thorough content analysis was conducted on these reports by the author. Using a single coder having sufficient training can ensure consistency and reliability of coding considering the subjectivity involved in content analysis.

## 5.4 Findings of the Study

**Table 5.1** is the disclosure checklist for coding the values of 40 individual items under eight content elements. The detailed scores are presented in Table 5.1, which includes the total score obtained by each university and the intermediate scores (subtotal for each content element) for each category of the checklist. The score obtained in each category and in total are shown in absolute terms and in percentage form (in relation to the maximum possible score of that content element).

The overall score of all content elements for the sample Japanese universities

**Table 5.1** Disclosure Checklist

| Item No. | Disclosure Items | Chiba University of Commerce | Okayama University | Hiroshima University | Tohoku University | Tsukuba University | Hokkaido University | By Content Element | Overall Score |
|---|---|---|---|---|---|---|---|---|---|
| | **Content Element 1: Organizational Overview and External Environment; Maximum Possible Score = 15** | | | | | | | | |
| 1 | Organization's mission, vision, and culture | 3 | 1 | 3 | 3 | 3 | 2 | | |
| 2 | Principal activities and markets | 3 | 2 | 3 | 3 | 3 | 2 | | |
| 3 | Ownership and operating structure | 3 | 2 | 2 | 3 | 2 | 1 | | |
| 4 | Competitive landscape | 2 | 1 | 2 | 2 | 1 | 2 | | |
| 5 | External environmental analysis | 2 | 1 | 2 | 2 | 2 | 1 | | |
| | **Organizational Overview and External Environment: Sub-total** | **13** | **7** | **12** | **13** | **11** | **8** | **64** | |
| | **Sub-total in percentage** | **86.67** | **46.67** | **80** | **86.67** | **73.33** | **53.33** | **71.11** | |
| | | | | | | | | | |
| | **Content Element 2: Governance; Maximum Possible Score= 15** | | | | | | | | |

| # | | | | | | | | | |
|---|---|---|---|---|---|---|---|---|---|
| 6 | Organization's leadership structure | 1 | 0 | 2 | 1 | 2 | 1 | | |
| 7 | Executive/non-executive roles and responsibilities of management | 1 | 0 | 2 | 1 | 2 | 0 | | |
| 8 | Disclosure on decision making process | 1 | 0 | 1 | 0 | 2 | 1 | | |
| 9 | Risk management process | 1 | 0 | 0 | 0 | 1 | 0 | | |
| 10 | Linking remuneration and incentives to value creation | 0 | 0 | 0 | 0 | 1 | 0 | | |
| | **Governance: Sub-total** | **4** | **0** | **5** | **2** | **8** | **2** | **21** | |
| | **Sub-total in percentage** | **26.67** | **0** | **33.33** | **13.33** | **53.33** | **13.33** | **23.33** | |
| | | | | | | | | | |
| | **Content Element 3: Business Model; Maximum Possible Score=15** | | | | | | | | |
| 11 | Explaining business model: (Identification of key elements of business model, disclosure with diagram/ narrative) | 3 | 2 | 2 | 1 | 3 | 0 | | |
| 12 | Relating and disclosing capitals with value creation (Narrative disclosure only, narrative with supporting quantitative disclosure) | 2 | 2 | 2 | 1 | 3 | 0 | | |
| 13 | Connecting KPIs with value creation | 2 | 2 | 2 | 2 | 3 | 2 | | |

| # | Description | | | | | | | | |
|---|---|---|---|---|---|---|---|---|---|
| 14 | Relating stakeholders with value creation | 2 | 2 | 2 | 2 | 3 | 2 | | |
| 15 | Changing business model to adapt with organization's external environment | 2 | 1 | 1 | 1 | 2 | 1 | | |
| | **Business Model: Sub-total** | 11 | 9 | 9 | 7 | 14 | 5 | **55** | |
| | **Sub-total in percentage** | 73.33 | 60 | 60 | 46.67 | 93.33 | 33.33 | **61.11** | |
| | | | | | | | | | |
| | **Content Element 4: Risks and Opportunities; Maximum Possible Score= 15** | | | | | | | | |
| 16 | Disclosure on significant risks and impacts | 2 | 0 | 1 | 1 | | 1 | | |
| 17 | Specific steps taken to manage risks | 2 | 0 | 1 | 1 | | 0 | | |
| 18 | Identification of opportunities for value creation and benefits there in | 1 | 2 | 1 | 1 | | 0 | | |
| 19 | Specific steps taken to create value from opportunities | 1 | 2 | 1 | 1 | | 0 | | |
| 20 | Stakeholder engagement in identifying material risk or opportunities | 1 | 1 | 1 | 1 | | 0 | | |
| | **Risks and Opportunities: Sub-total** | 7 | 5 | 5 | 5 | 0 | 1 | **23** | |
| | **Sub-total in percentage** | 46.67 | 33.33 | 33.33 | 33.33 | 0 | 6.67 | **25.56** | |
| | | | | | | | | | |

| | Content Element 5: Strategy and Resources Allocation; Maximum Possible Score= 15 | | | | | | | | |
|---|---|---|---|---|---|---|---|---|---|
| 21 | Organization's short, medium, and long-term strategic objectives | 3 | 1 | 2 | 3 | 3 | 2 | | |
| 22 | Plans to achieve strategic objectives | 2 | 1 | 2 | 2 | 2 | 1 | | |
| 23 | Resource allocation plans (stakeholder engagement) | 2 | 1 | 1 | 2 | 2 | 1 | | |
| 24 | Linking KPISs with strategic objectives | 2 | 1 | 2 | 2 | 2 | 1 | | |
| 25 | Environmental and social considerations embedded into the organization's strategy | 1 | 1 | 2 | 2 | 2 | 1 | | |
| | **Strategy and Resources Allocation: Sub-total** | 10 | 5 | 9 | 11 | 11 | 6 | **52** | |
| | **Sub-total in percentage** | 66.67 | 33.33 | 60 | 73.33 | 73.33 | 40 | **57.78** | |
| | | | | | | | | | |
| | Content Element 6: Performance; Maximum Possible Score=15 | | | | | | | | |
| 26 | KPIs: Key Quantitative Information (financial, non-financial and with trends) | 2 | 2 | 3 | 3 | 3 | 2 | | |

| No. | | | | | | | | Total |
|---|---|---|---|---|---|---|---|---|
| 27 | Strategic objectives for the period and achievement | 2 | 2 | 2 | 2 | 3 | 2 | |
| 28 | A complete view of performance (strategic, financial, and environmental) | 2 | 2 | 2 | 2 | 2 | 2 | |
| 29 | Both positive and negative effects on the capitals | 1 | 1 | 1 | 1 | 1 | 1 | |
| 30 | KPIs that combine financial measures with other components or monetizing certain effects on the capitals | 2 | 1 | 2 | 2 | 2 | 1 | |
| | **Performance: Sub-total** | 9 | 8 | 10 | 10 | 11 | 8 | **56** |
| | **Sub-total in percentage** | 60 | 53.33 | 66.67 | 66.67 | 73.33 | 53.33 | **62.22** |
| | | | | | | | | |
| | **Content Element 7: Outlook; Maximum Possible Score= 15** | | | | | | | |
| 31 | Expectations about external environment (General/ Organization-specific disclosure) | 2 | 0 | 2 | 2 | 2 | 1 | |
| 32 | Linkages between past and present performance, and outlook | 2 | 0 | 2 | 2 | 2 | 2 | |
| 33 | Potential implications of future uncertainties on capitals | 1 | 0 | 1 | 1 | 1 | 1 | |

| No. | Description | | | | | | | | |
|---|---|---|---|---|---|---|---|---|---|
| 34 | Ways for measuring outlook (General/ Organization-specific disclosure) | 1 | 1 | 2 | 2 | | 1 | | |
| 35 | Preparedness for future uncertainties | 2 | 1 | 1 | 2 | 2 | 1 | | |
| | **Outlook: Sub-total** | 8 | 2 | 8 | 9 | 6 | 6 | **39** | |
| | **Sub-total in percentage** | 53.33 | 13.33 | 53.33 | 60 | 40 | 40 | **43.33** | |
| | | | | | | | | | |
| | **Content Element 8: Basis of Preparation and Presentation (Maximum Possible Score= 15)** | | | | | | | | |
| 36 | Disclosure on the preparation method, and contents of the report | 1 | 0 | 3 | 3 | 3 | 1 | | |
| 37 | Disclosure on materiality (determination process and stakeholders' engagement) | 1 | 1 | 0 | 0 | 0 | 1 | | |
| 38 | Impact of material matters on organization's value creation process | 1 | 0 | 0 | 0 | | 0 | | |
| 39 | People involved in the preparation and review of the papers | 0 | 1 | 0 | 1 | 1 | 0 | | |
| 40 | Uncertainty related to data presented in the report | 0 | 0 | 0 | 1 | 1 | 1 | | |

| | | | | | | | |
|---|---|---|---|---|---|---|---|
| **Basis of Preparation and Presentation (Sub-total)** | 3 | 2 | 3 | 5 | 5 | 3 | **21** |
| **Sub-total in percentage** | 20 | 13.33 | 20 | 33.33 | 33.33 | 20 | **23.33** |
| **TOTAL (All Content Elements)** | 56 | 38 | 61 | 62 | 66 | 39 | |
| Total Score in percentage | **46.67** | **31.67** | **50.83** | **51.67** | **55** | **32.5** | **44.72** |
| Maximum possible score (Total) (15*8= 120) | | | | | | | |

Notes: This disclosure index is adapted from the IIRC report (2013). No disclosure = 0; Limited and narrative disclosure only = 1; Both narrative and quantitative disclosure with a link to other elements = 2; Both narrative and quantitative disclosure with a link to other elements and with information on trends = 3.

ranges from 31.67% to 55% and the average disclosure rate is 44.72%. It shows a poor to moderate rate of disclosure of these universities' integrated reports where three universities' reports have scored less than 50% and three others scored more than 50%. Of the eight content elements, "Organizational overview and external environment" has the highest level of disclosure, with an average disclosure level of 71.11%, followed by "Performance", with an average of 62.22%. This finding is similar to that of (Mauro *et al.*, 2020) for Italian public universities and (Sun *et al.*, 2023) for selected South African and Japanese universities' reporting quality. With reference to the first content element, that is, "Organizational overview and external environment", universities performed within a range of 86.67% to 46.67% of disclosure with an average disclosure of 71.11%. Sample universities in general, discussed the mission, vision, key values of the organization, and competitive environment. Under content element "Performance", all these reports have communicated their KPIs and mostly with trends. Every organization has specific strategic objectives to fulfill in their midterm and long-term planning. However, these reports rarely communicate any negative information about organizational performance.

Overall, the disclosure quality of three elements (Organizational overview and external environment, Business model, and Performance) has an average score higher than 60%, while the disclosure quality of three other elements (Governance, Risks and opportunities, and Basis of preparation and presentation) has an average score lower than 30%. The lowest level of disclosure is both for the "Basis of preparation and presentation" and "Governance", with an average of 23.33% for the sampled reports. "Risks and opportunities" is another neglected element that has an average disclosure of only 25.56%. These reports failed to communicate on their leadership structures, governance mechanisms, or risk management process. The "Risks and opportunities" section has provided a partial overview on current and future risks with a very insignificant amount of information on opportunities of the organization. Another important aspect of the IIRC framework is materiality-related disclosure, which is almost nonexistent in these reports. Low disclosure in these content elements were noticed not only in HEIs, but also in other sectors as well (Akhter *et al.*, 2022).

Tsukuba University has obtained the highest overall score with a disclosure level of 55%. Among the eight content elements, it has the highest compliance in "Business model" with 93% disclosure. For "Governance" and "Basis of preparation and presentation", Tsukuba University scored 53.33% and 33.33%, respectively, whereas the other universities have scored very low. Tohoku University has the second-highest overall disclosure of 51.67%; "Organizational overview and external environment" and "Strategy and resource allocation" are the two most disclosed elements of this university with 86.67% and 73.33% of disclosure, respectively.

In contrast, Okayama and Hokkaido Universities scored the lowest overall disclosure rates of 31.67% and 32.5%, respectively. Okayama University reported the minimal and only summarized information in its English version integrated report. "Governance"-related disclosure is almost nonexistent in its 2022 English integrated report. The report has a minimum of 13.33% disclosure on content elements, "Outlook" and "Basis of preparation and presentation". Hokkaido University discussed its vision, mission, and strategic goals, but did not explicitly explain the business model and its capitals. Use of KPIs is limited and their relationships with other elements are also not established. These resulted in relatively low scores in the elements "Business model" and "Performance" in comparison with other reports. In addition, this university has extremely low disclosures on "Governance" and "Risks and opportunities" (13.33% and 6.67%, respectively).

In general, it seems that the original versions of these reports in Japanese have provided more information for the stakeholders that is not available in the summarized English versions. For example, Okayama University has provided the least information in their English version integrated report for the sample year 2022 and has the lowest overall disclosure rate of 31.67%. Checking the Japanese version of the Okayama University integrated report shows that the university has provided much more required information as per the IIRC framework in that version.

## 5.5 Conclusion

Academia has recently focused on higher education institutions arguing that universities could play an important role in sustainable development by promoting education for sustainable development and introducing active policies for achieving sustainability goals, including effective communication of information. It is believed that this reporting practice also has the potential to significantly improve corporate reporting by presenting a complete overview of the corporate value creation process and thereby exhibit integrated thinking of the organization. This is also applicable to public sector organizations or educational institutions, such as universities. Based on these assumptions, this study wants to investigate the extent and quality of disclosure by some selected universities in Japan. In line with the existing research, this study has used the content analysis method and analyzed the contents of six Japanese universities' integrated reports against the IIRC framework. Only these integrated reports are available in English for the year 2022. To the best of the author's knowledge, this study is one of the few studies that examines IR practice in the HEI sector in Japan.

The overall disclosure score (of eight content elements) for the sample Japanese universities ranges from 31.67% to 55%, with an average disclosure rate of 44.72%. The three most disclosed content elements are Organizational overview and external environment, Business model, and Performance, with average disclosure rates of 71.11%, 61.11%, and 62.22%, respectively. In contrast, elements such as Governance, Risks and opportunities, and Basis of preparation and presentation have the lowest disclosure rates of 23.33%, 25.56%, and 23.33%, respectively. Although the Japanese versions of these reports appear to have better information on these content elements, these elements still require significant improvements in reporting.

Even with a small sample, this study could demonstrate the IR practice of Japanese universities and applicability of this reporting system to HEIs. Through integration of information, this reporting practice could be a mechanism for universities to transform their annual reports from ordinary sources of financial and nonfinancial information into tales of a university's value creation to the broader stakeholder groups. The findings of this study will be of interest to university administrators, policymakers and regulators, and other stakeholder groups of universities.

There are several limitations of the present study. First, the sample size is small as it contains only six integrated reports for the year 2022. Only six universities have published reports in English along with the original reports in Japanese. Second, only English versions of the six universities' reports have been taken into consideration. The Japanese versions of the same universities' reports could provide better disclosures for the same year. Therefore, this study is unable to produce any generalized conclusions about the IR practice of Japanese universities. Future research can extend the current findings with an increased sample size, or by investigating the reasons for universities to adopt this reporting practice.

● References

Adams, C. (2018). Debate: Integrated reporting and accounting for sustainable development across generations by universities. *Public Money and Management*, 38(5), 332-334. https://doi.org/10. 1080/09540962.2018.1477580

Adams, R., Martin, S., & Boom, K. (2018). A Conceptual Framework for Designing, Embedding and Monitoring a University Sustainability Culture. In *World Sustainability Series* (pp. 465-482). Springer. https://doi.org/10.1007/978-3-319-67122-2_27

Adhikariparajuli, M., Hassan, A., Fletcher, M., & Elamer, A. A. (2020). Integrated reporting in higher education: insights from Scotland, Northern Ireland and Wales. *Social Responsibility Journal*, 17(3), 321-342. https://doi.org/10.1108/SRJ-01-2019-0031

Ahmed Haji, A., & Anifowose, M. (2017). Initial trends in corporate disclosures following the introduction of integrated reporting practice in South Africa. *Journal of Intellectual Capital*, 18(2), 373-399. https://doi.org/10.1108/JIC-01-2016-0020/FULL/PDF

Akhter, T., Haider, M. B., & Ishihara, T. (2022). A comparison of integrated reporting practices in Japan and the UK. *Corporate Narrative Reporting*, 151-170. https://doi.org/10.4324/ 9781003095385-12

Aras, G., Kutlu Furtuna, O., & Hacioglu Kazak, E. (2022). Toward an integrated reporting framework in higher education institutions: evidence from a public university. *International Journal of Sustainability in Higher Education*, 23(2), 426-442. https://doi.org/10.1108/IJSHE-12-2020-0504

Arul, R., de Villiers, C., & Dimes, R. (2020). Insights from narrative disclosures regarding integrated thinking in integrated reports in South Africa and Japan. *Meditari Accountancy Research*, 29(4), 720-739. https://doi.org/10.1108/MEDAR-06-2020-0934/FULL/XML

Barth, M. E., Cahan, S. F., Chen, L., & Venter, E. R. (2017). The economic consequences associated with integrated report quality: Capital market and real effects. *Accounting, Organizations and Society*, 62, 43-64. https://doi.org/10.1016/J.AOS.2017.08.005

Brusca, I., Labrador, M., & Larran, M. (2018). The challenge of sustainability and integrated reporting at universities: A case study. *Journal of Cleaner Production,* 188, 347-354. https://doi.org/10.1016/j.jclepro.2018.03.292

BUFDG. (2016). *Helping universities tell their stories better.* www.sockmonkeyconsulting.com

Busco, C., Granà, F., & Achilli, G. (2020). Managing and measuring social impact through integrated thinking and reporting : The case of a European university. In *The Routledge Handbook of Integrated Reporting* (pp. 251-268). Routledge. https://doi.org/10.4324/9780429279621-17

Dumay, J., & Dai, T. (2017). Integrated thinking as a cultural control? *Meditari Accountancy Research*, 25(4), 574-604. https://doi.org/10.1108/MEDAR-07-2016-0067/FULL/XML

Feng, T., Cummings, L., & Tweedie, D. (2017). Exploring integrated thinking in integrated reporting–an exploratory study in Australia. *Journal of Intellectual Capital*, 18(2), 330-353. https://doi.org/10.1108/JIC-06-2016-0068

Garanina, T., & Dumay, J. (2017). Forward-looking intellectual capital disclosure in IPOs: Implications for intellectual capital and integrated reporting. *Journal of Intellectual Capital*, 18(1), 128-148. https://doi.org/10.1108/JIC-05-2016-0054

Guthrie, J., & Abeysekera, I. (2006). Content analysis of social, environmental reporting: what is new? *Journal of Human Resource Costing & Accounting*, 10(2), 114-126. https://doi.org/10.1108/14013380610703120

Hassan, A., Adhikariparajuli, M., Fletcher, M., & Elamer, A. (2019). Integrated reporting in UK higher education institutions. *Sustainability Accounting, Management and Policy Journal*, 10(5), 844-876. https://doi.org/10.1108/SAMPJ-03-2018-0093

Iacuzzi, S., Garlatti, A., Fedele, P., & Lombrano, A. (2020). Integrated reporting and change: evidence from public universities. *Journal of Public Budgeting, Accounting and Financial Management*, 32(2), 291-310. https://doi.org/10.1108/JPBAFM-08-2019-0120

IIRC. (2013). *The International <IR> Framework.* https://integratedreporting.ifrs.org/wp-content/uploads/2013/12/13-12-08-THE-INTERNATIONAL-IR-FRAMEWORK-2-1.pdf

IIRC. (2021). *International Integrated Reporting Framework.* https://integratedreporting.ifrs.org/wpcontent/uploads/2021/01/InternationalIntegratedReportingFramework.pdf

Jensen, J. C., & Berg, N. (2012). Determinants of Traditional Sustainability Reporting Versus Integrated Reporting. An Institutionalist Approach. *Business Strategy and the Environment*, 21(5), 299-316. https://doi.org/10.1002/BSE.740

Krippendorff, K. (2004). Reliability in Content Analysis- Common Misconceptions and Recommendations. *Human Communication Research*, 30(3), 411-433. https://doi.org/10.1111/j.1468-2958.2004.tb00738.x

Mauro, S. G., Cinquini, L., Simonini, E., & Tenucci, A. (2020). Moving from social and sustainability reporting to integrated reporting: Exploring the potential of Italian public-funded universities' reports. *Sustainability* , 12(8), 3172. https://doi.org/10.3390/SU12083172

Melloni, G., Caglio, A., & Perego, P. (2017). Saying more with less? Disclosure conciseness, completeness and balance in Integrated Reports. *Journal of Accounting and Public Policy*, 36(3), 220-238. https://doi.org/10.1016/j.jaccpubpol.2017.03.001

Miura, T., Furukawa, T., Harada, J., Hirano, Y., & Hashimoto, T. (2021). Evaluation of Universities' Integrated Reports Using Text Mining Technique. *2021 IEEE International Conference on Ser-*

*vice Operations and Logistics, and Informatics, SOLI 2021*. https://doi.org/10.1109/ SOLI54607.2021.9672410

Mohammed, N. F., Mahmud, R., Islam, M. S., & Mohamed, N. (2023). Towards achieving SDGs through integrated reporting in Malaysian public universities. *International Journal of Sustainability in Higher Education*, 24(5), 1002-1023. https://doi.org/10.1108/IJSHE-08-2021-0344

Nakagawa, K., Sashida, S., Kitajima, R., & Sakai, H. (2020). What Do Good Integrated Reports Tell Us?: An Empirical Study of Japanese Companies Using Text-Mining. *Proceedings - 2020 9th International Congress on Advanced Applied Informatics, IIAI-AAI 2020*, 516-521. https://doi. org/10.1109/IIAI-AAI50415.2020.00108

Nomura, K., & Abe, O. (2010). Higher education for sustainable development in Japan: Policy and progress. *International Journal of Sustainability in Higher Education*, 11(2), 120-129. https:// doi.org/10.1108/14676371011031847

Rowbottom, N., & Locke, J. (2016). The emergence of <IR>. *Accounting and Business Research,* 46(1), 83-115. https://doi.org/10.1080/00014788.2015.1029867

Stubbs, W., & Higgins, C. (2014). Integrated reporting and internal mechanisms of change. *Accounting, Auditing and Accountability Journal*, 27(7), 1068-1089. https://doi.org/10.1108/ AAAJ-03-2013-1279

Sun, Y., Ip, P. S., Arunachalam, M., & Davey, H. (2023). From ivory tower to a storyteller of value creation: integrated reporting at Japanese and South African universities. *Journal of Intellectual Capital*, 24(2), 580-597. https://doi.org/10.1108/JIC-01-2021-0008

The Institute of Directors in South Africa. (2016). *King IV: Report on Corporate Governance for South Africa 2016*. http://www.iodsa.co.za/?page=KingIVEndorsers

Veltri, S., & Silvestri, A. (2015). The Free State University integrated reporting: A critical consideration. *Journal of Intellectual Capital*, 16(2), 443-462. https://doi.org/10.1108/JIC-06-2014-0077

Chapter **6**

# Unravelling Mechanisms of Value Co-creation in Kinosaki Hot Spa:Based on Public Service Ecosystem

**Naoki Inoue**

**Shinichi Tanioka**

## Abstract

In recent years, tourism and community design has been promoted in Japan, but it has not been clarified what kind of value is created for the actors of tourism and community design by increasing the attractiveness of tourist destinations that are also places of residence. In this study, we focus Kinosaki Hot Spa, where many actors are involved in tourism and community design and examine what kind of value is co-created through tourism and community design. For the history of Kinosaki Hot Spa, reference is primarily referenced through the history of Kinosaki Town, while the current tourism and community design in Kinosaki Hot Spa is based mainly on the basic plan for the revitalisation of the city centres in the Kinosaki Town. In addition to the previous literature study, an interview survey was conducted with the relevant parties who are actively involved in the town development of Kinosaki Hot Spa. In Kinosaki Hot Spa, the values of co-existence and co-prosperity have long existed, as the hot springs are regarded as natural capital shared by the local residents and the limited amount of spring water is utilised. In the tourism and community design of Kinosaki Hot Spa, which is promoted based on the principles of co-existence and co-prosperity, tourists are not only expected to use Kinosaki Hot Spa, but also to be involved as actors in tourism and community design to maintain the atmosphere and landscape of the area. We positioned tourism and community design as a public service to be implemented through public-private partnerships and organised the values of Kinosaki Hot Spa resort tourism and community design according to public service logic. To promote value co-creation, the dimensions of value and value creation at four levels in the public service ecosystem (institutional, service, individual and belief levels) and the interactions across these levels must be understood.

**Keywords:**
Co-existence and co-prosperity, Town Management Organisation, Tourism and Community Design, Value Co-creation, Public Service Logic

## 6.1 Introduction

In Japan, tourism GDP, which is the value added by domestically produced tourism services, was approximately 11.2 trillion yen in 2019, accounting for only 2% of the total economy, a large difference compared to the average of the G7 countries and the average of seven Western countries. However, it is expected to expand its economic and social spillover effects in the future (Japan Tourism Agency, 2023). The value brought by tourism is not the material or monetary value of the product or service itself, but the psychological and sensory effects and satisfaction gained through the experience of using it, which is defined as experiential value (Schmitt & Zarantonello, 2013). For example, it has been shown that Japanese guests value the extraordinary experience in a *ryokan*, while foreign guests value a series of unique Japanese cross-cultural experiences related to their stay at a *ryokan*, such as access to the *ryokan* and walking around the area, in addition to the experience at the *ryokan* itself (Morishita, 2022).

There are many previous studies (e.g. Yuan & Wu 2008; Wu *et al.* 2018) from the perspective of tourism service providers enhancing the value of tourists' experiences. However, travel agencies, transport operators, governments, town development companies (TMOs: Town Management Organisation), and DMOs (Destination Management Organisation or Destination Marketing Organisation: It has not been clearly defined what value can be created by various actors, such as tourism management organisations, transport companies, public administrations, town management organisations (TMOs), destination management organisations or destination marketing organisations (DMOs) and residents' associations, by working together to enhance the attractiveness of tourism destinations. For example, following the UNWTO (2007) guidelines for promoting DMOs, which defined an institutional framework, the Japan Tourism Agency, together with the UNWTO Office in Japan, has developed a set of "Sustainable Tourism Guidelines for Japan" in accordance with international standards to enable local authorities and DMOs to carry out sustainable tourism destination management. The Japanese Sustainable Tourism Guidelines were developed in accordance with international standards to enable local authorities and DMOs to conduct sustainable tourism management. The Japan Tourism Agency/UNWTO Office in Japan (2020) stated that "in order to promote the development of a "good to live in, good to visit" tourism region that takes into consideration not only tourists but also local residents, local culture and the environment, not only local governments and DMOs but also all stakeholders in the region related to tourism (stakeholders) need to work together to promote sustainable tourism". The report recommends that, to promote sustainable tourism, not only local governments and DMOs, but also all stakeholders in the region need to take the promotion of sustainable tourism as their own business and work together to achieve this.

However, in the same guidelines, the values related to each actor and local resource are appended, but each value is not explained in detail. This situation is similar in previous studies on tourism region development. For example, a case study analysis of Atami City (Hori & Sano, 2019), which is home to one of Japan's leading hot spring resorts, analysed changes in the state of cooperation among tourism region development organisations due to cooperation promotion measures, as well as the effects and challenges of cooperation, and explained that "the conservative attitude of existing organisations and the difficulty of striking a balance between tourism and town development were found". However, there is no concrete indication of what value is created for whom by increasing the attractiveness of tourism destinations, which are also residential areas for local actors involved in tourism.

In recent years, there has been a growing body of previous research on the value of public services. For example, Eriksson *et al.* (2020), from a new model of care for older people with multiple chronic illnesses, found that a coordinator with a cross-organisational mission, vertical and horizontal support structures, trust established through relationships and the integration of the service system within the social system are crucial to the ability of public service organisations to develop a collaborative value proposition. Virtanen & Jalonen (2024) also presents an integrative conceptual framework that contributes to an understanding of public value creation flows in the context of politics and public service outcomes. These reflections on public service value are based on public service logic. Public service logic is a framework that explores the production of public services, their use ("consumption" (i.e. engagement with services by users), and the characteristics and processes of value creation in public service delivery (Osborne, 2018). Public Service Logic draws on Grönroos's work on service logic that value can only ever be created by the service user and the service organization cannot ever deliver value, but only offer a value proposition for the user and/or resources for the creation of value by the service user (Osborne, 2018). However, Service Logic (SL)(in all its guises) can be applied across both the commercial and public sectors equally, and with little differentiation (Grönroos, 2019), while public service logic takes a different stance from service logic. For example, the arguments of service logic for the commercial sector (that it is in the consumption of a service that value is created) is that production is only ever a means to an end and has no intrinsic value though the production and delivery of public services is a way in which public policy (and by implication societal values) is made extant and is also a value creation process in its own right (Osborne, 2021). In other words, value creation and value co-creation in both the production and use of public services is the core argument of public service logic.

Despite the involvement of diverse actors from the public and private sectors, there are not many previous studies that consider tourism and community design as a public service and the value it brings. Therefore, in this study, tourism and community design is positioned as a public service, and the public service logic is used to focus on the relationship between the production and use of tourism and community design and to identify a value framework for the process of public service delivery to individuals, service systems and society. In this study, Kinosaki Hot Spa Resort is used as a case study, as it is one of the most famous tourist destinations in Japan and many actors are involved in tourism and community design. For the purposes of this paper, actors are defined as town development companies, people involved in commerce and industry such as the inn industry, providers of public services such as the former town of Kinosaki, and users of public services such as tourists and residents. The aim of this study is to analyse the results of a literature review and an interview survey on tourism and community design in Kinosaki Hot Spa, and to clarify the mechanism by which value is co-created through tourism and community design by examining the results.

## 6.2 Research Methods

As discussed below, many of the residents of the former Kinosaki Town are engaged in the tourism industry at the Kinosaki Hot Spa in the town. Although the terms Kinosaki and Kinosaki Hot Spa are sometimes taken almost synonymously, in this study, when referring to the former Kinosaki Town, the name of the local government, and when referring to Kinosaki Hot Spa, the central town or community of Kinosaki Hot Spa, centred on the hot spring resort, which is the subject of tourism and community design.

The Great Hokutan Earthquake occurred on 23 May 1925 destroyed many historical documents relating to Kinosaki. In this study, the description of the history of Kinosaki Hot Spa is mainly based on a town history compiled by the Kinosaki Town History Compilation Committee.

In addition, the description of the current tourist town development in Kinosaki Hot Spa is mainly based the basic plan for the revitalisation of the city centres in Kinosaki Town. The city centres revitalisation system is a system under which the Prime Minister approves the 'basic plan for the revitalisation of city centres' drawn up by municipalities in accordance with the Law on the Revitalisation of Central City Areas, to comprehensively and systematically promote the enhancement of urban functions and economic vitality in the city centres. Municipalities draw up plans with town development companies, associations of commerce and industry, local residents and others, and the relevant ministries and agencies work together to provide focused support for the plans that have

146

been approved. The former Kinosaki Town issued a basic plan for the revitalisation of the city centres in December 2004, just before the merger, with the name "Kinosaki Kono Saki 100 Year Plan". (Kinosaki Town, 2004) explains that "Kinosaki Kono Saki 100 Year Plan will grow along with the growth of Kinosaki as a town", and that the plan consists of 33 projects and is expected to function as a compass, prescription and scenario for town planning even after the former Kinosaki Town becomes part of Toyooka City. It is expected to serve as a compass, prescription and scenario for town planning.

In addition to the previous literature study, the authors conducted a qualitative study by means of an interview survey: interviews were conducted at the Kinosaki Hot Spa Tourism Centre on 11 March 2024 with four people who are proactively involved in the town development of Kinosaki Hot Spa. As shown in **Table 6.1**, the interview survey was conducted by sending a questionnaire on the value co-creation of Kinosaki Hot Spa in advance and conducting semi-structured interviews on the day of the survey according to the questionnaire. The interview survey did not deal with personal information or information on personal preferences, behaviour, environment, body and mind, etc. Adequate informed

**Table 6.1** Questionnaire on Value Co-creation in Kinosaki Hot Spa

| I. Collaborative Community Development in Kinosaki Hot Spa | Question 1: History of Collaborative Community Development |
| --- | --- |
| | What actors have been involved and what initiatives have been implemented in the town development of Kinosaki Hot Spa? |
| | Question 2: Current Collaborative Community Development |
| | What actors are currently involved and what initiatives are being implemented in the town development of Kinosaki Hot Spa? |
| | Question 3: Characteristics of Town Planning in Kinosaki Hot Spa |
| | What are some of the features of Kinosaki Hot Spa town planning that distinguish it from other spa resorts? |
| II. Community Development and Value Co-creation | Question 4: Values on Community Development |
| | What values have been important to you in the development of Kinosaki Hot Spa? |
| | Question 5: Plan to Co-create New Value |
| | Do you have any plans to create new values for the town of Kinosaki Hot Spa together with collaborative town development actors? |

Source: Prepared by the Authors.

consent was given for the interviews, and only those who gave their consent were asked to sign a consent form before the interview survey was conducted.

The interview surveys were recorded and automatically coded by NVivo 14, developed by Lumivero, for each sentence in the thematic verbatim transcripts. **Table 6.2** shows the top seven codes with the highest coding frequency. While focusing on these codes with a high coding volume, manual coding was conducted for each question item, as described below, and analysed from the perspective of value co-creation.

Table 6.2　Thematic Automatic Coding Results for the Interview Survey

|  | **Inn** | **People** | **Town** | **Association** | **Sightseeing** | **Cooperation** | **_Yukata*_** |
|---|---|---|---|---|---|---|---|
| Question 1 | 0 | 0 | 2 | 0 | 0 | 3 | 1 |
| Question 2 | 4 | 1 | 1 | 4 | 1 | 3 | 0 |
| Question 3 | 5 | 3 | 3 | 2 | 3 | 1 | 0 |
| Question 4 | 7 | 4 | 0 | 2 | 4 | 0 | 6 |
| Question 5 | 0 | 2 | 3 | 1 | 0 | 0 | 0 |
| Total Amount | 16 | 10 | 9 | 9 | 8 | 7 | 7 |

Source: Prepared by the Authors Using NVivo 14.
* Light cotton kimono worn in the summer or used as a bathrobe.

Based on the analysis of previous literature studies and interview survey results, the mechanism of value co-creation in Kinosaki Hot Spa Resort is elucidated using public service logic. In many previous studies, the research question is to increase the value of tourists from the perspective of producers for tourism service providers and from the perspective of service users for tourists. However, in this study, to clarify the mechanism of value co-creation by public service logic, value is considered by the perspective of service users in tourism and community design. Osborne (2021), as shown in **Table 6.3,** defines the concept of value for public services as value-in-exchange, value-in-production, value-in-use and value-in-context, and describes a value framework for the process of public service delivery to individuals, service systems and society, focusing on the relationship between production and use. The public service delivery processes are (i) public policy (values), (ii) pre-production (experiences and expectations of all actors), (iii) production (co-design of public services as resources, capital and training), (iv) co-production (creating value through production - for users and citizens), and (v) use (creating value for public service users by their use), where a feedback loop is said to exist (Osborne, 2021).

**Table 6.3** The Dimensions of Value for Public Service Delivery in Relation to the Process of Public Service Delivery

| Dimension of value | Individual | Service system | Society |
|---|---|---|---|
| Value-in-exchange | Value as the price that a public service user will pay (exchange) for a public service | Value as the price that a PSO will either pay for inputs into a public service or the charge to service users for that service | Value as the price that a society will pay for public service in the form of taxation |
| Position in the public service delivery process | Either at the policy stage (taxation) and/or point of production/co-production (fee/charge) | At the point of production/co-production (price/charge) | At the policy stage (taxation) |
| Value-in-production | Value-added, derived from the experience of being involved in the co-design and/or co-production of a public service (as a service user or significant other) and independent of its outcomes | Value-added derived from being involved in the co-design and/or co-production of a public service (as a public service worker within a PSO) and independent of its outcomes | Value-added, derived from public services making extant societal values and beliefs |
| Position in the public service delivery process | Either at the co-design and/or co-production stage | At the co-design, production and/or co-production stage | Either at the production and/or co-production stage |
| Value-in-use | Value-added derived from the experience of using a public service, either in terms of its short- or medium-term effect upon well-being or of its impact upon the holistic lived experience of service user | Value-added derived from the experience of being involved in the production of a public service for public service workers, in terms either of its short or long-term effect upon well-being | Value-added derived from the increase in societal well-being and/or inclusion as a result of public services |

| Position in the public service delivery process | At the use stage, and in relation to prior experience and expectations (established at the pre-production stage) | At the use stage, and in relation to prior experience and expectations (established at the pre-production stage) | At the use stage, and in relation to societal beliefs and values |
|---|---|---|---|
| Value-in-context | Value-added derived from how a service impacts upon the needs of a service user, in the context of their lived experience | Value-added derived from how a public service is improved as a result of iterative learning within the service ecosystem | Value-added derived from how a public service impacts upon identified social or economic needs |
| Position in the public service delivery process | Primarily at the use stage, but also possibly at the co-design/co-production stage | At the co-design, production and co-production stages | Primarily at the use stage |

Source: Osborne (2021, 76-77).

In addition to the value framework for public service delivery processes, Osborne *et al.* (2021) describe public service ecosystems as ecosystems that are not created solely by public service organisations or networks of organisations, but are shaped by interactions aimed at survive, through organisational learning and subsequent system They describe public service ecosystems as systems that attempt to survive through organisational learning and subsequent systemic improvement. Osborne *et al.* (2022) also present the concept of public service ecosystems across four levels (institutional, service, individual and belief levels) and describe the dimensions of value and value creation within public service ecosystems at each level and the interactions across levels.

As diverse actors are involved in tourism and community design, the concept of a public service ecosystem is used to organise the interrelationships between actors and clarify the conditions necessary for value co-creation in the tourism and community design of Kinosaki Hot Spa Resort.

## 6.3 Value Co-creation in Kinosaki Hot Spa

### 6.3.1 Historical Background

Currently, the former Kinosaki Town merged with one surrounding city and four towns in April 2005 and became part of Toyooka City. The former Kinosaki Town is located in the north-east of Hyogo Prefecture, approximately three hours from Kyoto, Osaka and Kobe by express train or car. In winter, many tourists visit Kinosaki Hot Spa for the crabs from the Sea of Japan and the hot springs.

According to the Kinosaki Town History Compilation Committee (1988), Kinosaki Hot Spring has a history of approximately 1,300 years. In the Edo period (1603-1867), a bathhouse was built near the source of the spring in the present-day hot spring resort of Yushima, Kinosaki-cho, and six outlying bathhouses were set up as public bathhouses that could be used free of charge by local residents, thus forming the form of Kinosaki Hot Spa as we know it today. Later, in addition to inns called *ryokan*, local landlords called masters offered their houses free of charge as lodgings when no inns were available, but these later evolved into today's inns, which charge a fee for accommodation. In terms of hot spring management, before the Edo period, the out-spa was managed and operated by an innkeepers' association called yukata, but in 1895 the Yushima Property District was established, which included the hot springs and forests. The Yushima Property District was established in 1895, including the hot springs and forests, and has since become a property district, a special local public body as defined in the Local Autonomy Law. Thus, in Kinosaki Hot Spa, the springs continued to be managed and operated based on their character as common property of the local residents.

According to the preface to the Kinosaki Town History, Mr. Teiroku Nishimura, the mayor of the former Kinosaki Town at the time, mentioned the recovery from the Great Hokutan Earthquake and the resolution of the Indoor Baths Disturbances as events that would guide future development plans (Kinosaki Town History Compilation Committee, 1988), as well as the merger of towns and villages. In particular, the Indoor Baths Disturbances is detailed in a separate chapter of the Kinosaki Town History and is considered to be a notable historical fact for the former Kinosaki Town that should be passed on to future generations. How these two events influenced the formation of the value concept in Kinosaki Hot Spa and lead to the current value co-creation is discussed below.

### 6.3.1.1 Great Hokutan Earthquake

According to the Kinosaki Town History Compilation Committee (1988), the Great Hokutan Earthquake of 23 May 1925 was a magnitude 7.0 earthquake with its epicentre in the Tajima region, where the former Kinosaki Town is located. In Kinosaki Hot Spa, many houses where people were cooking before noon collapsed and were almost completely consumed by fire, killing more than 400 people, making it a disaster of unprecedented scale in the Tajima region. Most buildings at the time were wooden and did not have the earthquake-proof technology for buildings that we have today, so the fire and other damage caused by the great earthquake also devastated the hot spring resort. The original hot springs remained largely unaffected, but all six out-spa baths were damaged by the earthquake. According to Kinosaki Town History Compilation Committee (1988), then Mayor Nishimura took into account the broad interests of the middle class in the former Kinosaki Town, including small and medium-sized inns and product shops, and actively implemented public works projects to rebuild the spa town, mainly through the reconstruction of the out-spa baths. The earthquake triggered a large-scale rezoning plan, whereby roads and the Otani River, which runs through the centre of the town, were extended to improve transport links, while all landowners were to provide the town with 10% of the publicly offered area free of charge to prepare against fire and flood damage.

After a hiatus during the Second World War, the rezoning project, which was completed in 1950, led to the formation of the current townscape of Kinosaki Hot Spa, which is representative of Kinosaki Hot Spa, with its rows of willow trees along, three-storey wooden inns and seven outdoor hot springs.

### 6.3.1.2 Indoor Baths Disturbances

According to the Kinosaki Town History Compilation Committee (1988), in Kinosaki Hot Spa, where the amount of spring water was low, it was customary and forbidden for each inn to build indoor baths, called *uchiyu*, on their premises to prevent the original hot spring water from drying up, thus allowing the culture of outside hot springs to take root. However, before World War II, some inns insisted on installing bathtubs on their premises and allowing indoor baths using the hot spring water that gushes from their premises. Disputes arose over the right to use the hot springs with other inns that had previously operated on the premise of an outside hot spring, leading to litigation between some inns and the Yushima Property District.

Litigation, both criminal and civil, continued until 1950, when a settlement and conciliation was reached, ending a dispute that had lasted 23 years. The installation of indoor baths was permitted, but the Kinosaki Hot Spa Utilisation Ordinance stipulated fees for the use of indoor baths, standards for approval of bathtub installation, penalties, etc., and all sources were to be centrally controlled by the Yushima Property District. After the Indoor Baths Disturbances, Japan's first centralised hot spring distribution system was introduced in 1956, and hot spring water was distributed to inns. Today, almost 100% of the inns in genuine need of hot spring water are already considered to be inns equipped with indoor baths (Kinosaki Town History Compilation Committee, 1988).

### 6.3.1.3 History of Collaborative Community Development

Question 1 of the interview survey asked about the history of collaborative town planning and investigated the initiatives undertaken by the actors involved. Based on the results of the automatic coding, an analysis was conducted on the responses concerning the Great Hokutan Earthquake and the Indoor Baths Disturbances.

The Great Hokutan Earthquake and the Indoor Baths Disturbances had a significant impact on the tourism and community design of Kinosaki Hot Spa. The interview indicates that the actors involved in tourism and community design in Kinosaki Hot Spa have become more aware of the practice of coexistence and co-prosperity, with the idea of coexistence and co-prosperity further heightened after the Great Hokutan Earthquake and the Indoor Baths Disturbances.

The townscape of Kinosaki Hot Spa, which suffered extensive damage from the Great Hokutan Earthquake, was reset, and the public and private sectors worked together to create a new landscape for the whole town. The reconstruction project that all the landowners of Kinosaki Hot Spa gave up part of their private property to start new town planning is a manifestation of the philosophy of co-existence and co-prosperity that has now taken root in the town planning of Kinosaki Hot Spa. The town, which was designed for the convenience of tourists while the actors themselves prepared for disasters, can be considered a pioneer in the creation of a tourist region that is "good to live in and good to visit".

The Kinosaki Town History Compilation Committee (1988) states that "The settlement of the indoor baths' lawsuit was reached because of many sacrifices and efforts by the people of Yushima Ward and both parties in the spirit of love for the town and the traditional Kinosaki Hot Spa philosophy of 'co-existence and co-prosperity'. At the time of the settlement, it was confirmed that, although the ownership of the land for the private springs was recognised as private, the right to use the hot spring water gushing from the springs was entirely owned by the Yushima Property District. The Kinosaki Hot Spa Utilisation Ordinance was promulgated, which clearly defined the former Kinosaki Town's spa business as a public enterprise, and the centralised management of Kinosaki Hot Spa usage rights came into effect". The historical fact that the culture of out-spa hot springs took root in Kinosaki Hot Spa due to the practice of not allowing the use of in-spa hot springs, and that the centralised management and distribution of hot springs started after the Indoor Baths Disturbances shows that the concept of the value of coexistence and co-prosperity in town development was formed by regarding hot springs as natural capital shared by local residents and by the property district protecting the source, the original hot spring. This is an example of the value concept of coexistence and co-prosperity town development.

### 6.3.2   Community Development for Co-existence and Co-prosperity

The idea of co-existence and co-prosperity is also reflected in Kinosaki Town (2004) and discussions towards the preparation of this plan were conducted by the Kinosaki Kono Saki 100 Year Conference. The council is a consultative body consisting of residents, NPOs, the former Kinosaki Town Yushima Property District, the former Kinosaki Town Chamber of Commerce and Industry, the Kinosaki Hot Spa Ryokan Cooperative Association and the Kinosaki Hot Spa

Tourist Association, along with external experts such as Professor Haruhiko Goto of Waseda University and students from the Massachusetts Institute of Technology.

The former Kinosaki Town is also a member of the council, but commerce and industry, particularly inns, are responsible for the preparation, implementation and ongoing management of the plan, while the administration plays a supporting role by preparing and implementing ordinances necessary for the maintenance and management of the landscape and providing subsidies. In the following, the current collaborative town planning in Kinosaki Hot Spa and its characteristics will be clarified by organising the relationship between the town management organisation and regional management organisation whose business purpose is to promote the basic plan for the revitalisation of the city centres. It also examines how the actors of tourism and community design in Kinosaki Hot Spa, while sharing the values of co-existence and co-prosperity, collaborate with external stakeholders, such as tourists, and attempt to co-create new values.

### 6.3.2.1  Town Management Organisation and Regional Management Organisation

Like many depopulated areas in Japan, the current situation in the former Kinosaki Town is that of a super-aged society, with the proportion of elderly people aged 65 and over in the total population exceeding 21%, and with a declining birthrate and an ageing population. According to the census conducted in 1965, when the former Kinosaki Town had the largest population, and the most recent census conducted in 2020, as shown in **Table 6.4**, the number of

**Table 6.4**  Number of Households, Population and Percentage of Population by Three Age Groups in the Former Kinosaki Town

|  | Number of Households | Total Population | Ratio of Juvenile Population | Ratio of Working Age Population | Ratio of Elderly Population |
|---|---|---|---|---|---|
| 1965 | 1,565 households | 6,262 persons | 23.8% | 68.0% | 8.2% |
| 2020 | 1,377 households | 3,125 persons | 9.7% | 48.7% | 41.6% |

Source: National Census.

households and total population in 2020 compared to 1965 were 88.0% and 49.9% respectively, the ratio of the juvenile population (aged 0 to 14) decreased 14.1 percentage points, the working-age population (aged 15 (aged 0 to 64) decreased by 19.3 percentage points, while the proportion of the elderly population (aged 65 and over) increased by 33.4 percentage points.

While many other well-known hot springs in Japan have resort hotels run by large corporations whose owners live in other towns rather than in the hot spring resort area, around 80% of the local population is employed in the tourism industry in Kinosaki Hot Spa. For many residents, Kinosaki Hot Spa is characterised as both a place of work and a place of residence. Therefore, the falling birthrate and ageing population will directly lead to a shortage of labour in Kinosaki Hot Spa and will also affect the vitality of the local community.

Kinosaki Town (2004) defines the area covered by the basic plan for the revitalisation of the city centres as "the area within which tourists can walk around the hot spring resort", which roughly corresponds to the area where the approximately 80 tourist inns and other facilities affiliated with the Kinosaki Hot Spa Ryokan Cooperative Association are located. The Kinosaki Town History Compilation Committee (1988) describes the topographical features of Kinosaki Hot Spa and the awareness of the local people towards hot springs: "The topography is narrow and surrounded on three sides by steeply sloping mountains, making it an inhospitable environment for agriculture. If there had been no hot springs, the village would probably have been absorbed by the neighbouring cities and towns. Therefore, there was a subconscious awareness that the only way to survive was to depend on the hot springs", it explains.

In 2012, a town development company called Yunomachi Kinosaki Co. was established to implement and manage the basic plan for the revitalisation of the central city area by utilising the natural capital of hot springs, taking into account the ongoing low birthrate and ageing population, the integration of work and residential areas and the topographical features of the area. The company is a private company established in 2008 to implement and manage the implementation of the basic plan for the revitalisation of the central city area, and is funded by nine local tourism, commerce and industry-related organisations, including the Kinosaki Hot Spa Ryokan Cooperative Association and the Kinosaki

Hot Spa Tourist Association. In Kinosaki Hot Spa, the management of inns has been passed down from parent to child for generations. Many of the directors of the town development company are descendants of local landlords, known as masterssince the Edo period, and are the owners of inns in Kinosaki Hot Spa.

### 6.3.2.2 Current Collaborative Community Development

Questions 2 and 3 of the interview survey asked about the general situation of current collaborative town planning and its characteristics, and investigated the initiatives undertaken by the actors involved and how they differ from other spa destinations. Based on the results of the automatic coding, it was assumed that the current collaborative town planning and its characteristics are related to the integration of the place of work and the place of residence and the existence of the town management organisation, and the answers related to these issues were analysed.

According to the interviews, residents in Kinosaki Hot Spa explained that because business and life are almost the same, they inevitably cannot only think about making money, but also take part in various community events. For example, in Kinosaki Hot Spa, the PTA presidents of successive generations of elementary and junior high school PTAs have always been inn owners and other people involved in commerce and industry, and many of the fire brigade members are also involved in commerce and industry, and people working in the tourism industry are often leaders and members of the community. In other words, in Kinosaki Hot Spa, there is a lot of overlap between local issues and tourism and community design issues, so solving local issues is linked to promoting tourism and community design.

Although Yunomachi Kinosaki Co. is a for-profit town development company, the profits earned from its business activities are used as a resource for tourism town development for the benefit of tourists and Kinosaki Hot Spa as a whole. All of the company's directors are unpaid to manage the town development company and carry out projects for tourism and town development. As many residents are engaged in the tourism industry in the spa resort, it is a characteristic of Kinosaki Hot Spa that the main actors in the tourism town development and the directors of the regional management organisation are the same people. Therefore, the value of co-existence and co-prosperity, which is a tradition of Kinosaki Hot Spa, is shared not only in tourism and community design, but also in the activities of the regional management organisation. The fact that the town development company and the regional management organisation share many common actors and share the values of co-existence and co-prosperity and are the main actors in tourism town development and community development is a characteristic of Kinosaki Hot Spa Resort.

### 6.3.2.3   Value Co-creation with Tourists

The Kinosaki Hot Spa Tourism Association website introduces Kinosaki Hot Spa as having the concept of "the whole town as one big inn". The idea is that the JR Kinosaki Hot Spa Station is the entrance to the town, the streets are the corridors, the inns are the guest rooms, the out-spa is the baths, the souvenir shops are the shops and the restaurants are the restaurants, and not only the guests at the inns and shops, but the whole town welcomes all guests with care. A walk from the *ryokan*, dressed in *yukata* and clanking clogs, through the willow trees along the Otani River and the three-storey wooden *ryokan* street to the seven out-spa baths has become the standard way to enjoy Kinosaki Hot Spa.

To maintain the landscape of Kinosaki Hot Spa, which was created in the process of reconstruction after the occurrence of the Great Hokutan Earthquake, some of the projects listed in the basic plan for the revitalisation of the city centres in the former Kinosaki Town include those that require the cooperation of tourists. Kinosaki Town (2004) states in its project to familiarise itself with the Otani River, which creates the symbolic landscape of Kinosaki Hot Spa, such as preserving the trees planted along the river and introducing night-time lighting to enrich the atmosphere of the town: "It is required of Kinosaki Hot Spa, the residents who live in Kinosaki and the visitors to Kinosaki that this atmosphere and nature is maintained for the next 100 years".

In the soundscape project, which refers to soundscapes such as the sound of wooden clogs called *geta* echoing through the hot spring resort, the murmur of the Otani River, the rustling of willows, the cries of cicadas and festival music, it is explained that "the 'soundscape' and 'local culture' are closely related, and the landscape given meaning by each individual's sensibility creates the image of the landscape of the entire town. It can be said that the landscape that is signified by the sensibility of everyone creates the image of the landscape of the town as a whole". In other words, the plan is based on the hope that tourists will not only use Kinosaki Hot Spa but will also be involved in maintaining the atmosphere and landscape of Kinosaki Hot Spa as actors in the development of the tourism town.

### 6.3.2.4 Values in Town Planning and New Value Co-creation Plan

Questions 4 and 5 of the interview survey explored the values of town planning and the plans for new value co-creation. Based on the results of the automatic coding, we analysed the responses regarding these values, focusing on the existing town planning values of co-existence and co-prosperity, and the new attempted value co-creation relationship with external stakeholders.

According to the interviews, it was explained that the pride of those working in Kinosaki Hot Spa is to keep the landscape intact and protect the atmosphere of the town, and at the same time, this is the value that customers perceive in this town. The actors in Kinosaki Hot Spa town development, including residents who are not involved in the tourism industry, have naturally developed a sense of hospitality. For example, there are no litter bins in the streets of Kinosaki Hot Spa, but there is hardly any litter on the streets. Tourists come to Kinosaki Hot Spa expecting to see a clean town, so the custom of cleaning up the streets before local festivals and other events has naturally developed. Based on the principles of co-existence and co-prosperity, Kinosaki Hot Spa has fostered a culture of taking the initiative in doing things for the town, without asking for anything in return from others.

In Kinosaki Hot Spa, where the entire town is regarded as a large inn and has a unique atmosphere and landscape, tourists are not expected to cause nuisances such as throwing rubbish in the streets, which can be likened to corridors, or making noise in the streets. To co-create the values of Kinosaki Hot Spa with tourists who feel sympathy for tourism and community design, a new tourism and community design plan for the next 100 years is being prepared in the former Kinosaki Town.

### 6.3.3 Analysis of Value Co-creation Mechanisms through Public Service Ecosystem

Using the framework by the process of public service delivery and the associated value dimensions of public service delivery, it is possible to organise the values of Kinosaki Hot Spa in tourism town development, as shown in **Table 6.5**.

**Table 6.5** Values in Tourism and Community Design of Kinosaki Hot Spa by Value Dimensions of Public Service Delivery

| Dimensions of value | Individual | Service system | Society |
|---|---|---|---|
| Value-in-exchange | Value as the price paid by tourists for tourism services. (e.g. the price of a night's accommodation at an inn). | Value as either the amount of money that the town planning company puts into tourism and community design as an input or the amount paid by the tourist. (e.g. costs incurred by the town management organisation). | Value as the price paid by society for tourism and community design in the form of taxes. (e.g. subsidies from the prefecture to promote universal tourism to Kinosaki Hot Spa). |
| Value-in-production | Value added from the experience of being involved in the co-design and/or co-production of tourism and community design. (e.g. improving the image of the town's landscape by touring the out-spa baths wearing yukata and geta). | Value added from co-design and/or co-production of tourism and community development services. (e.g. cleaning activities and snow shoveling to improve the image of the town's landscape). | Value added by tourism and community development services that create existing social values or beliefs. (e.g. tourism region development that considers both tourists and local residents and the local culture and environment). |
| Value-in-use | Added value of the experience of using tourism and community design as an effect on the life experiences of tourists. (e.g. unusual | Value added from the experience of being involved in the production of tourism and community design (e.g. increased satisfaction of tourists | Value added from increased social wellbeing and/or inclusion because of tourism community development services. (e.g. rediscovering the |

| | experiences in inns and city centres). | and constituents) | attractiveness of the town, increasing the number of people involved). |
|---|---|---|---|
| Value-in-context | Value added from the impact of tourism and community design services on the needs of tourists. (e.g. increased willingness to participate in tourism and community design). | Value added from improved tourism and community design services because of iterative learning within the service ecosystem. (e.g. raising awareness of the need to promote coexistence and co-prosperity in tourism and community design). | Value added by the impact of tourism and community development services on identified social and economic needs. (e.g. increased tourism GDP) |

Source: Prepared by the Authors.

Experiential value as defined by (Schmitt & Zarantonello, 2013) is relevant in public service logic to the process of public service delivery for individuals and falls under value-in-use as a value dimension. Value-in-use for individuals is only part of the value in the public service, tourism and community design; as Osborne 2018 suggests, in public service logic, value creation in the production, use and delivery of public services not only for individuals but also for service systems and society and processes in the production, use and delivery of public services, not only for individuals, but also for service systems and societies. **Table 6.5**, based on the Public Service Logic framework, shows that users of tourism and town development services, such as tourists, commercial and industrial actors and residents of Kinosaki Hot Spa, not only find value in the use of services, but also co-create value by being involved in the production of services.

It is also possible to organise the roles of the various actors participating in the development of the tourist town of Kinosaki Hot Spa in terms of a public service ecosystem. **Figure 6.1** shows the implementation and progress management system of the basic plan for the revitalisation of the city centres in Kinosaki Town (Kinosaki Town, 2004).

**Figure 6.1**   Implementation and Management of Basic Plan for the Revitalisation of
City Centres in Kinosaki Town

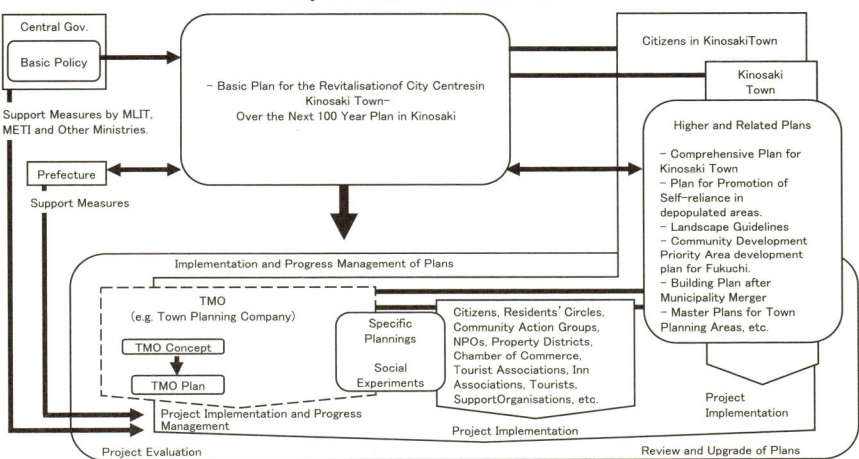

Source: Kinosaki Town (2004, 5).

At the institutional level, this applies to national and prefectural measures to support tourism and community design. For the interior renovation of inns and the promotion of universal tourism, the state and prefectures provide assistance in the form of subsidies and funding on favourable terms. At the service level, as mentioned above, while town development companies whose members are related to commerce and industry play a central role in tourism town development, Toyooka City, of which the former Kinosaki Town became part as a result of the merger, has enacted an ordinance to maintain the landscape of the three-storey wooden inn area and to create a lively atmosphere in Kinosaki Hot Spa resort at night during summer months. Support is provided for setting off fireworks. On an individual level, the various commercial and industrial players are working to make the whole town a major hotel that tourists can feel valued by. Behind this is a shared awareness of the need to utilise the town's precious natural capital, its hot springs, to promote tourism and community development for co-existence and co-prosperity at the level of belief, and the cooperation of the residents. Although the tourism and town development actors involved may not explicitly have such awareness, the basic plan for the revitalisation of the city centres in Kinosaki Town has a lot in common with the public service ecosystem and is being implemented and progressively managed.

## 6.4   Conclusion

As a value related to tourism, the experiential value brought about by the effects and satisfaction gained through the experience of use has been the subject of consideration. In recent years, tourism and community design or tourism region planning has been promoted, but the value created by increasing the attractiveness of tourism destinations, which are also places of residence for local actors, has not been clarified. The study therefore focuses on Kinosaki Hot Spa, where many actors are involved in tourism and community design and examines what kind of value can be co-created through tourism and community design.

In Kinosaki Hot Spa, which has a history of approximately 1,300 years, the values of co-existence and co-prosperity have long existed, as the hot springs are regarded as natural capital shared by residents and the limited quantity of spring sources is utilised. After the Great Hokutan Earthquake and the Indoor Baths Disturbances, the value concept of coexistence and co-prosperity town planning solidified by the property district protecting the original hot spring through centralised management and distribution of hot spring water. In the tourism and community design of Kinosaki Hot Spa, which is being promoted based on the principles of co-existence and co-prosperity, tourists are not only expected to use Kinosaki Hot Spa, but also to be involved as actors in tourism and community design to maintain the atmosphere and landscape of the area.

We positioned tourism and community design as a public service implemented through public-private partnerships and used public service logic to elucidate the mechanism of value co-creation in Kinosaki Hot Spa. Focusing on the relationship between production and utilisation in tourism and community design, we organised the value of tourism and community design in Kinosaki Hot Spa using a framework with five public service delivery processes for individuals, service systems and society, and four value dimensions of related public service delivery. Experiential value, which is considered in much of the previous literature, corresponds to value-in-use for individuals in the public service logic. As Osborne (2021) indicates, to promote value co-creation, at the four levels of the public service ecosystem (institutional, service, individual and belief levels) value and the dimensions of value creation, as well as the interactions across levels, need to be understood.

## ● References

Eriksson, E., Andersson, T., Hellström, A., Gadolin, G. & Lifvergren, S. (2020). Collaborative Public Management: Coordinated Value Propositions among Public Service Organisations. *Public Management Review*, 22(6), 791-812.

Grönroos, C. (2019). Reforming Public Services: Does Service Logic Have Anything to Offer? *Public Management Review*, 21(5), 775-788.

Hori, K. and Sato, Y. (2019). Effectiveness and Challenges of Measures to Promote Collaboration in Tourism and Community Design. *Journal of Tourism Research*, 30 (2), 39-51.

Japan Tourism Agency and UNWTO Office in Japan (2020). *Guidelines for Sustainable Tourism in Japan*.

Japan Tourism Agency (2023). *White Paper on Tourism 2023*.

Kinosaki Town History Compilation Committee (1988). *Kinosaki Town History*.

Kinosaki Town (2004). The Basic Plan for the Revitalisation of the City Centres in Kinosaki Town.

Morishita, S. (2022). Examining the Experience Value of Japanese Inns through Analysis of Foreign Visitors View. *The Tourism Studies*, 34, 109-115.

Osborne, S. P. (2018). From Public Service-Dominant Logic to Public Service Logic: Are Public Service Organizations Capable of Co-production and Value Co-creation? *Management Review*, 20 (2), 225-231.

Osborne, S. P. (2021). *Public Service Logic: Creating Value Public Service Users, Citizens, and Society through Public Service Delivery*. Routledge.

Osborne, S. P., Nasi, G., & Powell, M. (2021). Beyond Co-production: Value Creation and Public Services. *Public Administration*, 99 (4), 641-657.

Osborne, S. P., Powell, M., Cui, T., & Strokosch, K. (2022). Value Creation in the Public Service Ecosystem: An Integrative Framework. *Public Administration Review*, 82 (4), 634-645.

Schmitt, B. & Zarantonello, L. (2013). Consumer Experience and Experiential Marketing: A Critical Review, Malhotra. *Review of Marketing Research*, 10, 25-61.

UNWTO (2007). *UNWTO Guidelines for Institutional Strengthening of Destination Management Organisations* (DMOs).

Virtanen, P. & Jalonen, H. (2024). Public Value Creation Mechanisms in the Context of Public Service Logic: An Integrated Conceptual Framework. *Public Management Review*, 26(8), 2331-2354.

Yuan, Y. H. & Wu, C. K. (2008). Relationships among Experiential Marketing, Experiential Value and Customer Satisfaction. *Journal of Hospitality and Tourism Research*, 32 (3), 387-410.

Wu, H. C., Cheng, C. C., & Ai, C. H. (2018). A Study of Experiential Quality, Experiential Value, Trust, Corporate Reputation, Experiential Satisfaction and Behavioral Intentions for Cruise Tourists: The Case of Hong Kong. *Tourism Management*, 66, 200-220.

Chapter **7**

# Value Creation and Performance Evaluation in Japanese Local Governments: Focusing on the Case of Usuki City

**Fumiaki Himawari**

**Daisaku Sakai**

**Abstract**

In recent years, the term "value" has been used more frequently in public management. The term "value co-creation" has come to be used in government and central ministry documents. However, there is no clear definition of value in public management. Influenced by New Public Management (NPM) since 1990s, various administrative reforms have been implemented in Japanese local governments. NPM-based administrative methods emphasize economy, efficiency, and effectiveness. Municipal services have been improved from this perspective. Among the various methods, performance evaluation, which has been adopted by many local governments in particular, has become a central tool for administrative reform in Japanese local governments.

On the other hand, in recent years, there has been criticism of such NPM-based administrative reforms and value recognition; Moore (1995) and Osborne (2021) are representative studies, and changes are occurring in the concept of value in public management. This paper analyzes administrative reform in Japan, taking Usuki City, Oita Prefecture, as a case study. Usuki City is one of the first cities to reform public accounting and introduced performance evaluation early on. Usuki City has been working on administrative reform based on NPM. However, in recent years, the city established a system for comprehensive performance improvement and has begun a new stage with evaluation by citizen and citizen participation. Through a case study of Usuki City, the past administrative reforms in Japan will be examined, and it will become clear that evaluation by citizens and citizens participation are important for future local government management for value creation.

**Key Words:**
Performance Evaluation, New Public Management, Public Value, Public Service Logic, Citizen Participation

## 7.1 Introduction

The term "value" has been used by Japanese administrative organizations since the 1990s, when administrative and fiscal reforms influenced by New Public Management (NPM) were implemented. The debate over what value means in local governments has intensified since the introduction of NPM, but a clear conclusion has not yet been reached regarding value and value creation in local governments.

Based on recent research findings, this study first examines the meaning of value and value creation for local governments. Next, as a specific case study, we examine the reform process in Usuki City, Oita Prefecture, which has been working to improve the value of its service provision. We aim to identify and examine specific efforts to improve services, which are the source of value provided by local governments; this is done not only through internal management improvements but also by incorporating service recipients' perspectives into performance evaluation. Finally, we clarify the importance of the role of citizens, not only as service recipients but also as co-creators of those services. The aim is to help local governments create more value for citizens in the future.

## 7.2 Value in Local Governments

### 7.2.1 Value created by local governments

The term "value" has been used frequently by local governments in recent years.

However, there is no clear definition of the type of value that local governments create. For example, the term "value-added" has long been used in the business world. In the classical context, value-added provides a productivity-centered idea of how much value is added to the resources invested in an organization; it is generally derived from accounting figures. In a prominent study related to value-added, Michael Porter first introduced the concept of the value chain (Porter, 1985). His study discussed the creation of value by companies/organizations through the investment of resources.

The classical view about value is that value in business is expressed in terms of the amount of profit generated from the investment of resources. In the case of local governments which do not operate for profit, it is difficult to express value in terms of such accounting figures; therein lies one of the reasons for the difficulty in articulating the concept of value for local governments.

Despite these difficulties, NPM is characterized by the fact that it views value in the same way that businesses do (Osborne, 2021). As Hood (1991) and other studies have shown, one of NPM's propositions is to incorporate private companies' management methods into local governments' operations. Neoliberal pressure for efficiency in public administration has created the background for NPM. Under these circumstances, administrative reform has also been introduced in Japan, to eliminate uneconomic and inefficient services, and improve the remaining ones. Among the various methods, the one that was introduced the most was the performance evaluation. Many local governments have been using a performance evaluation tool based on linear cause-and-effect relationships; it is called "the logic model" that is used to examine the economic efficiency and effectiveness of services. In other words, under NPM, the criterion for value is whether the services are created economically and efficiently.

The definition of value based on NPM has been critically evaluated in recent years. The idea of Public Value (PV) that the value of public services is enriching society, and that administrative management should be based on this value, is gaining ground. Moore and Benington are considered to be proponents of this idea (Moore, 1995; Benington, 2009; Benington and Moore, 2011; Moore, 2013). Moore (1995, 2013) have suggested that the value provided to individuals as consumers in the private sector is different from the value provided in various forms to individuals and society as a whole in the public sector. Society is a group formed by members of the public, and their evaluations are referred to as public value. Benington (2009) states that public value connotes value addition into the public sphere. It includes not only economic value but also ecological, political, social, and cultural values. In addition, it is not only the government that is responsible for creating public value, but also the private and voluntary sectors, informal organizations, and others.

Osborne (2010) discussed New Public Governance and emphasized the importance of networks in public services. Osborne (2010) clarified the limitations of government monopolies in providing services, and highlighted the importance of networks in public services. Osborne (2021) proposed Public Service Logic (PSL) as a new logic for evaluating value in the public sector. He highlights that the problem with conventional NPM-based administrative management methods is that they are inclined toward a product-dominant technical approach, rather than the essence of service. He states that an administrative management method that understands the essence of service is important. He also notes that users should not be regarded as passive recipients of services, but should be emphasized as co-creators of value.

PV and PSL methods are both critical of administrative methods based on NPM that focus on economy and efficiency. PSL criticizes easy value evaluations based on linear logic, and focuses on how administrative services create value by mainly focusing on the nature of the service. These discussions on value in local governments show that it is important to measure value broadly and comprehensively; and that citizens must be viewed as active entities. Their evaluation and participation in value creation must be encouraged, instead of simply defining value in terms of administrative outputs.

### 7.2.2　Value creation and internal management

In 7.2.1, we examined the value created by local governments based on recent studies. In these studies, value does not refer to the products (or services) produced by local governments themselves, but rather to the social changes and impacts created by them.

The logic model that captures the linear flow of inputs, outputs, and outcomes has had a significant influence on NPM-based administrative management. Based on discussions on value, the logic model has a certain affinity with value creation in terms of outcomes. However, NPM-based administrative management has tended to focus on inputs and outputs and prioritized economy and efficiency. On the one hand, it may not be appropriate to dismiss all NPM-based administrative management to date by relying solely on PV and PSL. While it is extremely important to be aware of these other methods in the evaluation of final outcomes and values, NPM-based administrative management can contribute to certain areas, especially when focusing on the internal management of local governments.

Anthony's management control theory has long been used as a framework for examining organizational management (Anthony, 1965,1988; Anthony and Young, 2003); for classifying the organization control process into planning control, management control, and operational control; and clarifying that the decisions to be made, and the subjects to be considered differ according to the hierarchical classification of the organization. He highlighted the importance of management control, which links both planning control and operational control.

Linking Anthony's theory to previous discussions on value, planning control may determine the value to be created and set the direction which the organization should move forward on. Based on this premise, management control is the process of examining specific methods for creating value, communicating them to the field, and managing them. Given this, operational control is considered the process of appropriately producing services at each site. Therefore, it is necessary to be keenly conscious of the value on planning control and management control. Simultaneously, NPM-based methods are needed to run services economically and efficiently in management control and operational control. On the other hand, PSL is characterized by its emphasis on value at the field-level because it focuses on services; appropriate operational control can be simultaneously achieved by being aware of this during management control. This awareness of value at the field-level is also a characteristic of PSL as it focuses on services.

In summary, this discussion suggests that the value that local governments should provide is the one propagated by PV and PSL. However, from the perspective of municipal management, it is important not to reject NPM-based administrative management altogether, but to integrate all these ideas. Value-oriented planning and internal management are necessary to provide the public with true value. Internal management tools include the financial statements and performance evaluation that have been used in the past. For internal management, it is necessary to seek a value perspective rather than simple economic and efficiency. To this end, as Osborne (2021) highlights, a mechanism for citizens to be involved in these activities, and accountability information that can capture citizens' evaluations, are important.

## 7.3 Value Creation Initiatives in Usuki City

Thus, to create value for citizens, it is necessary to redefine the concept of value and establish an internal management system and citizen participation based on this redefinition. This study considers the case of Usuki City, Oita Prefecture, to examine the administrative and fiscal reform efforts of local governments in Japan. Usuki City was the first city in Japan to create the balance sheet, and has been working to create financial statements and a performance evaluation system appropriate for local governments. The city has not only adopted these NPM-based methods but has also incorporated the perspective of citizen participation, an approach that is in line with the value discussion of recent years. However, this does not necessarily imply that they are functioning faultlessly or smoothly; there are some issues remaining that need to be addressed. Through a case study of Usuki City, it is possible to observe the fusion of NPM-based methods and modern values, their achievements, and challenges.

First, we systematically organize examples of public accounting and municipal reforms that began with the creation of Usuki City's financial statement and examine their processes and significance. We examine how the Usuki City Service Verification System, the performance evaluation system functions to improve the quality of administrative services and create new service value. We also discuss how the services can be further developed. One of the co authors of this study had worked in Usuki City Office for many years, and the description of the case of Usuki City is based on his experiences during that time.

### 7.3.1   Outline of Usuki City, Oita Prefecture

Usuki City is located in the southeastern part of Oita Prefecture, facing the Bungo Channel of Kyushu, and is designated as the Nippo Kaigan Quasi-National Park. The town has a population of approximately 35,000 and is surrounded by mountains and the sea.

The present city center was built by Otomo Sorin, a Christian feudal lord who ruled the entire Kyushu area during the Warring States Period, in the 16th century. It was known as a port designated for trade with Spain and Portugal, and used as a base for Christian missionary work. Since then, it has become an important political and economic center. At the time, Usuki was regarded an international city that imported Western culture. The castle town landscape formed around Usuki Castle remains well preserved, and the unusual town layout still exists.

In November 2021, the city was recognized as a member of the UNESCO Creative Cities Network[1](food culture) in recognition of its activities to preserve and spread its traditional food culture. As a food culture creation city, the city aims to promote industries that make the most of its diverse food culture.

### 7.3.2   Preparation of the Balance Sheet

In summary, the local government is a place where services are provided for citizens. In other words, the local government produces services, which form the basis of the value. Local governments build and own city halls, schools, sports facilities, community centers, and roads; through use by the public, and over time, this infrastructure products services and eventually creates value.

Local governments have many employees, and personnel costs account for a large proportion of municipal expenditures. Some employees provide services direct to citizens, such as health promoters, whereas others indirectly provide services, such as the levying and collecting of taxes. The nature of their work varies, but the bottom line is that they are all engaged in providing municipal services. Employees provide value to citizens through their services, whether directly or indirectly. The major characteristic of local governments is that they produce only services. This is a completely different characteristic from that of ordinary private sector companies. In addition to producing products, private companies generate profits, pay dividends from their profits, pay taxes, and accumulate capital. The purpose of private companies is to maximize profits, and the production and sale of products are merely means to that end. Local governments produce only services and aim to maximize them. As previously mentioned, this factor complicates the value provided by local governments. At the root of the various initiatives that Usuki City has undertaken is the idea that the local government produces only services and aims to maximize services; thus, these initiatives have been undertaken to understand and improve the provision of value through these municipal services.

There are two positions from which to judge whether municipal services have been adequately provided. One is the perspective of the local government as the service provider, and the other is the perspective of citizens as the service recipients. Citizens need information to decide whether services are satisfactory, so the city, as a supplier, needs to report the kinds of services it has aimed for and implemented. Financial statements are necessary for this fundamental evaluation; thus, the first step that the Usuki City undertook was to develop them. The most fundamental factor in judging the value of services is to evaluate the kind of services provided and whether the funds (public tax revenues) used to pay for them have been satisfactorily used. No matter how much pride the local government takes in providing services, it cannot be judged as a good service unless the citizens who consume them are not satisfied. Therefore, the supplier must always be evaluated by the recipient and produce results that meet the recipient's expectations. Local governments' preparation of financial statements is a fundamental effort when residents evaluate the value of their local government.

From this perspective, Usuki City decided to create the balance sheet, which had not been created by any other local government in Japan. The reason for Usuki City's decision to create the balance sheet was their poor performance with regard to financial indicators for 1994. Usuki City's ordinary account balance ratio of 93.0%, bond expense ratio of 20.7%, and debt limit ratio of 15.7%, were not only the worst among the 58 local governments in Oita Prefecture, but also the second worst among the 93 cities in the Kyushu Area, and the seventh worst among the 663 cities in Japan. Japanese Local governments that still use single-year cash-based accounting are now required to prepare the balance sheet on a supplementary basis; however, around 1994, there was no concept of local governments preparing the balance sheet in Japan. However, Usuki City decided to prepare the balance sheet to allow its residents to evaluate the value of Usuki City, and Usuki City to assess the value of its own services. In preparing the balance sheet, Usuki City aimed to explain the use of taxes in a more concrete and easy-to-understand manner to its citizens. It was planned that the balance sheet would show what kind of financial resources were used for asset formation, in addition to providing information on single-year cash-basis accounting.

### 7.3.3  The Service Formation Account[2] (Statement of Administrative Costs)

To demonstrate the value created by the local government, it is not only necessary to clarify the balance sheet, which shows asset formation and use of funds, but also the cost of the services which are basis of value. Following the creation of the balance sheet, Usuki City began to create the Service Formation Account to clarify who bore the costs of the services. This statement is equivalent to profit and loss statements in corporate accounting. Asset formation can be gauged from the balance sheet, but to clarify ordinary expenses such as personnel and administrative costs, and the types of municipal services and their costs and financial burdens, the Service Formation Account was considered necessary to show how the services were formed.

The Service Formation Account is required to analyze services, clarify how much they cost and who paid for them; thereafter, the information is widely disclosed, so that city officials are themselves aware of the cost and result of each service. The purpose of creating the Service Formation Account was to clarify the content and cost of the service and who bore its cost.

For the local government to improve its services and the value they provide, it needs to explain or clarify who paid for those services and provide details on the content, quantity, and cost of the services. In addition, they must also be evaluated by citizens. The Service Formation Account is an attempt to organize such information. The features of the Service Formation Account of Usuki City are as follows.

Like the balance sheet, it is classified into six categories by purpose: Living, Environment, Welfare, Education, Industry, and General Affairs. It is structured to show what kinds of expenses were incurred in providing municipal services. In addition, the Detailed Sheet of the Service Formation Account, which shows the expenses for each service in detail, was prepared. This clarifies the specific costs of projects closely related to citizens, such as daycare and civic centers, and provides material for examining future administrative projects and efficiency improvements. This information is available to the public and in fact served as a decision-making tool when public nursery schools were outsourced to the private sector in 1999. Information from the Service Formation Account is also used when assembling service projects in the budgeting process.

By organizing these financial statements, disclosing information, and receiving evaluations, a foundation has been established for understanding value and making improvements. However, at the root of these efforts is a structure in which the local government provides value through their services, and citizens receive them. And these efforts are based on the idea of incorporating corporate accounting methods into local governments operations. There is still no idea of citizen participation here. At this stage, it can be said that they remain limited to NPM-based value recognition. However, these efforts by Usuki City were epoch-making in Japan at a time when the basic approach to organizing financial information had not yet been implemented.

## 7.4 Creating a Mechanism to Evolve Services - Creating Service Value -

### 7.4.1 Use of financial information and service improvement

The balance sheet and the Service Formation Accounts are the most basic information disclosures, which can explain the process of policymaking to the citizens; such as why a project was implemented and why a certain method was adopted, along with financial information. To improve services for citizens, it is necessary to make use of the information contained in these financial statements. By creating the balance sheet, Usuki City can take action with specific goal-setting to improve its financial structure. Furthermore, the information obtained from the financial documents can be used to make decisions on policies and other matters as part of the process of "Creating Local Government that is Useful for Citizens."A moot point is not so much that financial statements, such as balance sheet and Service Formation Accounts were created, but rather that internal capacity building was achieved in the process of creating them, with the support of related partners. This is believed to have triggered the creation of new value in the services that followed.

On the other hand, the preparation of the financial statements was a collaborative effort: experts and the Planning and Management Department within Usuki City performed the work, and the staff of the Finance Section did all the calculations. It is difficult to improve services successfully if only a few staff members within an organization perform cost accounting, and publicly announce it as part of the closing documents after the project is completed. Therefore, to share this knowledge and experience with all departments and employees, the Service (Cost, Financial Burden, Purpose, and Performance) Verification System described in the next section was established, and all the staff are now working to improve value by enhancing citizen services, while making efforts to restore government finances.

### 7.4.2  Comprehensive Systems for Performance Improvement

With the aim of improving the value provided to citizens through services, Usuki City has started creating the Service Verification System. This system is prepared since 2000 to utilizes information from the balance sheet and Service Formation Account and other sources. This system is designed to determine whether or not the services were effective to utilize future service development. This system requires all staff members who make the decisions to be proficient in its use.

The Service Formation Account created in 1999 made it possible to organize the costs, financial resources, and financial burdens for various services. This enabled the city to calculate and disclose the costs for all the city's projects and the six departments of Living, Environment, Welfare, Industry, and General Affairs, as well as to organize and disclose the costs and financial resources for the major projects of each department. Based on this cost information, Usuki City has begun systematizing the Service Verification System as a performance evaluation system. In this performance evaluation system, administrative activities, which are the smallest units of internal affairs, were set as the unit of evaluation. This system places the "Improvement of Services for Citizens" as the top priority goal. In the process of implementing the evaluation, the system is being built with the objective of comprehensively promoting, the Usuki City Comprehensive Plan, thorough accountability, an administrative shift to result-oriented administration, and the realization of citizen-oriented administration. Therefore, the purpose of introducing the Service Verification System can be summarized as follows:

- Improve municipal services
- Systematic, efficient, and comprehensive promotion of the Comprehensive Plan
- Thorough accountability of administrative results to citizens
- Shift to a result-oriented administration based on the citizens' perspective
- Realization of citizen-oriented, efficient, and high-quality public administration

The contents of the evaluation of administrative activities were contained in a single A4-size sheet to prepare for the evaluation and its utilization as efficiently and effectively as possible. The evaluation was conducted from three perspectives (Necessity, Effectiveness, and Efficiency) and was based on an understanding of the relationship with the Comprehensive Plan; it contains non-financial information to consider the degree of achievement of action and performance as well as the costs derived from the financial statements. Furthermore, the evaluation was composed of items indicating "understanding of administrative problems and issues" and "specific improvement plans," which are considered the most important items in performance evaluation. It is a NPM-based performance management evaluation system structured from the perspective of necessity, effectiveness, and efficiency with an awareness of the inputs, outputs, and outcomes. This evaluation system, which targets administrative activities as the smallest unit of internal administration, contributes to management control and operational control. Although it may be criticized as an NPM-based performance management evaluation system, it is indispensable from the viewpoint of improving internal management for value creation.

Furthermore, the evaluation of measures, which is the basis for evaluation of the entire organization, has been conducted since 2006. While the evaluation of administrative activities mainly seeks results in the form of improvement of operations and the fostering of cost awareness among employees, the evaluation of the measures is conducted mainly for the purpose of verifying measures positioned as the objectives of administrative activities. It is meant as a progress management tool for the comprehensive plan, and for fulfilling the accountability of operations to citizens and other stakeholders. In addition to external accountability, these measures contribute to management control and planning control.

The performance evaluation that Usuki City undertook was based on the major objective of evolving services or improving the provision of value through services, and was positioned to play a major role in managing the progress of the comprehensive plan, and as a method of promoting administrative and fiscal reform. In addition to the evaluation of administrative operations, the introduction of measure evaluation has resulted in a system in which all employees, from those in charge of administrative operations to the managers in charge of the measures, are evaluated. The development of these internal management environments provides a foundation for efforts to understand and improve value through service provision.

## 7.5   Internal Management Cycle

### 7.5.1   Premise for Internal Management Cycle Formation

In Usuki City, the Service Verification System is used within the organization to evaluate and verify whether a project is truly necessary and if it is being implemented efficiently and without waste. However, to improve and enhance municipal services, it is essential for both the citizens and local government, as recipients and providers of the services, respectively, to evaluate the services. Therefore, since 2002, Usuki City has been conducting an awareness survey (citizen questionnaire) titled "Usuki City Better City Planning Questionnaire" via mail; it asks for citizens' perspectives on the city's policies and measures.

This questionnaire was designed as the citizen awareness survey to survey citizens' level of need and satisfaction with 53 measures (the Second Usuki City Comprehensive Plan). It categorizes each measure into: the review area (low need and high satisfaction), consideration area (both need and satisfaction are low), the improvement area (both need and satisfaction are high, so improvement or maintenance is desired), and the enhancement area (high need and low satisfaction, so enhancement of initiatives is desired). In particular, the measures of the enhancement area are those where the level of need and satisfaction are higher and lower than the average, respectively. They are thus judged to have a high level of importance and priority as areas where enhancement is desired. In previous NPM approaches, performance was monitored and improved, mainly from the supply side perspective. However, as discussed in Osborne's study and others, the user perspective is indispensable in discussing value in service provision.

Specifically, these evaluations are compiled as external evaluations, and together with internal evaluations conducted by the local government itself, they are used by the "Usuki City Administrative and Financial Revitalization Promotion Committee,"[3] which consists of citizen representatives from various

Figure 7.1  Service Verification System Flow

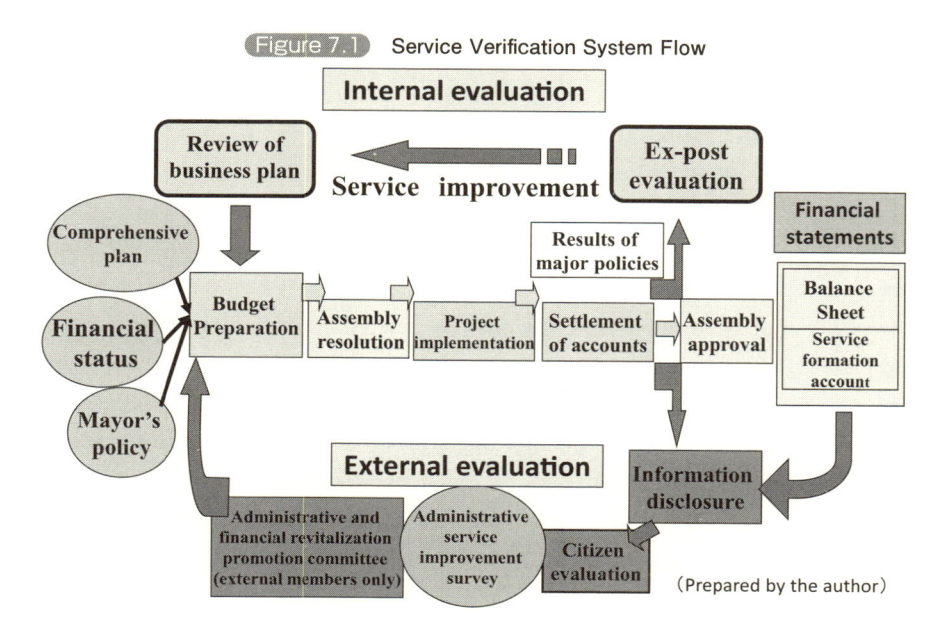

(Prepared by the author)

fields and social spectrum. At committee meetings, measures and policy evaluations are discussed and evaluations and recommendations are made regarding the priorities for project implementation. The results of the 2020 survey indicate that the following are the most important issues for the city: "support for stable and independent living," "environmental improvement for disaster prevention and disaster mitigation," "fostering and attracting local businesses," "improving basic academic skills," "improving convenience of public transportation," "abuse prevention and countermeasures." It is important to note that this initiative involves not only the evaluation perspective but also the participation of citizens who are service users in the basic decisions of local government management. This initiative, which not only evaluates performance from an external perspective, but also incorporates the perspective of participation, can be seen as a step forward from NPM-based management perspective to the value-creation perspective discussed in PV and PSL.

### 7.5.2 Usuki City Service Verification System for value creation

In order for the Usuki City Service Verification System to become a performance evaluation system that leads to further value creation, it is necessary to refine the verification of the internal evaluation which forms the basis of the city organizations' systems, and the external evaluation which centers on citizen awareness surveys.

So far, the city has used external evaluation primarily as reference for projects that are listed in the enhancement area at measures level. So external evaluation is treated as a support for internal evaluation. This makes it difficult to expect the performance evaluations to lead to the creation of new value for the municipal services. This is why we believe that a new perspective is needed for the analysis and verification of each evaluation.

Measures in the enhancement area, as determined by the citizen awareness survey, are those that have not been effectively accepted by citizens. The measures in this area are highly necessary but deemed unsatisfactory. However, the city's decision is limited to "strengthening the measures in this area in the future with emphasis on the results of the survey." This means that the specific development of the project or activity cannot be expected, and it will be difficult to get close to achieving the objectives. Therefore, it is necessary to evaluate whether the specific development of the relevant project or activity can contribute to mission and value creation in the first place. We believe that it is necessary to shift to a comprehensive evaluation that refers not only to effectiveness, efficiency, and necessity but also to the degree of penetration and achievement.

Until now, Usuki City has been implementing the PDCA cycle (Plan → Do → Check → Action) for administrative improvement by continuing to implement the Service Verification System every year; including internal evaluations and external evaluations. Although the mechanism has been established, it is necessary to also examine the actions taken after the evaluation; that is, whether the evaluations are effectively reflected in the review of measures. If the action does not function effectively, the Plan → Do → Check process may be in vain.

The categories finally judged in the evaluation are broadly classified as "enhancement," "maintenance," and "review and consideration," but it is necessary to indicate how the measures will be reviewed based on these judgments in more detail. For example, how will measures that are judged to be "enhancements" be fundamentally revised, and used to implement projects? Can measures that are judged to be "maintenance," be further improved by, specifying or expanding the target population for services? For measures judged to be under "review and consideration," it is necessary to present specific improvement items that will bring the measures closer to achieving their objectives, such as how to transform them into better projects by fundamentally changing the way they are implemented. Furthermore, it is necessary to evolve the PDCA cycle into one that allows reporting on how the identified areas for improvement have been achieved. To create a flow of review items for commercialization and properly manage progress, it is necessary to clarify the content of the reviews.

Next, it is necessary to verify the need for a focused analysis and examination of measures where there is a discrepancy between internal and external evaluations. The measures with discrepancies in evaluation are those that the city judges as useful to residents in its internal evaluation, but the citizens' awareness survey shows low necessity or lack of satisfaction in the external evaluation.

Regardless of how diligently the city evaluates and implements measures, if it is not appreciated by the receiving citizens, it is necessary to return to the origin of the measure's purpose and consider how to bridge the gap in awareness, which will lead to the creation of value for new municipal services.

### 7.5.3   Issues of the Usuki City Service Verification System

We analyzed the current status of the Usuki City Service Verification System and will attempt to organize review items to make the system function better, so that municipal services can evolve and new service value can be created.

(1) Points for review

a. Through the implementation of the performance evaluation, rebuild the PDCA cycle with a strong awareness of items to be improved in the following year when evaluating measures and administrative activities.

b. For measures where the results of external and internal evaluations diverged for a long period, investigate the causes and implement countermeasures to make use of external evaluations in the decision-making (review) of the measures.

c. Clarify the linkage between evaluation results and budgeting to improve the accuracy of the evaluation and make the system more effective.

d. To achieve this, we re-examined the work content and time schedule associated with the PDCA cycle.

(2) Items for review

a. Improvements in internal evaluations

The evaluation criteria to date have been, effectiveness, efficiency, and necessity, and the performance of administrative activities and measures have been evaluated by reviewing the degree of achievement in terms of certain indicators. As a result of the evaluation, they have been evaluated as "enhancing," "maintaining," or "review and consideration," but no guidelines have been provided as to how the city plans to develop projects or activities based on the results of these evaluations.

For example, if it is "enhancing," can it be enhanced by reviewing the implementation methods? If it is "maintenance," how can the scope of service recipients be improved further? For "review and consideration," it is necessary to establish a cycle that considers the schedule for reporting specific improvements for the next fiscal year, such as how to transform the projects or activities by changing the implementation method, before starting the new project.

b. Incorporate a comprehensive evaluation to get closer to achieving the objectives

To achieve the objectives of the meassures, the understanding and cooperation of not only the local government but also the citizens or recipients of the services is necessary. Therefore, to bring a measure closer to achieving its objectives, it is necessary to verify whether the specific development of the measure can contribute to those missions and value creation in the first place.

To this end, we believe that internal evaluations must include not only evaluation criteria such as effectiveness, efficiency and necessity, but also a system that enables comprehensive judgments on the degree of progress, penetration, and contribution to the objective.

c. Verify valuation discrepancies

The gap between internal and external evaluations is a major challenge in the evolution of services. By examining the content of the issue, it is necessary to consider solution-based plans and methods, so that new value-creating can be developed to improve municipal services.

As a method of verifying discrepancies, the "Administrative and Financial Revitalization Promotion Committee," which is the verification committee for external evaluation, will deliberate on the evaluation of measures that have diverged based on the evaluation results of the most recent three years. In addition to the evaluation criteria used to date, the committee will also comprehensively scrutinize the measures, considering the degree of penetration and contribution of the projects, and offer advice and proposals to the city regarding new value creation and development for the improvement of services.

d. Linkage of evaluation results to budgeting

The suggested steps are:

a) Report to the mayor the results of internal review meetings based on internal evaluations and external evaluations by the "Usuki City Better City Planning Questionnaire" and the "Administrative and Financial Revitalization Promotion Committee."

b) Prepare a municipal and budgeting policy for the next fiscal year, which will be used as a guideline for budgeting for the new fiscal year.

c) Share the report and policies throughout City Hall and prepare the budget for the new fiscal year.

## 7.6 Conclution

We examined a performance evaluation system for evolving value creation in municipal services based on the case of Usuki City. We systematically organized cases of municipal reforms, such as the public accounting reforms that began with the creation of financial statement and the Service Verification Systems for performance evaluation, and then examined their processes and significance.

How can these go beyond verification toward creating value for the evolution of municipal services? By reviewing the Service Verification System, we examined measures for the evolution of citizen services and the value creation of new citizen services by refining the analysis of internal and external evaluations.

Osborne (2021, p. 2.) describes such tools as "they can only have real importance when understood within a framework that privileges 'service' and (external) 'value creation' as the cornerstones of public service management - 'Public Service Logic'." Further research should be conducted to determine how these reviews work in the actual cycle and by understanding the current situation and determining their effectiveness.

Usuki City's reforms began with the elaboration of accounting information, and the initial objective was to understand and improve performance of services. These are typical NPM-based methods, which shows that early administrative reforms were greatly influenced by NPM. However, a major characteristic of Usuki City's reforms is that they aim to construct a more comprehensive administrative management system that is not limited to NPM-based methods. In the construction of this system, Usuki City is strongly conscious of the evaluation by the citizens, who are the recipients of services. Usuki City is unique in that it not only evaluates the services by the administration as a provider, but also by citizens as recipients. In other words, the city has shifted from management based on NPM to value creation. Thus, the Service Verification System can be defined as an internal management mechanism built to utilize the citizens' evaluations, as recipients. As discussed in this paper, further improvements are required to appropriately link these two.

Additionally, it is important to understand that the results of citizen evaluations do not necessarily represent all public values. Citizens' evaluations tended to focus on whether they were satisfied with the services they received. However, to evaluate public value, it is necessary to look not only at the level of satisfaction with the services received, but also at whether society as a whole has benefited from the services and whether welfare has improved. To realize such an evaluation, it will be necessary for citizens to participate in the planning stage and become the bearers of responsibility.

Usuki City, which has been implementing NPM-based ethods, and is continuously making improvements to enhance public value, may serve as a good reference for establishing frameworks and methods for public value realization.

## Notes

1 UNESCO established this program in October 2004. It aims to promote the development of local creative industries through international cooperation among cities with creativity at its core, and to promote the "sustainable development" of cities. The Creative Cities Network has seven fields, with 295 member cities in 90 countries, including 49 member cities in the food culture field. Japan has 10 member cities in all fields (as of November 8, 2021).

2 At the 6th meeting of the "Balance Sheet Review Committee" established in July 1998, the committee decided to prepare a "Service Formation Account" to organize the movement of services to its citizens, in addition to the balance sheet which shows the movement of assets. The preparation of this account continued until the fiscal year 2006 settlement of accounts, as per Usuki City's original specification.

3 Composed of 10 representatives from various organizations in the city (industry, economy, finance, welfare, neighborhood associations, women's groups, councils), the committee verifies the "internal evaluation" conducted by the city and the "external evaluation" based on the "Usuki City Better City Planning Questionnaire" for policy-level projects, and conduct a comprehensive evaluation.

● References

Anthony, R. (1965). *Planning and Control Systems: A Framework for Analysis*. Harvard University

Press.

Anthony, R. (1988). *The Management Control Function*. Harvard Business School Press.

Anthony, R. N., Govindarajan, V., Hartmann, F. G., Kraus, K., & Nilsson, G. (2007). *Management Control Systems -12th edition*. McGraw-Hill.

Anthony, R., & Young, D. (2003), *Management Control in Nonprofit Organization -7th edition*. Mc-Graw-Hill.

Benington, J. (2009). Creating the public in order to create public value? *International Journal of Public Administration*, 32(3-4), 232-249.

Benington, J., & Moore, M. (2011). *Public value: Theory and practice*. Palgrave Macmillan.

Hood, C. (1991). A public management for all seasons? *Public administration*, 69(1), 3-19.

Moore, M. H. (1995). *Creating public value: Strategic management in government*. Harvard University Press.

Moore, M. H. (2013). *Recognizing public value*, Harvard University Press.

Osborne, S. (2010). *The New Public Governance? Emerging Perspectives on the Theory and Practice of Public Governance*. Routledge.

Osborne, S. (2021). *Public Service Logic: Creating Value for Public Service Users, Citizens, and Society through Public Service Delivery*. Routledge.

Porter, M. E. (1985). *The Competitive Advantage: Creating and Sustaining Superior Performance*. Free Press.


Himawari, F., Sakai, D., & Ishihara, T. (2013). Awakening with Balance Sheet : Balance Sheet Creation Began on Independence Day - Balance Sheet Go Beyond Public Accounting Reforms to Municipal Reforms, *CIPFA Japan Journal*, 7, 1-28, in Japanese.

# Chapter 8

# Perception of Value and its Center of Gravity in the Management Reform of SMEs: A Case of Japanese Ship Repair Industry

Hiroki Sekishita

◆

**Abstract**

This chapter aims to examine the perceptions of the value of SME managers as they engage in management reform and where they place the center of gravity of their managerial "value." It takes up case studies of SMEs engaged in management reform and reads about this from the words of senior management. In other words, the textual data of senior management, obtained by collecting published and published interview articles and other sources and by conducting semi-structured interviews, were classified and evaluated using text mining methods. The NVA model of Pepperd and Rylander (2006) was used to elucidate value linkages based on the data obtained.

As a result of the analysis, the author provides empirical evidence of which words are emphasized and the value linkages around them due to the text mining. The chapter confirms that words such as "SNSB" and "people" are used repeatedly in the company's management reforms and that these are central perception of value in the company's management reforms. It then uses the SOM developed from the extracted data to identify the extent to which the value linkages in the current situation are essential in how senior management talks about management reform.

This chapter attempts to extract perceptions of value from textual data capturing the words of senior management. It provides a unique perspective on SME management reform research, as although there are many studies on management strategies and individual methods, few have studied perceptions of value in SMEs.

**Keywords:**

Value Network, TPS, Gentani, Text mining, Perception of value

## 8.1 Introduction

Small and medium-sized enterprises (SMEs) in Japan account for 99.7% of all enterprises and produce approximately 50% of Japan's GDP in terms of value added (Small and Medium Enterprise Agency, 2024). Management reform of SMEs, which support the Japanese economy as a whole and local economies, is an urgent issue. The Japanese Government has developed and backed up various measures to encourage SME companies to undertake this management reform. Management to improve value creation is one such measure. However, "value creation" is polysemic and has different meanings from different perspectives. When referring to value in business management, many may refer to Corporate Value, while some studies highlight value-creating schemes through networks.

Matsuo *et al*. (2021), citing Lusch *et al*. (2006), Vargo *et al*. (2008), and Grönroos *et al*. (2014) for the concept of value co-creation, organizes Goods Dominant Logic (GDL), Service-Dominant Logic (SDL) and Service Logic (SL) are organized. In SDL and SL, services are intangible goods and also activities. As a fundamental characteristic of service goods, production, and consumption coincide, and service quality is formed when consumers participate in the production process (Matsuo *et al*., 2021).

Examining the linkages between values to identify their relationships in a framework is a prerequisite for value creation. Porter (1980, 1985) proposed the value Chain as a theory of the linkages between values. It has proved a very useful mechanism for portraying the chained linkage of activities that exist in the physical world within traditional industries, particularly manufacturing (Peppard and Rylander, 2006). It is heavily used in analyses in various places.

However, While in the Value Chain, there is a sequential and linear logic to the process organization in order to reach value creation, in the more fluid Value Network, the process does not have a rigid order but works at the same time in a network within which there are also external organizations (Ricciotti, 2019). However, there is no widely agreed-upon and defined ontology for value networks

(Leviäkangas and Öörni, 2020). Some of the most representative studies of value networks include Christensen *et al.* (1995), Stabell and Fjeldstad (1998), Normann and Ramirez (1993), and Allee (2008). In particular, Pepperd and Rylander (2006) state that the Value Chain does not take into account the nature of alliances, competitors, complementors and other members of the business network, while the Value Network focuses on the value creation system itself, in which various economic entities cooperate to co-produce value. In other words, a Value Network are the links between individuals, between individuals and companies, and between companies, whose interaction brings value to the group. A Value Network is now an example of an economic ecosystem in business. The actors within the network influence each other and create value. The author will explore management reform for SMEs using the logic of this value co-creation and Value Network as a lens.

To reform the management of SMEs, the perception of value of the management team, which significantly impact management, are thought to be essential. In SMEs, leadership has a strong influence; in this sense, the perception of value of the management team are essential. Therefore, this chapter questions where the center of gravity of "value" lies in SME management and its perception of value.

In this chapter, to ascertain managers' perceptions, the author sought to extract perception of value based on interviews and published articles—specifically, the words managers utter (directly or indirectly) are collected as text. The collected texts are analyzed using text-mining techniques.

The chapter is structured as follows: in Section 2, the research method provides an overview of the research and analysis subject and refers to the text mining analysis. Section 3 clarifies the method of collecting the text data to be analyzed and the analysis results. Section 4 discusses how the results are perceived to be valuable in light of the analysis framework and where the emphasis is placed, followed by conclusions in Section 5.

## 8.2 Methods

### 8.2.1 Methods of Analysis

Relevant data were collected to confirm management reforms and perception of value in SMEs, and an interview with the president was conducted with the cooperation of Mukaishima Dockyard Co., Ltd.

Interviews with the survey subjects were conducted on 8 May 2024 in a meeting room at the head office of Mukaishima Dockyard Co., Ltd. Concerning the interviews, permission was obtained from the Wakayama University Research Ethics Council, the subjects were informed that their cooperation in the survey was voluntary, and their consent was obtained after explaining that the survey results would only be used for research purposes. About the collection of relevant data, articles published in magazines and newspapers from 2023 to 2024 concerning Mukaishima Dockyard Co., Ltd, and text data extracted from the parts of statements made by the company's president, Mr.Tomohiro Kuno, in his speech transcripts and interviews, were collected for analysis. These text data were organized, and the external way of perceiving the company (news reports) and the internal top management statements were transcribed into text data and analyzed quantitatively using KH Corder.[1]

The company was selected for analysis for two reasons. First, because of Hammervoll. *et al*. (2014) use of Value Network as a value analysis of maritime clusters. Hammervoll. *et al*. (2014) treats co-creation as an' interaction between members of a Value Network'. "Following Borys and Jemison (1989), co-creation of value is defined as the process whereby the capabilities of value network members are combined such that cost or learning advantages are achieved" Hammervoll. *et al*. (2014). This definition is based on the SDL thinking of Vargo and Lusch (2004) and Lusch *et al*. (2010). This was a Value Network, yet the company wanted to identify the structure of value creation in the internal business model from the organization's internal network. Secondly, the company is working on improving company operations through TPS. The company's president is from the Toyota group and has been managing the company based on TPS. The company is not just superficially accepting TPS, as was the case with many companies that failed to introduce TPS, but is trying to rebuild the company from the ground up, as symbolized by the establishment of a basic unit (gentani: gen-tan-i).[2] This is because the author thought it was worth examining how transformation through TPS in SMEs affects value creation.

## 8.2.2   Subject of Analysis

The maritime industry, especially shipbuilders and repairers, is concentrated in the coastal areas from Onomichi and Fukuyama to Kure in Hiroshima Prefecture. A substantial maritime cluster centered on Imabari Shipbuilding Co., Ltd also exists in Imabari City on the northern coast of Shikoku. This city is also famous as a maritime cluster in the Seto Inland Sea region, including the coastal areas of Hiroshima Prefecture. The Mukaishima Dockyard, featured in this article, is one of the core companies of the maritime cluster in Onomichi City.

Mukaishima Dockyard Co., Ltd is a dockyard specializing in ship repairs in Onomichi, Hiroshima Prefecture, Japan. The cranes and floating docks can be seen in front of the JR Onomichi Station (across the Onomichi Channel). The company is a landmark in Onomichi. The company has a 70-year history as a current company, established in 1953. The company is an unlisted owner-operated (SME) with a capital of JPY 90 million, approximately 200 employees, and annual sales of JPY 5 billion. As a founder's business, the company was founded in 1929 as a shipbuilder. Due to a wartime control order during World War II, the predecessor company merged with another company and temporarily ceased to exist as a company. After World War II, Mukaishima Dockyard was re-established by taking over part of the merged company's facilities. Looking back over the company's history, it can be said that it has existed for about 100 years. The company ceased building ships in 1966. Since then, the company has specialized in ship repair and expanded its facilities to include two dry and two floating docks.

The company's customers are owners of domestic ships. Domestic vessels are vessels operating within Japan. Domestic shipping is an important distribution channel, accounting for approximately 40% of Japan's domestic logistics (Ministry of Land, Infrastructure, Transport and Tourism, 2024).

The company is characterized by the fact that, in addition to its dockyard business, it also operates a shipping business: it owns a fleet of 4 vessels and operates a ship chartering business. The vessels owned include state-of-the-art electric propulsion vessels, lithium-ion battery-powered vessels, diesel/motor hybrid propulsion vessels, electric propulsion container vessels, and conventional diesel-powered vessels. The company's value proposition to its customers is "Provide that enables stable navigation." These vessels are operated to meet the needs of their customers' shipowners. The company collects data on vessels in operation and uses it for repairs. It is unusual in Japan for a ship repairer to also operate a shipping business.

The company's president, Mr. Tomohiro Kuno, worked for Toyota-affiliated automobile parts manufacturer AISHIN SEIKI Co., Ltd (now AISHIN Co., Ltd), where he was vice-president of AISHIN Mexican subsidiary. He joined Mukaishima Dockyard in 2016. In 2021, he was appointed managing director; in July 2022, he was appointed company president.

Since his appointment, Mr. Kuno has been promoting operational improvements using the Toyota Product System (TPS), which he developed at Toyota-affiliated companies. Previously, the Mukaishima Dockyard did not have the standardization required for repair work. This standardization establishes a basic unit of work called the "Gentani" (See Yoshikawa, 2010).

Since joining the company, he has been working on the verbalization of tacit knowledge, which he calls KKD (K: Keiken (experience), K: Kan (intuition) D: Dokyo (courage)). He is not necessarily hostile to or averse to KKD based on the senses. Because it is a human part of the process, it contains the essentials of the work. He values this and has worked on the verbalization of knowledge in order to share it within the organization rather than keeping it personal. Through this verbalization, the basic unitization (Gentani-ka), work, and operations have been promoted.

This "gentani-ka" is considered an essential keyword in this analysis. He finds that the main reason why companies that try to introduce TPS fail is because they do not standardize work, or in other words, do not gentani-ka in the first place, even with the Kanban method, which is a typical TPS method, if the gentani is not set first, the amount of work and person-hours cannot be determined, and the

BOM (Bill Of Materials), which is the basis for costing the work required, cannot be calculated. The BOM, the basis for the work's cost, cannot be defined. In this sense, identifying gentani-ka is recognized as a lifeline for the company's reforms.

## 8.3   Results

### 8.3.1   Collected text data

In order to investigate the perception of value in the company's management, the author decided to take articles featuring the company and statements made by its management and analyze them. Author chose to focus on the statements made by the management, with a particular emphasis on the manager, Mr. Kuno, due to the strong influence managerial leadership in SMEs can have on management.

Textual data were collected through interviews and interview articles that recorded Mr. Kuno's direct words, questions, and answers in university lectures and indirectly adjusted linguistic data that were converted from interviews into articles, i.e., newspaper and magazine articles and summaries of university lectures, broadly classified. The list is presented in **Table 8.1**.

The division into direct text data and indirect text data is because direct text data, such as interviews, is less organized in terms of content than articles and the like. Therefore, at the stage of carrying out the text mining analysis, the text

**Table 8.1**   List of Textual Data Used in the Analysis

| Title | Source |
|---|---|
| Direct verbal text data | |
| Panel Discussion (6th Sep 2024) | MLIT Kinki Branch |
| Interview text data (8th May 2024) | Auther |
| Mail text data (9th May 2024) | Auther |
| Indirect verbal text data | |
| Lecture Sammary(Bingo Region Economics) text data | Fukuyama University |
| Article (2nd May 2024) | The Chugoku Shinbun (Local News Paper) |
| Article (19th Mar 2024) | The Japan Maritime Daily  (Business Press) |
| Article (Dec 2023) | Wedge (Business Journal) |

Source: Author.

data organized by the articles was combined and used in the analysis in a complementary manner. This is because it is thought that this will add an objective perspective to the organized content of the articles.

In applying the text data to text mining, the author organized the interview content as follows:

- Meaningless phrases such as interjections and exclamatory words were eliminated.
- The directive words were corrected so that they could be identified.
- Inconsistent terminology and contractions in the interviews were standardized where necessary.
- Parts of the text that did not make sence were corrected to extent that they did not change the meaning.
- Abbreviated words were connected where necessary to ensure that the meaning was understood.

## 8.3.2  Text mining results

The text mining was analyzed by combining interviews and other interviews containing the direct president's words and articles based on the interviews. The reason for studying the direct and indirect texts together was that, as mentioned above, the direct words alone are not organized in terms of content, which may lead to a lack of accuracy in understanding the company's business. Therefore, articles with organized content were combined and used in the analysis as a supplement to ensure objectivity.

The total number of extracted words, the number of different words, the mean number of occurrences, and the standard deviation of the number of occurrences are shown in **Table 8.2**.

**Table 8.2**  Mean and Standard Deviation of the Total Number of Extracted Words, the Number of Different Words, and the Number of Occurrences

| | |
|---|---|
| Total number of words extracted | 7,232 |
| Number of different words | 1,934 |
| The mean number of occurrences | 3.74 |
| The standard deviation of the number of occurrences | 13.35 |

Source: Author.

## 8.3.2.1   List of extracted terms (Table 8.3)

The terms extracted by KH Corder are as follows. Compound terms are picked up from the extracted terms and added as analysis terms. The reason for adding compound terms is that morphological analysis alone splits words that have meaning and are unsuitable for analysis.

**Table 8.3**   List of Extracted Words

| Extracted words | Occurrences | Extracted words | Occurrences | Extracted words | Occurrences |
|---|---|---|---|---|---|
| person | 100 | different (v) | 13 | change (n) | 10 |
| on sight | 50 | involved | 13 | business model | 9 |
| make (v) | 46 | occurrence | 13 | awareness | 9 |
| now | 44 | management | 13 | intuition | 9 |
| organzation | 41 | executive | 13 | relationship | 9 |
| story | 40 | plan | 13 | criterion | 9 |
| see (v) | 38 | result | 13 | customer | 9 |
| repair | 37 | Appearance | 13 | first | 9 |
| myself | 35 | advance | 13 | realization | 9 |
| value | 32 | ship owner | 13 | aggregation | 9 |
| change (v) | 29 | definition | 13 | correct | 9 |
| Mukaishima Dockyard | 28 | provide information | 13 | beyond | 9 |
| ship | 28 | engine | 12 | many | 9 |
| business field | 27 | values | 12 | provide | 9 |
| have | 26 | go (v) | 12 | get (v) | 9 |
| figure | 26 | use (v) | 12 | get in | 9 |
| significance | 26 | execution | 12 | part | 9 |
| company | 24 | crew | 12 | aim for | 9 |
| job | 24 | before | 12 | goal | 9 |
| natural | 23 | system | 11 | philosophy | 9 |
| eventually | 22 | data | 11 | improvement | 8 |
| task | 22 | trouble | 11 | include | 8 |
| stable navigation supply business | 21 | rev | 11 | Total happiness | 8 |
| mean | 21 | share | 11 | man-hours | 8 |
| technology | 21 | experience | 11 | navigation | 8 |
| gentani | 21 | reproducibility | 11 | industry | 8 |
| do (v) | 21 | era | 11 | specification document | 8 |
| environment | 20 | company employee | 11 | next | 8 |
| think | 20 | situation | 11 | emproyee | 8 |
| president | 20 | large | 11 | craftsman | 8 |
| enterprise | 19 | come (v) | 11 | world | 8 |
| happiness | 19 | good | 11 | institution | 8 |
| business | 19 | digital transfromation | 10 | production | 8 |
| shipbuilding | 19 | digital | 10 | phase | 8 |
| vessels | 18 | process | 10 | tool | 8 |
| change | 18 | stable | 10 | conception | 8 |
| year | 17 | assignment | 10 | understand | 8 |
| need | 17 | control | 10 | profit | 8 |
| dockyard | 16 | manager | 10 | client | 7 |
| appear | 16 | common | 10 | image | 7 |
| time | 16 | operation | 10 | communication | 7 |
| repairing business | 16 | inspection | 10 | safety | 7 |
| standardization | 16 | structure | 10 | action | 7 |
| KKD | 15 | send out | 10 | heading | 7 |

| timing | 15 | always | 10 | amount of work | 7 |
|---|---|---|---|---|---|
| words | 15 | human | 10 | concept | 7 |
| costal shipping | 15 | society | 10 | enhance | 7 |
| best | 14 | strategy | 10 | instructions | 7 |
| work (v) | 14 | electricity | 10 | sustainable | 7 |
| Onomichi | 14 | Japan | 10 | automobile | 7 |

Source: Author.

## 8.3.2.2 Co-occurrence networks

The co-occurrence network created by the analyzed data is as follows: from the co-occurrence network in **Figure. 8.1**, 12 groups could be recognized, as shown in **Table 8.4**.

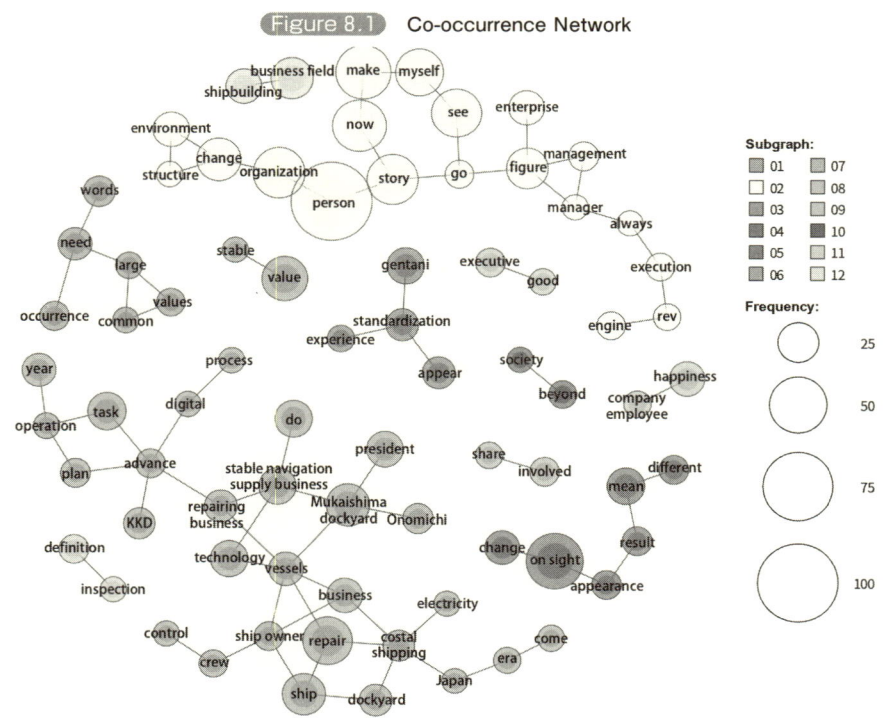

**Figure 8.1** Co-occurrence Network

Source: Author.

**Table 8.4**  Groups of Words Indicated by Co-occurrence Networks

| Group | number of Words | Words |
|---|---|---|
| Group 1 | 28 words | Mukaishima dockyard, Onomichi, president, stable navigation supply business, do, technology, vessels, repairing business, repair, costal shipping, electricity, dockyard, ship, ship owner, business, crew, control, advance, KKD, task, plan, operation, year, Japan, era, come, digital, process |
| Group 2 | 19 words | person, organization, change (v), environment, structure, now, make, myself, see, go, story, engine, turn, execution, always, manager, management, figure, enterprise |
| Group 3 | 6 words | values, common, large, need, words, occurrence |
| Group 4 | 6 words | on sight, change, mean, different, result, send out |
| Group 5 | 4 words | gentani, standardization, appair, experience |
| Group 6 | 2 words | value, stable |
| Group 7 | 2 words | share, involved |
| Group 8 | 2 words | good, executive |
| Group 9 | 2 words | company employee, happiness |
| Group 10 | 2 words | before, society |
| Group 11 | 2 words | difinition, inspection |
| Group 12 | 2 words | shipbuilding, industry |

Source: Author.

Group 1 is the largest in the co-occurrence network diagram, with 28 words. "Mukaishima dockyard", "stable navigation supply business (SNSB)" and "repair" are the most frequently occurring and core values. "Mukaishima Dockyard" and "SNSB" are combined and can be identified as the company's core values. These two words are central to the company's core business of "repair" and the "technology" required to "repair" "vessels." "Repairs" are carried out following the wishes of the "shipowner." The company's customers are almost exclusively "domestic vessels." The environment surrounding "domestic vessels" indicates that power systems that replace fossil fuels, such as "electric" propulsion vessels, are being promoted to counter climate change, indicating that an "era" is "coming" to "Japan," where new power systems will be supported. The report also highlights that shipowners face the challenge of "managing" their "crews" in the face of a declining population. They are also "moving forward" with the "digitalization" of "KKD" "processes," which are tacit knowledge in the workplace. It also expresses the need to advance "work," "planning", and "operations."

Group 2 is the second largest after Group 1, with 19 words. This group sees "people" as a core value. An interesting consequence is that to change "people" and "organization," the "environment" and "structure" must be changed. This is also in line with what the President repeatedly asserted in interviews and speeches. It also expresses that the "managers" in charge of "management" must understand "figures" such as business performance. He also insists that the reforms must be "constantly" "implemented," like "revving up" an "engine."

Group 3 contains words and deeds related to the company's culture and values. They consider it "necessary" to have "common" values. This indicates that various changes "happen" as a result.

Group 4 is dominated by language relating to workplace changes brought about by management reforms. This group of words questions the "meaning" of "change" in the "workplace" and explains that the "results" of change are "produced."

Group 5 is a series of terms related to the basic unit of work. It makes sense that it is linked to "standardization," which is the essential effect of "gentani (basic unit)." Through "standardization", "experience," and other factors that were tacit knowledge of employees are made "visible." The word "experience" here is thought to have a connection with "KKD" but was not displayed in the data.

Group 6 outputs words representing perception of value. In this group, "value" is combined with "stability." This "stability" represents SNSB, which indicates that the company's key perception of value is in SNSB.

Group 7 combines "sharing" and "getting involved." It indicates that the "sharing" of values, knowledge, and skills changes the relationship between the different sectors.

Group 8 combines "good" and "management." These words frequently occur in discussions of situations where management is improving the environment within the company. In other words, they indicate that they are used in the context of management's internal improvements, such as "management improving internal communication" and "building a good company."

The value of "happiness" is a significant feature of Group 9. Happiness is linked to "employees." Thinking about employees' happiness is considered to have a social impact. This may be because Mr Kuno used the term "total amount of happiness" in his interview. This is a unique expression by the president, who expresses happiness in terms of quantity and sees its expansion as the creation of value.

Group 10 combines "beyond" and "society." The former is a word that emerged about the period, while the latter represents a contribution to "society." The results for this group did not show a strong association as far as the text was checked.

Group 11 combines "definition" and "inspection". This "definition" is a definition of the amount of work, which stems from the fact that ship repairs are synonymous with carrying out "inspections." This is because many ships carry out "repairs" at the timing of periodic "inspections" and are coupled to that "definition" via the volume of construction work.

Group 12 is coupled with "shipbuilding" and "industry." This indicates that the shipbuilding industry was mentioned more frequently. The ship repair industry is also closely related to "shipbuilding" industry.

Overall, there are a relatively high number of internal descriptions of the company. Alternatively, the agenda-setting of the interviews etc. reflects the fact that the focus is on the company's internal and the president's personal thinking. In management, the interviews are shown to be more conscious of the company's internal reforms, etc.

## 8.4   Findings and Discussion

The Value Network is examined here to identify the company's perception of value and its focus; Peppard and Rylander (2006) present a five-stage Network Value Analysis (NVA). However, the survey did not reach the stage where nodes and links could be identified. Therefore, it was decided to clarify the terms, etc. that form the basis for examining the Value Network from the relationship between each extracted vocabulary and the co-occurrence network described above. In addition, as the current study was mainly based on extracts from interviews with the president, some external value associations were identified, but they were not captured in detail. Therefore, it was decided to examine value linkages within the organization and their focus in a limited way this time.

Constructing a Value Network in Peppard and Rylander (2006) is a step-by-step process from Step 1 to Step 5.

- Step 1: Define network goals.

    The company's core network goal can be defined as SNSB from the co-occurrence network described above.

- Step 2: Identification and definition of network participants

    The company's employees, shipowners as customers, seafarers, shipping operators, and shipbuilders are raised from the co-occurring network. Suppliers are also important, although they do not appear in the co-occurrence network.

- Step 3: Identification of the value dimensions of the network participants

    To identify the value dimension, the interviews are limited to "perceived value" within the company, as the interview subjects are limited to the company itself. Here, the "SNSB" created internally from the bottom-up by the employees can be identified as valuable to the employees.

- Step 4: Definition of value linkage

    Value is created through exchanging goods and services, affection and favor, information and ideas, and influence and power (Pepperd and Rylander 2006). Considering this assumption, maintaining good relationships between departments and individual employees and sharing values can be defined as value linkage.

- Step 5: Analysis and illustration

    A Network Value Map (NVM) is useful for presenting an overview of the network; Pepperd and Rylander (2006) present a diagram with nodes and links, but as the survey of external network participants was not sufficient for this study, for convenience, a Self-Organising Map (SOM) was used. The above definition, identification and text mining data can be shown in **Figure. 8.2**.

The SOM categorized eight areas from A to H. Although the relationships between each other do not appear clearly from the SOM, it is possible to recognize the size of the current areas, with area F being the largest at 78 hex. This is where tacit knowledge is being converted into data, a pressing concern at the company. It is an area where the backbone of the company's management reform

Figure 8.2   Self-Organizing Map (SOM)

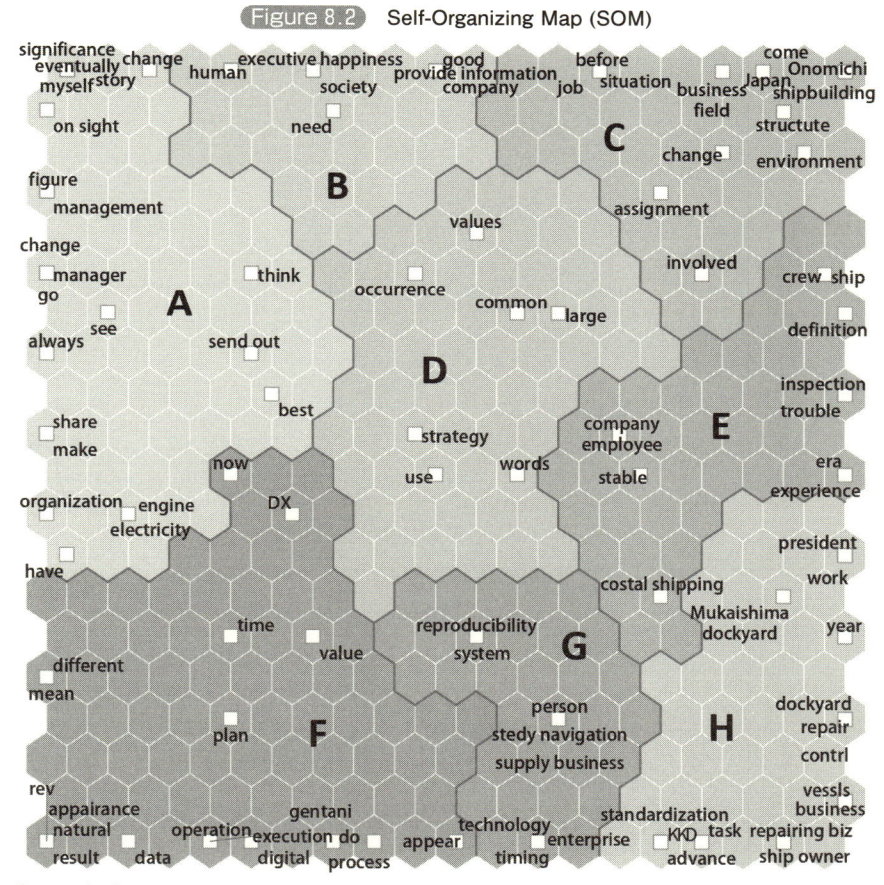

Source: Author.

is being built, as the company is building up the gentani and improving on-site work through it. Area A, at 70 hex, is the area for promoting "management by quantification" and training the next generation of managers. It can be recognized that this area is also in the process of implementing management reforms by receiving the results of area F.

On the other hand, SNSB, which area G has identified as a core value, is a smaller area overall at 32 hex. This can be taken as an indication that SNSB was created as a slogan in the previous year of the survey and that the organization has started to move in this direction.

Based on the above analysis, the following four points should be noted, particularly as observations from the discussion. Firstly, the Stable Navigation Supply Business (SNSB). The slogan "SNSB" was adopted on the company's 70th anniversary. It can be recognized that these words are placed at the heart of the value. Although not connected to the slogan, the foundation for a SNSB is the standardization of operations through basic unitization. This, too, could be read from the co-occurrence network. Gentani is the engine of concrete value creation, and the standardization of operations based on gentani and standardization creates stable operations, leading to the creation of stable value creation and an increase in the "total amount of happiness." This can be positioned as value creation for internal (employee value) and external (customer value).

Secondly, the possibility of applying the SECI model in the company. The basic unitization and standardization of work mentioned earlier can be seen as an innovation in knowledge management at the company. Drucker foresaw the arrival of the "knowledge society" in the 1950s. "In a knowledge society, the key issue is how to encourage knowledge creation within the organization" (Shoji, H., 2019). Apart from the president intentions, the SECI model (Nonaka, 1994) appears to have been realized in the company. From the interviews, the tacit knowledge in the workplace is transformed into formal knowledge by verbalizing it. Formal knowledge is consolidated by combining it. Internalizing the organized formal knowledge can be reacquired by employees through learning and then retained. Innovations in knowledge management are considered to lead to value creation as they improve the relationships between each other. This area could also be clarified by further research as a case study.

Third, the company's "strategy." Mukaishima Dockyard has a company policy (course of action) and slogans but does not have a clear corporate strategy. This can be seen from the fact that the word "strategy" does not appear in the co-occurrence network. The word "strategy" appears in the extract, but this is due to the answer to a question the interviewer dared to ask. The president's reasons for not developing a strategy say that the company takes a strategy for granted. From the interview with the president, it was confirmed that the company does have what might be called a "strategy." For example, the fact that the company is not only in the repair business but also in the SNSB, which provides total support for ships from a safety perspective, is a sufficient "corporate strategy." However, while making changes is an autonomous decision, it can also be seen as a reflection of the company's environment.

Finally, the fourth is about "stakeholders." The company is a small or medium-sized enterprise and not a listed company. As such, it reacts differently to stakeholder perceptions than listed companies. The company's stakeholders are, naturally, the founding family but also, in terms of importance, customers, employees, and suppliers. This can be seen from the company president's statement that the company does not need to care about the outside world as much as it should, as it does not have the wide range of shareholders that a public company has. Employees, in particular, are the driving force behind the company, and from the president's perception, the gaze directed towards them is full of enthusiasm.

In summary, the company does not explicitly state a "corporate strategy," but it implements a substantial strategy based on a sense of "taken for granted." In addition, the strategy is driven by the management vision of SNSB, which permeates the company internally. This is probably due to the clarity of the vision. In addition, the analysis revealed that, as the company is not a public company, customers and employees are considered to be the central stakeholders. These may be in line with the recent trend of an increasing number of companies conducting MBOs and delisting.

## 8.5　Conclusion

Section 8.1 presents the problem, and Section 8.2 describes the analysis methodology. In Section 8.3, a text-mining analysis was conducted on the collected text data. Section 8.4 attempted to identify the perception of value and its focus on the company from the text mining analysis. The results show that the company formulates and implements strategies, rather than calling them strategies, based on a sense of taking them for granted. In addition, the promotion of the strategy is progressing due to the internal penetration of the management vision. This is probably due to the clarity of the vision. In addition, the analysis revealed that, as a non-public company, the company is aware of its customers and employees as stakeholders.

This study has two limitations. First, it is limited to a textual analysis of only one company. The author feel that further case analysis is needed. Second, external relationships and value creation need to be analyzed in more detail and examined through the creation of a Value Network Map (Pepperd and Rylandar, 2006).

To study Value Networks in the broader maritime industry, as Hammervoll *et al.* (2014) states, Value Networks in the maritime industry is necessary to refer to the following observations, "this is also interesting for further research on learning and innovation in clusters, because by addressing specific type of service and service exchange, there is a potential to redirected discussion from broad to specific notions of learnig and innovation in cluster". Value Network research based on value co-creation in the maritime industry needs to be promoted.

## Notes:

1 Quantitative analysis of texts such as newspaper articles has been conducted in the social sciences for many years, and one method that has been devised, used, and continuously improved is "content analysis". The software developed based on this content analysis method is KH Coder (Higuchi, 2020), and the analysis in this chapter is based on this concept. The analysis results can be compared.

2 Gentani (Gen-tan-i: the basic unit) is a standard quantity of materials, person-hours, and labor required to produce one product unit.

## ● References

Allee, V. (2008) Value Network analysis and value conversion of tangible and intangible assets, *Journal of Intellectual Capital*, 9(1), 5-24.

Borys, B. and D. B. Jemison (1989) Hybrid Arrangements as Strategic Alliances: Theoretical Issues in Organizational Combinations, *The Academy of Management Review*, 14(2), 234-249.

Christensen, C. M. and R. S. Rosenbloom (1995) Explaining the attacker's advantage: technological paradigms, organizational dynamics, and the value network, *Research Policy*, 24, 233-257.

Hammervoll, T. L. L. Halse and P. Engelseth (2014) The role of clusters in global maritime value networks, *International Journal of Physical Distribution & Logistics Management*, 44(1/2), 98-112.

Grönroos, C. and J. Gummerus (2014) The service revolution and its marketing implications: service logic vs service-dominant logic, *Managing Service Quality*, 24, 206-229.

Higuchi, K. (2020) *KH Corder Official Book*, Nakanishiya Shuppan.

Idle, T. (2014, November 3) How Toyota uses gentani to optimize performance and cut waste, *TRELLIS*, https://trellis.net/article/how-toyota-uses-gentani-optimize-performance-and-cut-waste/ Final Access Date: 05th August 2024.

Leviäkangas, P. and R. Öörni (2020) From business models to value networks and business ecosystems: What does it mean for the economics and governance of the transport system?, *Utilities Policy*, 64, 101046.

Lusch, R. F. and S. L. Vargo (2006) Service-Dominant Logic: Reactions, Reflections and Refinements, *Marketing Theory*, 6(3), 281-288.

Matsuo, R., H. Sekishita, S. Hosomi and T. Ishihara (2021) Integrated framework of concepts on value co-creation, *CIPFA Japan Journal*, 5, 3-11.

Ministry of Land, Infrastructure, Transport and Tourism (2024) *White Paper on Land, Infrastructure, Transport and Tourism in Japan*.

Normann, R. A. and R. Ramírez (1993) From value chain to value constellation: designing interactive strategy, *Harvard Business Review*, 71(4), 65-77.

Nonaka, I. (1994) A Dynamic Theory of Organizational Knowledge Creation, *Organization Science*, 5(1), 14-37.

Organization for Small and Medium Enterprises and Regional Innovation (2023), *Survey on DX Promotion in Small and Medium Enterprises (2023): Questionnaire Report*.

Peppard, J. and A. Rylander (2006) From Value Chain to Value Network: Insights for Mobile Operators, *European Management Journal*, 24(2-3), 128-141. Network Value Analysis Approach.

Porter, M. (1980) *Competitive Strategy: Techniques for Analyzing Industries and Competitors*. Free Press, New York.

Porter, M. (1985) *Competitive Advantage: Creating and Sustaining Superior Performance*. Free Press, New York.

Ricciotti, F. (2019) From value chain to value network: a systematic literature review, *Management Review Quarterly*, 70(2), 191-212.

Shoji, H. (2019) How Can We Facilitate Kansei Value Creation?, *10th Conference of Transdisciplinary Foundation of Science and Technology*. (Japanese only)

Stabell, C. B. and Ø. D. Fjeldstad (1998) Configuring Value for Competitive Advantage: On Chains, Shops, and Networks, *Strategic Management Journal*, 19, 413-437.

The Small and Medium Enterprise Agency (2024) *2024 White Paper on Small and Medium Enterprises in Japan*. (Japanese only)

Vargo, S. L. and R. F. Lusch (2004) Evolving to a New Dominant Logic for Marketing, *Journal of Marketing*, 68, 1-17.

Vargo, S. L., P. P. Maglio and M. A. Akaka (2008) On value and value co-creation: A service systems and service logic perspective, *American Review of Public Administration*, 36, 41-57.

Yoshikawa, T. (2010) Cost Accounting Standard and Cost Accounting System in Japan: Lessons from the Past-Recovering Lost Traditions, Accounting, *Business and Financial History*, 11(3),269-281.

World Bank Group (2024) Small and Medium Enterprises (SMEs) Finance, https://www.worldbank.org/en/topic/smefinance Final Access date: 6th June 2024.

Chapter **9**

# Deriving a Multilayered Logic Model in Public Management:A Comprehensive Community Care System in Japan

## Ryoji Matsuo

◆

**Abstract**

The paper proposes the multilayered logic model as a new model of policy formation in the public through a case study analysis of a comprehensive community care system in Japan. The paper also examines the effectiveness of the various elements of the multilayered logic model and the effectiveness of value creation. The results of the verification confirmed that the multilayered logic model consists of multiple layers and that value is created.

In addition, at each layer or between layers, the multi-layered logic model is posed from the perspective of policies, or measures, projects and services. At each layer, the resources, technology and know-how possessed by each actor are combined through the coordination function of the value co-creation coordinator. Individual and organizational values related to "economy", "efficiency" and "effectiveness" are then co-created. This particular policy, etc. is linked to related policies, etc. in the "same layer" or "other layers" through value co-creation coordinators and actors. The accumulation of multiple individual and organizational values then creates "social value" related to "impact".

**Keywords**

Value co-creation, Ecosystem, Multilayered logic model

## 9.1 Introduction

### 9.1.1 The importance of public management based on diversity and regionalism

In the public sector, in addition to traditional policy formation based on Public Administration (PA), New Public Management (NPM), which took the world by storm around 2000, has promoted the participation of diverse actors including private companies in the public sector. Today, in addition to these methods, policy formation based on governance logic by a variety of actors, such as New Public Governance (NPG) and Public Service Logic (PSL), is being developed.

As policy-making methods in the public sector continue to evolve and diversify, Osborne describes public management as "an essential process by which social values and beliefs underpinning public services are debated and established, and social norms are embedded in public services," and as "manifesting the underlying values of society" (Osborne 2021, p.44). In addition, "social work, health care, education, economic and business support services, and community promotion and revitalization are all services rather than tangible products in that they are intangible, process-oriented and committed to be delivered in advance." (Osborne 2021, p.41). Osborne argues for the importance of viewing them in a service logic rather than a product-dominant logic based on manufacturing.

In the public, based on the needs and demands of the individuals and organizations that make up society, there is a "regionality" that is specific to each country, region and other characteristics. Under regionality, diverse policies, measures, projects and services (hereinafter referred to as "policies, etc.") are developed by diverse actors in diverse fields.

Thus, "diversity" and "regionality" are considered keywords in recent public management.

### 9.1.2 Linear Logic Models and Their Challenges

In the public, "diversity" and "regionality" are considered as keywords. On the other hand, in research on public management, which should be the norm, the linear logic explained by the "good dominant logic" derived from the manufacturing industry (hereinafter referred to as "linear logic") is often discussed in previous studies. Linear logic is a logic in which resource inputs produce outputs and outcomes, and is a useful logic for a simplified and formulaic view of a project and service. However, the activities carried out in the public sector are in fact complex and diverse. Linear logic is an extremely simplistic description of the reality of the situation, or of the methods used to formulate projects centered on government-led service provision. For example, Osborne writes, "Too often it seems, a closed production model has been employed by Public Service Organizations (PSOs) that has seen public services as produced through a linear production model of turning inputs into outputs, and then delivered onto their users" (Osborne, 2021, p. 2).

In actual policy formation and service development, there are cases that can be explained using linear logic. However, many of the services and projects that make up policies and measures are intertwined with diverse activities by a wide range of actors. Therefore, it is important to view the logic of public policy from an areal or three-dimensional perspective.

In addition, services and projects developed in the public are not limited to activities conducted by the government. In addition to the government, a variety of actors such as private companies and Non-Profit Organizations (NPOs) participate in the public sector. Policy areas in the public sector cover a wide range of fields, for example, industry, transport, tourism, welfare and healthcare. Some policy areas are developed by government actors, while others are provided by private companies and establishments. In many cases, policies and other measures are co-created through public-private partnerships and the division of roles between the public and private sectors.

In a way, public services are a complex of diverse projects and services developed by diverse actors in a public-private co-creation. Public policy needs a logic to explain the complexity with diverse actors in mind, including the "government", but also private companies, NPOs, volunteers and users.

In Japan, policy development used to be centralized based on the PA. In 2000, the Law on Decentralization was enacted and a system to promote the entry of private companies in public services came into force. Nowadays, rather than public services co-created by the public administration, the private sector and users, and private-sector-led public services are expanding.

As public services co-created by the public and private sectors are expanding, a linear logic model that assumes the linear "public administration" as the subject finds it difficult to explain the rich reality of policy formation and service development by various public and private actors in the public domain, and is also not useful in management practice.

Osborne describes the recent shift in policy formation from public services as products produced by linear production processes to value created in the ecosystem (Osborne, 2021, p.116). He also views the linear model as a product-dominant logic and points out three problems with it. First "that production and consumption are discrete processes that are ruled by different logics." Second, "and consequently, that the costs of production and consumption are distinguishable and separate." Finally, "that customers are largely passive in the process." Product-dominant logic "none of these asumptions hold for public services because they fail to recognize the core elements of public services as services" (Osborne, 2021, p. 9).

In light of these arguments, an areal and layered logic that goes beyond linear logic is called for. In other words, as a new model for policy formation in the public sphere, it is important to consider public space as diverse and multilayered, and the logic that develops in a multifaceted ecosystem with various constituent elements. This multilayered logic has already been developed in various fields. An example of a distinctive public-private partnership that is "regional" in addition to "diverse" is the "community-based comprehensive care system" in Japan.

### 9.1.3 Overview of Community-based Comprehensive Care System in Japan

In Japan, a community-based comprehensive care system is defined as "a system in which a variety of lifestyle support services, including not only medical and nursing care but also welfare services, are appropriately provided in daily living areas to ensure safety, security, and health in daily life, based on the provision of housing that meets the needs of the residents" (Ministry of Health, Labor and Welfare website).

Under the national government's institutional design, local governments, medical and long-term care professional associations, service-providing organizations, and other diverse actors design policies, including frameworks and rules, according to regional characteristics. These policies are then promoted through collaboration among the actors involved. Furthermore, concrete projects and services at the field level are developed through co-creation among related actors, including users and stakeholders, in order to realize the policies. In other words, policies, measures, projects, and services are developed through co-creation among the actors involved, while maintaining mutual consistency. Interaction between actors beyond the layers of "measures" and "projects and services" also takes place in diverse forms. Value is co-created through interactions between actors in a multilayered "ecosystem" that is not linear but complex and diverse.

In developing public management, it is important to promote value co-creation by diverse actors and focus on user outcomes, as well as creating value and impacting society, including "social value". In addition, a "multi-layered logic model" based on an ecosystem that addresses the complexity of the public sector is needed. This chapter examines the elements of the value co-creation process in the policy-making ecosystem through a case study analysis of a comprehensive community care system in Japan with regard to value co-creation and ecosystems in the public sector. It then derives a "multilayered logic model" and a framework for policy formation based on it, with a view to applying it to the public sector in general.

## 9.2   Analysis of Community-based Comprehensive Care System in Japan

### 9.2.1   Organization of Key Concepts in Case Analysis

In a community-based comprehensive care system, "value co-creation" in which medical care, nursing care, prevention of nursing care, housing, and lifestyle support services are comprehensively provided among various actors, and "ecosystem" as a place where policies are formed, are assumed to be the core concepts. In analyzing case studies of community-based comprehensive care systems, this analysis reviews previous studies on "value co-creation" and "eco-systems". In particular, the "ecosystem" is a system that constitutes the elements of a "multilayered logic model," which is an alternative to the linear logic model. In addition to extracting such elements, this study also propose a framework of "value types" regarding the content and value evaluation of the value created through the logic model, which can be a management goal.

### 9.2.2 Value Co-Creation

Public services, including community-based comprehensive care systems, bring value to stakeholder organizations and users. When considering the "multi-layered logic model," it is important to consider the logic of co-creating "value" in a clear manner.

According to Osborne, Value creation is a dynamic process where value is created through the use of public service and with the service user as its arbiter. This can involve both value co-creation, where the service user interacts with the PSO and its staff to create value, and value creation, where the service user in their own needs and expectations (Osborne, 2021, p.88). In other words, public policy outcomes are explained in terms of "value". Value is ultimately created by users in a value creation process based on co-creation through interaction between diverse actors, and is also created on the provider side in that process.

Regarding value co-creation, Grönroos states that "Co-creation of value can take place only if interactions between the firm and the customer" (Grönroos, 2011, p.290) Vargo *et al.* state "The customer is always a co-creator of value." "Value is always uniquely and phenomenologically determined by the beneficiary". (Vargo *et al.*, 2008, p. 148). Thus, value co-creation is considered to be created when policies, etc. proposed by diverse actors are used by customers as users.

Osborne proposes a public service logic (PSL) based on the previous research of Grönroos *et al.* Osborne describes the process of value co-creation as the evolution or deepening of value, using three value concepts: value in production, value in use, and value in context (Osborne, 2021, pp. 120-123).

Public policies, measures, projects, and services are developed in a "public ecosystem" consisting of various actors, their resources, organizational culture, and other elements. In the "co-creation area" where the "supply side" proposing public services and the "demand side" receiving public services intersect, "value in production," "value in use," and "value in context" are created through co-creation among actors, and further new services are created through a feedback cycle. The co-creation process of business and services is not something that is created only by front-line, field-level actors. For example, front-line level services are usually provided under laws, social systems, rules within or between organizations, and external environments. Taking medical services in a community-based comprehensive care system as an example, "policies" such as basic rules for medical care are co-created among various actors, including governments, professional associations, and academic experts, by combining the resources possessed by each actor. Policies are then formed according to the regional characteristics necessary for their implementation.

Then, "measures" as coordination and enhancement measures for medical care, long-term care, care prevention and livelihood support that realise the "policies" are co-created between actors such as the government and professional associations, and shared with actors of service implementing organizations such as each medical institution. Then, the actors at the frontline level co-create the "services" by combining the resources possessed by professionals and the needs of patients. The services are then developed as useful projects for each actor to develop their services. In this way, a multilayered place with a hierarchy of "policy layer," "measure layer," and "project and service layer," as well as relationships among layers, can be understood.

### 9.2.3   Public Ecosystem

#### 9.2.3.1   Ecosystem Definition and Hierarchy

Ecosystem, originally meaning "ecosystem" in biology, has been studied in various fields of business administration as a concept to explain various activities in business. However, there is no clear definition or what can be called a settled theory at this time (Fujimaki, 2020, p.2). Fujimaki cites Moore (1996) as an early study of ecosystems, who defines a business ecosystem as "an economic community supported by a foundation of interacting organizations and individuals" (Fujimaki, 2020, p.2).

As Osborne *et al.* state, "PSOs are now part of complex public service delivery systems where their mission-critical objectives require the successful negotiation of relationships within these systems – with policy makers, other PSOs, service users, citizens, and indeed a range of service system elements and stakeholders." (Osborne *et al.*, 2015, p.2). The "public ecosystem" in which diverse actors, both public and private, work together, must function organically to promote solutions to public issues.

Petrescu notes that "Considering the multiple levels at which stakeholders co-create and find value in public services, the base of analysis should focus on the micro, meso, and macro levels, emphasized by an ecosystem framework that captures individual and collective aspects." (Petrescu, 2019, p.1736), pointing to the existence of a multilayered hierarchy. Ciasullo *et al.* also use the example of the ecosystem of healthcare services, where each actor at the mega (Government agencies, Health funding body, Regulatory bodies, etc), macro (State health authorities, Professional associations, Unions in health care sector, etc), meso (Hospitals, Clinics, Local health support agencies, Care homes and hospices), and micro (Focal patients, Clinitians, Nursing staff, Allied health professional, Families, friends, other patients) levels forms the services through value co-creation (Ciasullo *et al.*, 2017, p. 225). Some previous studies have taken each level of the hierarchy from the perspective of actors, but policies and other services are formed through the interaction of resources and other resources possessed by actors and through the combination of resources, etc.

Assuming the formation of policies and other services at each level as proposed by Ciasullo *et al.* In the macro level, policies that take regional characteristics into account, in the meso level, measures for implementing services and projects, and in the micro level, services and projects are considered to be formed. Howlett *et al.* refer to the content of policy at each level, with "macro" being Governance Arrangements, "meso" being Program level operationalization, and "micro" being Specific on the ground measures (Howlett *et al.*, 2017, p. 6). If the hierarchy is viewed from the perspective of such policy formation, the "policy layer" corresponds to the "macro" layer, the "measure" layer to the "meso" layer, and the "project and service layer" to the "micro" layer.

## 9.2.3.2 Ecosystem Components

A "public ecosystem" is composed of diverse actors and elements such as the actors resources, organizational culture, and environment. With regard to the components of an ecosystem, Sano points out the diversity of components of an innovation ecosystem in a region, including (1) funds, (2) facilities, equipment, and materials, (3) human resources, (4) knowledge and information, (5) technology and capacity, (6) networks, and (7) intermediate support (Sano, 2020, p.9). In "public ecosystems," including community-based comprehensive care systems, it is thought that the same diversity of components exists as in the ecosystems envisioned in these regions, given the "diversity" and "regional characteristics" that characterize public policy. In particular, the term "intermediary support" is defined as "any action that supports the promotion of activities by connecting individuals and organizations with other individuals, organizations, and resources," and "any organization or specialized institution within or outside the region that provides any kind of intermediary support to individual players and the ecosystem as a whole" (Sano, 2020, p.12).

In addition, Yokozawa states that the diversity of components is important for a business ecosystem, because "value that cannot be created by a single company is created when diverse companies cooperate with each other" (Yokozawa, 2013, p.65). As an example of the diversity of components, Yokozawa cites the Silicon Valley ecosystem, which is composed of a variety of entities and customers, including companies, universities and research institutions, venture capitalists, support infrastructure, a global pool of talent, pioneering spirit, customers, and lead users (Yokozawa, 2013, p.67). He also states that "indirect interactions among entities are important for value creation and value acquisition," and that "platform leader companies that play a core role need to provide leadership to complementary vendors," pointing out the importance of the presence of coordinating actors (Yokozawa, 2013, p.65). He also noted that ecosystems have "boundaries based on geographical conditions" and that different countries and regions are characterized by "regional characteristics," with the best ecosystems differing depending on the country or region (Yokozawa, 2013, p. 67).

Osborne states that "PSOs do not act in isolation in their relationships with citizens, but rather are part of service delivery ecosystems" and that these ecosystem includes "both service-specific elements (PSOs, citizens, technology, etc) and broader elements including the societal context, values, and expectations that surround and legitimate these ecosystem" (Osborne, 2021, p.85). The components of a public service ecosystem include "the key individual actors and stakeholders to a public services," "the organizations involved in the ecosystem," "the resources that go into the production of a public service by PSO," "the public service infrastructure," "the processes both service enactment and use and of value creation". The diversity of components is pointed out (Osborne, 2021, p.117).

Thus, the components of the "public ecosystem" are diverse, and there is a multilayered logic in which the resources possessed by the actors, organizational culture, and networks within the ecosystem are organically combined to form policies, etc. and co-create value. In addition, taking into account the points made by Sano (2020) and Yokozawa (2013), it is believed that in value co-creation, value is created through the organic combination of resources possessed by individual actors.

Therefore, in public management as well, the existence of actors who provide intermediary support and coordinate value co-creation, so to speak "value co-creation coordinators," is considered important.

### 9.2.3.3　Value Types

In public management, value is co-created through the formation of policies by combining the resources of diverse actors, etc. Matsuo *et al.* (2021) organized the types of value created as shown in **Table 9.1**.

First, value is divided into "individual and organizational value," which is brought to individuals and organizations, and "social value," which brings change to society. Then, individual and organizational value is subdivided into "economy" which is defined as a decrease in costs and input resources, "efficiency," which is defined as an increase in the volume of services and opportunities, and "effectiveness," which is defined as an increase in satisfaction. Social value is then explained in terms of "impact," which is indexed by what is involved in solving social issues. In a multilayered logic model, compared to a linear model, it is necessary to assume a wider range of resources, etc. possessed by various actors. Economy, efficiency and effectiveness are created by the actors in the user's position through interactions between diverse actors. The accumulation of these factors creates the "impact" that brings about social change.

**Table 9.1**  Value Typology

| Value Typology | | Examples of Indicators |
|---|---|---|
| Individual and organizational value (narrowly defined) | economy | Decrease in cost<br>Decrease in input resources, etc. |
| | efficiency | Increase in the volume of services<br>Increase in opportunities, etc. |
| Individual and organizational value | effectiveness | Increase in satisfaction<br>Increase in improvement<br>Increase in revenue<br>Improvement of indicators and skills, etc. |
| social value | impact | Solving Social Problems<br>Solving structural problems<br>Improvement of public finances, etc. |

Source: Modified from Matsuo. R. *et al* (2021), pp. 3-11.

## 9.3  Case Analysis and Discussion

### 9.3.1  Assumptions of the Elements of the Multi-Layered Logic Model

In the previous chapter, a review of previous studies on value co-creation and ecosystems in the public sector is conducted to extract the elements of the multilayered logic model.

The first element of the multilayered logic model extracted from the review is "multilayered". In the multilayered logic model, the ecosystem consists of a "policy layer," a "measure layer" and a "project and service layer". At each layer, resources and other elements are combined through the interaction of diverse actors, policies and other elements are formed and value is co-created.

Second is "regionality". As Osborne (2021) argues, ecosystems differ from country to country and from region to region, and the ecosystems that form optimal policies, etc. will differ from region to region.

Third is "diversity of components". As Sano (2020) and Yokozawa (2013) point out, in an ecosystem, resources, know-how, etc. possessed by diverse actors are combined through co-creation in a network among actors. The elements that facilitate this are organizational culture and environment.

The fourth factor is the existence of value co-creation coordinators. Such as the existence of an intermediate support function in the ecosystem as pointed out by Sano (2020) and the existence of entities with leadership as pointed out by Yokozawa (2013), which are important for value co-creation. Co-creation is facilitated by "value co-creation coordinators" positioned between actors.

In this chapter, we will analyze a case study of a community-based comprehensive care system in Japan based on these elements of the multilayered logic model, and verify the validity of the components through case study analysis. Furthermore, we will analyze the value brought about through the ecosystem and consider the effectiveness of policy formation in the multilayered logic model.

### 9.3.2　Framework for Case Analysis

As a framework for the case study analysis, we first analyze the hierarchical structure of the multilayered logic model. Then, we will examine how the various elements of the multilayered logic model function in policy formation. Finally, we analyze the value created. The analytical framework is shown in **Table 9.2**.

The hierarchical structure of the multilayered logic model will be analyzed by identifying each hierarchy and analyzing the value co-creation that takes place within each hierarchy, and its characteristics and outline will be summarized.

Next, in order to verify the validity of the elements of the multilayered logic model, (1) the diversity of the components and (2) the existence of value co-creation coordinators, we will clarify how each element functions specifically in the case study.

Then, we will clarify the contents of value co-creation through the multilayered logic model. In this analysis, the process from individual value to organizational value and social value will also be analyzed, and the value co-creation process in the multilayered logic model will be discussed.

In this section, we will organize our findings on the basic framework of the multilayered logic model in public management through comprehensive analysis and discussion of community comprehensive care systems.

Table 9.2   Case Analysis Framework

| Hierarchical structure of the multilayered logic model | Characteristics and overview of each tier |
|---|---|
| Elemental analysis of the multilayered logic model | (1) Diversity of components<br>(2) Existence of value co-creation coordinators |
| value analysis | Economic, efficiency, effectiveness, impact<br>Value in Production, value in use, value in context<br>Individual value, organizational value, social value |

Source: Prepared by the author

### 9.3.3   Analysis and Discussion

### 9.3.3.1   Hierarchical Structure of the Layered Logic Model

The Government of Japan defines the basic matters such as system design for the community comprehensive care system. Prefectures and municipalities then establish the system according to local conditions. The relevant parties are supposed to work together to develop services such as "medical care", "nursing care", "care prevention", "housing" and "livelihood support". The hierarchy of the community-based comprehensive care system in Japan can be explained as follows: the aforementioned "policy layer", "measure layer," and "project and service layer".

The "policy layer" is the layer that plans concepts and systems related to the direction and policies of the policies and services of the community-based comprehensive care system. The "policy layer" is the layer in which each actor plans visions, concepts, and systems by combining resources under the leadership of the value co-creation coordinator, while taking into account the organizational culture, systems, and external environment in the area where the policy is to be implemented. Within the "policy layer", for example, it is envisioned that a network with the government as the value co-creation coordinator, focusing on the development of laws and regulations, and another network with research institutions as the value co-creation coordinator, focusing on academic research, will interact and share roles to organically plan and formulate a set of policies. In a comprehensive community care system, the government is assumed to be the main actor in policy formation.

The "government" forms the basic direction, policies and other policies for the country as a whole concerning the various systems that make up the community-based care system, such as medical care, long-term care and livelihood support. "Local government" formulate policies, measures and administrative tasks, such as basic directions and policies, according to regional characteristics. The "measure layer" concretizes the policies formed in the "policy layer" to a level where they can be practically deployed in the "project and service layer" as services such as medical care, nursing care, prevention of nursing care, and lifestyle support. The "measure layer" is responsible for the implementation of policies formulated in the "policy layer" to a level where they can be practically deployed as services for medical care, long-term care, prevention of long-term care, and support for daily living. In the "project and service layer," "value in production" is created through the interaction between service providers and users, and "value in use" is created through the use of services.

### 9.3.3.2　Elemental Analysis of the Multi-Layered Logic Model

9.3.3.2.1　Diversity of components and various activities at each layer

The base of the multilayered logic model is the ecosystem. In an ecosystem, resources and know-how possessed by various actors are combined through co-creation in a network among actors. In the "policy layer", the "government" is an organization with a concentration of resources and authority, including financial resources, organizational capacity and human resources to formulate rules, information necessary to implement measures, and networks with related organizations, and it possesses various elements necessary for the ecosystem. Policies are planned, designed, and implemented under an organizational structure and staffing that includes divisions responsible for medical care and long-term care, as well as divisions that oversee both. "Professional associations" have elements such as human resources with professional expertise and the ability to propose issues. While interacting with the government, medical institutions, nursing care facilities, and other related organizations, they propose policies and create policies to implement projects in their own organizations as well.

In the "measure layer," the "government" possesses diverse elements such as financial resources, organizational and human resources with the ability to plan services, and networks with related community-based organizations. Based on such diverse elements, the planning and designing of specific medical and long-term care services to realize the policies, as well as the planning and designing of rules and human resource development measures necessary for comprehensive service provision, are carried out through interaction with medical and long-term care actors. The "service-providing institutions" such as medical and long-term care facilities have diverse elements such as funds, human resources, information on users, and networks with various actors. They co-create measures for service provision with the government while interacting with the government and professionals at the field level.

In the "project and service layer," there are diverse elements such as professionals with the knowledge necessary for service provision and users who have service needs. Professionals design proposals to users for service implementation, reflect their needs through dialogue with users, and co-design services. They then deliver the services and create "value in production."

In addition, government organizations and professional associations, in cooperation with each other, co-design specific projects such as human resource development measures and measures to secure human resources based on policies, and through implementation of the projects, create "value in production"through interaction with users such as participants.

### 9.3.3.2.2   Value Co-Creation Coordinator

In policy formation, coordinating organizations and people are always necessary, and in each layer of the multilayered logic model, "value co-creation coordinators"promote the combination of resources among actors and co-create value. In the "policy layer", the actor that serves as a value co-creation coordinator when developing laws and rules related to the community-based comprehensive care system is the "government". The actor that serves as a value co-creation coordinator in the case of compiling knowledge related to medical science is an academic organization, etc. The organization that serves as a "value co-creation coordinator" differs depending on the content of the policy formation.

In the case of wide-area infrastructure development and human resources development based on regional characteristics, the value co-creation coordinator is the "prefectural government." For example, in the area of wide-area medical infrastructure development, prefectures promote the development of infrastructure that meets diverse medical needs, such as medical provision systems for emergencies and daily medical provision systems, through interaction with medical associations, core medical institutions and others. For human resource development measures, etc., through interaction with professional associations from the planning stage, value in production are created that improve design capabilities of professional associations, such as the design of training programs, and value in use are co-created when training programs are actually held and attended by professionals.

In the "measure layer," the value co-creation coordinator for planning specific measures to implement services is the "local government". Local government develop care services, care prevention services and livelihood support services through interaction with local comprehensive support centers, medical institutions and care service organizations, and materialize improvement measures. Value is co-created through the development of those services at the "project and service layer."

In the "project and service layer," the value co-creation coordinator for the development of specific services is the "professional. For example, care managers interact with users, combine their own knowledge with the needs of users, and plan services that support users" independence. They then co-create value by providing services to users in cooperation with medical and nursing professionals, volunteers and others.

As described above, at each level of the multilayered logic model, there are "value co-creation coordinators" who coordinate among the various actors in accordance with various policy groups, measures, and services.

### 9.3.3.3 Value Analysis

The value analysis is based on the PSL proposed by Osborne and the value categories presented by Matsuo *et al.*, 2021, such as "economy," "efficiency," "effectiveness," and "impact". We will analyze the "value in production" at the stage of receiving value propositions from key actors, the "value in use" of using them, and the "value in context" of improving and increasing their value through interactions among users or actors. The values brought to individuals and users are analyzed as "individual value," those brought to organizations as "organizational value," and those that lead to social change as "social value".

First, at the "policy layer", the government, as a value co-creation coordinator, co-designs policies related to community-based care systems such as medical and long-term care, while interacting with actors such as professional associations and academic experts. In addition, the Government creates "value in production," which forms new knowledge and perceptions among stakeholders through the improvement of the system through laws and institutional amendments to the system that have been proposed for improvement. Then, at the stage when the system is enforced, the stakeholders operate the system based on the system and "value in use" is created. These are sublimated and generated as "value in context" in the process of establishing and improving the system, etc., among the stakeholders. In these processes, "social value" is created through the development of projects and services at the field level, which ultimately result in an "impact" that is a social transformation, such as a reduction in the rate of care required certification or a reduction in social security costs.

In addition, the government, as a value co-creation coordinator responsible for policy formation in the region, creates "value in production" such as service improvement measures and human resource development in collaboration with medical and nursing care professional associations, etc., and "value in use" is created through the use of such value by participants and other stakeholders. Stakeholders create "value in context" by adding their own knowledge and forming know-how to improve services.

Finally, "social value" is created through the improvement of the service infrastructure, resulting in various "impacts".

In the "measure layer", the government, as a value co-creation coordinator, creates "value in production" in cooperation with professional associations, community support centers, medical institutions, care service organizations, etc., through the design of service provision know-how and human resource development measures, etc., to enhance their knowledge and expertise. "Value in use" is created when professional associations, medical institutions, etc. use such know-how and initiatives to enhance their knowledge. Ultimately, this will increase "effectiveness," which is an increase in organizational value, such as an increase in the organizational policy-making capacity of governments, professional associations, medical institutions, etc. It also improves "economy" through the sharing of resources possessed by multiple actors, thereby reducing the input resources of each actor. Furthermore, the improvement of the quality and competence of actors improves "efficiency," and through such improvements in "effectiveness," "economy" and "efficiency," "organizational value" is created.

In the "project and service layer", Health and care professionals, who are value co-creation coordinators, make value proposals to service users. The service users reflect their needs and other aspects of the value proposition through interaction with the professionals, and create "value in production" that leads to an increase in their own satisfaction. They then accept the value from the use of the service and create "value in use". Value in context created through these activities include, firstly, "effectiveness," such as improving the health status of service users and maintaining and improving independent living. Then, "individual value" is created through "economy," such as the reduction of resource inputs among various actors, and "efficiency," such as the improvement of the quality of service providers. The accumulation of such "individual value" leads to change through the resolution of social issues, and ultimately to the creation of "social value."

## 9.4   Conclusion

### 9.4.1   Multilayered Logic Model in Public Management

In the previous chapter, we examined the effectiveness of the various elements of the multilayered logic model and the effectiveness of the model itself in creating value through a case study analysis of a comprehensive community care system in Japan. The validity of each of the elements was confirmed, and the following framework can be proposed for the multilayered logic model in policy formation.

First, it was confirmed that the multilayered logic model consists of multiple layers. The policy hierarchy in public administration includes "policies," "measures," and "projects and services". Broadly classifying them by function, we can divide them into three functional layers: the "policy layer" corresponding to "policy," the "measure layer" corresponding to "measures," and the "project and service layer" corresponding to "projects and services.

The "policy layer" is the layer that plans concepts and systems related to the direction and policies of policies and services. The "policy layer" is the layer that plans visions and concepts by combining resources under the leadership of the value co-creation coordinator, while taking into consideration the organizational culture, institutions, and external environment in the area where the policy is to be implemented. For example, within the macro layer, it is possible to envision a network in which the government is the value co-creation coordinator with a focus on the development of laws and regulations, and a network in which research institutions are the value co-creation coordinators with a focus on academic research, and through interaction and role-sharing, a set of policies can be planned and formulated organically.

The "measure layer" is the layer where the policies formed in the "policy layer" are concretized to a level where they can be practically managed in the "project and service layer" and commercialized. It is also the layer that secures the resources required for the micro-layer, such as training and securing human and financial resources necessary for the implementation of projects. Therefore, it may be necessary for the value co-creation coordinator of the "measure layer" to play a central role in dialogue with actors in the policy layer and the business/service layer.

The "project and service layer" is the layer that implements the projects conceived in the "measure layer" and commercialized in the "policy layer," and is the layer that is at the forefront of value co-creation with users. In this layer, for example, the value co-creation coordinator who coordinates plans for service provision with users co-creates "value in production" with users, and "value in use" is created by using services from actors who actually provide services in accordance with the plans. Then, "value in context" is created as users increase their satisfaction through continuous use of the service. These values created by users are "individual values" that lead to improvements in "economy," "efficiency," and "effectiveness" among the various actors. The "organizational value" is that which is enjoyed by the organization through multiple users, and the "social

226

value" is that which leads to the "impact" of society as a whole.

Next, a multilayered logic model in public management can be posed if we look at each policy or measure, or project and service separately at each level or between levels. At a certain layer, the resources, technology and know-how possessed by each actor are combined by the coordinating function of the value co-creation coordinator, influenced by the organizational culture, system and environment, in order to form and develop a certain "policy" or "measure" or "project and service". Individual and organizational values related to "economy", "efficiency" and "effectiveness" are then co-created. The value co-creation process is based on the coordination function of the value co-creation coordinators. This specific policy, etc. is linked to related policies, etc. in the "same layer" or "other layers" through value co-creation coordinators and actors, and "social value" related to "impact" is created through the accumulation of multiple individual and organizational values.

Therefore, the flow of policy formation based on this logic model is as follows: First, a vision/concept is established, and the resources, technology, and know-how possessed by public and private actors involved in policies to realize the vision,

**Figure 9.1** Multidimensional Logic Model at Each Layer or Between Layers

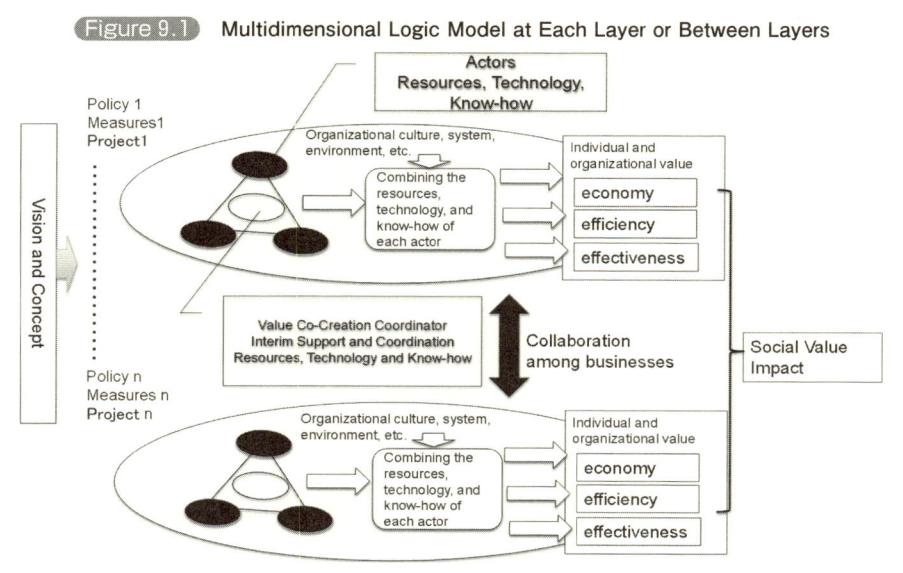

Source: Prepared by the author

etc., are identified. Next, the core actors act as value co-creation coordinators to analyze the organizational culture and environment, and combine the resources, technology, and know-how of all actors to co-create value, while taking into account the relationship with other policies. Evaluate whether value equivalent to the realization of the vision has been created, and reflect improvements in policies and other measures. A multifaceted logic model is envisioned that involves the public and private actors described above.

### 9.4.2  Implications for Future Research

Public-private co-creation has already spread as a basic method in public management, regardless of the type of policy, such as software or hardware. In the private sector, there is also a growing trend toward CSV (Creating Shared Value) -based management and the perception of the public as a business opportunity. In order for public-private co-creation to take root, it is essential for public actors to take the lead and set up opportunities and venues for co-creation. It is also expected that the public sector will formulate and implement policies and other measures to more actively utilize the resources, technology, and know-how possessed by the private sector, and that the private sector will accelerate its participation in and contribution to public management, even on the premise of securing profits from its core business.

● References—————————————————————

Ciasullo, M. V., Cosimato, S., Palumbo, R., & Storlazzi, A.(2017). Value co-creation in the health service ecosystems: The enabling role of institutional arrangements, *International Business Research,* 10(12), 222-238.

Fujimaki S.(2020). Ecosystem to wa nanika. (in Japanese), *Syogakukenkyukakiyou,* 90, 1-20.

Grönroos, C. (2011). Value Co-Creation in Service Logic: A Critical Analysis. *Marketing Theory.*

Grönroos, C. and Gummerus, J.(2014). The service revolution and its marketing implications: service logic vs service-dominant logic, *Managing Service Quality*, 24, 206-229.

Howlett, M., Kekez, A. & Poocharoen, O.(2017). Understanding Co-production as a policy tool: Integrating New Public Governance and Comparative Policy Theory, *Journal of Comparative Policy Analysis,* 19(2), 1-15.

Sano, J. (2020). Naihatutekitiiki inovation ecosystem no kouzou. (in Japanese), *Syakai Kagaku,* 50(1), 1-32.

Ministry of Health,Labor and Welfare web site Establishing The community-based Integrated

228

Care System' https://www.mhlw.go.jp/english/policy/care-welfare/care-welfare-elderly/dl/estab-lish_e.pdf, :accessed 1 April,2024.

Matsuo R., (2018). Chihojichitai ni okeru seisaku no keisei to jissen no ronri - NPM to NPG no yugo - [Logic of Policy Formation and Practice in Local Government-Fusion of NPM and NPG-] (in Japanese).

Matsuo, R., Sekishita,H., Hosomi,S., & Ishihara,T.(2021). An Integrated Framework of Various Concepts Related to Value Co-Creation, *CIPFAJ Journal,* 5, May 2021, 3-11.

Moore, J. F.(1996). The death of competition: Leadership and strategy in the age of business eco-systems, New York, NY: HarperCollins.

Osborne, S. P., Z. Radnor, T. Kinder and I. Vidal (2015), "The Service Framework: A Public-service-dominant Approach to Sustainable Public services," *British Journal of Management,* 26(3), 1-15.

Osborne, S. P.(2021). Public service logic: creating value for public service users, citizens, and soci-ety through public service delivery. *Routledge.*

Petrescu, M.(2019). From marketing to public value: towards a theory of public service ecosystem, *Public Management Review.* 21(11), 1733-1752.

Porter, M. E & Kramer, M. R.(2011), Cresting Shared Value: How to reinvent capitalism and un-leash a wave of innovation and growth, *Harvard Business Review.* 62-77.

Strokosh, K. & Osborne, S. P.(2020), CO-experience, co-production and co-governance: an ecosys-tem approach to the analysis of value creation, *Policy & Politics.* 48(3), 425-442.

Vargo, S. L., Maglio, P. P., & Akaka, M. A. (2008). On value and value co-creation: A service systems and service logic perspective. *European management journal,* 26(3), 145-152.

Yokozawa, Y.(2013). "Business ecosystem no gainen ni kansuru rironteki kentou."(in Japanese), *Okayama syoudai ronshu* 48(3) Febrary, 61-76.

Chapter **10**

# Value Co-creation by Regional University and Regional Venture Company: Perspective of Solving Social Issues

**Toshio Araki**

◆

## Abstract

In Japan, as the declining birthrate and aging population accelerate, the significant population outflow from rural areas to urban areas, particularly around the Kanto region, has become a major issue, leading to the deterioration of regional economies and communities. Given these circumstances, approximately half of regional private universities are struggling to meet their enrollment capacities, resulting in a challenging business environment. These universities are expected to fulfill various roles in their respective regions, such as maintaining educational opportunities as public institutions and serving as hubs for the revitalisation of the local economy and society. Under this situational recognition, it is imperative for regional universities to enhance their value, actively contribute to their communities, and pursue sustainability in their management.

On the other hand, amidst declining population in rural areas and the consequent exhaustion of the local economy and community, there are many social issues (regional issues) that need to be resolved in the region. Despite various initiatives by the Japanese central and local governments, significant challenges remain. In light of such circumstances, this chapter focuses on the social implementation of innovative social issue-solving projects between the regional private university and the regional venture company in Japan from the perspective of solving social issues and revitalising local communities. And through case studies, it clarifies the roles of regional private universities and regional venture companies in regional revitalisation, provides insights into the importance of "value co-creation" by various actors in the region, and elucidates the value creation process by diverse actors and their concrete contributions to the region.

**Keywords**

regional university, regional venture company, value co-creation, social impact, regional revitalisation, ecosystem

## 10.1 Introduction

As the declining birthrate and aging population accelerates, the population in rural areas is declining, especially in rural areas as people move to urban areas to enter universities or find employment, and revitalising local economies and local communities has become a major social issue. In such a situation, due to the population decline in rural areas, private universities, especially located in rural areas, are facing a difficult business environment.

However, regional universities are expected to play a variety of roles that differ depending on the region, such as maintaining educational opportunities as public institutions in the region and serving as bases for revitalising the local economy and local communities, including human resource development. In addition, as the core of regional revitalisation, regional universities are expected to utilize the intellectual resources (distinctive resources) that each regional university possesses to form a regional platform that involves various related actors and to play an important role as one of the core elements of that platform (MEXT, Higher Education Bureau, 2020).

Despite this expected role of regional universities, there have been a number of mergers and closures, particularly of small private universities and private women's universities and junior colleges in the region.

### 10.1.1 Fulfilment of enrolment capacity at private universities

In Japan, the population decline is particularly serious in rural areas. As a result, the management of regional universities, especially small private universities in rural areas, is in an extremely difficult situation. According to the press release by

MEXT on 20 December 2023, there are 810 universities in total, of which 86 are national universities, 102 are public universities, and 622 are private universities (MEXT website, 2023).

According to the Promotion and Mutual Aid Corporation for private schools of Japan (2023), among the 600 four-year private universities surveyed in Japan, the percentage of universities with unfilled enrollment quotas increased by 6.0 points, reaching 53.3% (Promotion and Mutual Aid Corporation for private schools of Japan, 2023, p.2). In addition, there are considerable differences in the fulfilment of an enrolment capacity not only by the size of the enrolment capacity, but also between different regions (p. 8). If this situation continues, there is a possibility that the number of universities falling into financial crisis will increase rapidly. If such a situation occurs, as mentioned at the outset, the pressing issue will be how to secure educational opportunities in rural areas and how they can fulfil their role of revitalising the local economy and local community. About one third of universities are concentrated in the Kanto area, namely Tokyo, Saitama, Chiba and Kanagawa prefecture (118 universities in Tokyo, 26 in Saitama, 26 in Chiba and 27 in Kanagawa - 197 universities in total (FY2023)(Promotion and Mutual Aid Corporation for private schools of Japan, 2023, p.8). In this chapter, universities outside these Kanto areas are assumed to be regional universities.

This chapter focuses on the social implementation (including entrepreneurship) of the new social issue-solving project between the regional private university and the regional venture company in Japan, from the perspective of solving social issues (regional issues) and revitalizing local communities, considering the current situation in Japan. Specifically, the role of the regional private university and the regional venture company in regional revitalisation is demonstrated through examples of advanced initiatives for value co-creation by the regional university and the regional venture company. The aim is then to identify the value creation process by diverse actors and their specific contribution to the region.

## 10.2 Literature Review

### 10.2.1 Public Service Logic and Public Service Ecosystem

As this chapter studies examples of value co-creation by diverse local actors to solve local problems, the whole system is seen as an ecosystem. In relation to the "ecosystem" that is the focus of this chapter, Vargo and Lusch (2017, p.50) indicated that the role of actors in the ecosystem and how to make the service ecosystem function are important research topics and require further exploration. On the other hand, Osborne (2021) applies the Service Marketing and Management theory that has been developed in the private sector to administrative organisations in the public sector and proposes the concept of Public Service Logic (PSL).

PSL is a framework that supports the fundamental principles of the public service management, namely "service" and (external) "value creation" (Osborne, 2021, p.2). Petrescu (2019) discusses the ecosystem in its PSL framework as "Public service ecosystems incorporate a comprehensive, 360-degree view of all the individuals, technologies, and institutions involved in the creation and delivery of value generated through the public system and adjacent private stakeholders" (p.1734). The public service ecosystem (PSE) is a framework whose components include public service providers (public service organisations), service users (residents, etc.), and contractors (Osborne, 2021, p.117, Table 5.1). Strokosch and Osborne (2020), in relation to the PSE and value creation, state that "The value of public services is associated with the outputs, outcomes and experiences for various individuals and groups in society (e.g. individual citizens, public service users, taxpayers, communities) but is also pursued by the organisations delivering services" (p.429). As Osborne (2021) points out that public service agencies and their staff are central to value co-creation in the service ecosystem, the role and function of intermediary support organizations as coordinators to promote value co-creation will be necessary.

Osborne (2021) also presents value-in-production, value-in-use and value-in-context as three dimensions of value in the PSE (p.122). And, among others, in relation to social impact, which is discussed in the next section, Osborne (2021) indicates *"An indirect societal impact of a public service"* (p.123, Table 5.3) as the social component of value in the dimension of value-in production. Osborne (2021) identified the seven ecosystem components in public services (for details, see p.117, Table 5.1).

The research objective of this study is to clarify the value creation process and specific contributions to the region by diverse actors, including the government, from a case study of an advanced approach to value co-creation by the regional private university and the regional venture company. Therefore, the PSL and PSE, which are the concept and the framework of value co-creation in public services, will be used to address the research question.

### 10.2.2   Socially responsible investment (SRI) and social impact investment

This section origanised previous research on socially responsible investment and social impact investment in the Japanese context.

#### 10.2.2.1   Socially responsible investment in Japan

Tanimoto (2006) defines socially responsible investment as "basically a method of evaluating corporate activities not only from a financial perspective but also from a social and environmental perspective and deciding where to invest and finance" (p. 110). Matsumoto and Mizuguchi (2005) also point out that, although the impression of SRI differs depending on the focus, one way of looking at it is "to evaluate and invest in companies that better fulfil their CSR" (p. 5). Omuro and Ohira (2013) focus on the investment motive of social change among socially responsible investors and conduct a study on the behavioral change of investors. Omuro and Ohira (2013) point out that a key difference between general investment and SRI is that SRI leads to social change (p.42).

#### 10.2.2.2   Social impact investment and evaluation

Kobayashi (2021) states that, although interest in social impact investment is growing in Japan, it is recognized that "it is difficult to say that a common understanding of impact investment has been formed among policy makers, practitioners and researchers" (pp. 1-2). Based on this recognition, Kobayashi (2021) states that not only practitioners but also researchers need to advance academic research on this topic as a research agenda (p.13).

Additionally, Kobayashi (2021) organaises the issues related to the concept and definition of impact investment and the process of how impact investment has developed historically and suggests challenges in the current situation and the direction of future development. And Kobayashi (2021) points out that the definition of impact investment as "investments made with the intention to generate positive, measurable social and/or environmental impact alongside a financial return" (GIIN website) has been accepted in general (p.2).

On the other hand, Kobayashi (2021) points out that several issues have become apparent regarding social impact investment and raises the question of how to measure social impact and how to distinguish it from socially responsible investiment (pp. 2-3).

### 10.2.2.3  Summary

From the perspective that regional universities in particular are expected to play a role and function as bases of regional revitalisation, one initiative to fulfil this role, such as socially responsible investment, could well be an option. From the perspective of regional revitalisation, specific examples of how socially responsible investment targeting local communities is creating a concrete social impact may be sought. In organising these, the dimensions of value creation and the societal element of value within the PSE as presented in Osborne (2021) may be useful (p.123, Table 5.3).

## 10.3  Research Question and Research Design

### 10.3.1  Research question

Based on the above-mentioned problem awareness and background, and the research objective of this chapter, which is "to clarify the value creation process by diverse actors and the concrete contribution to the region from examples of advanced value co-creation initiatives by regional universities and regional venture companies," the following research questions were derived from the current situation in local society and regional universities and from previous research.

"What functions can regional universities fulfil as intermediary support organisations to solve social issues (regional issues)? How can regional venture companies involve diverse local actors to solve social issues? What kind of the ecosystem is needed to achieve this?"

### 10.3.2　Research Design

In this study, the PSL concept (Osborne 2021) and the PSE framework are used for discussion and analysis. The reasons for using this framework are (i) the focus is on regional universities and regional venture companies, and the focus is on the intermediary support functions and intermediary support organisational forms that link various regions. (ii) It refers to the higher education policy in Japan as a form of public policy and considers value co-creation with diverse actors. In view of these factors, it was decided to use the PSL concept and the PSE framework described above.

Based on the previous research review, the following two perspectives of analysis based on the PSL concept, and the PSE framework are set out.

(1) Ecosystems and assumed internal components

(2) Specific value creation as societal impact

### 10.3.3　Case Study

The case study will focus on a collaborative project to solve social issues between a regional university, local communities, and various local actors such as intermediary support organisations, local credit unions, and local residents. Specifically, based on the research results of the Research Centre for the Local Public Human Resources and Policy Development (LORC) of Ryukoku University, a public policy theory and practice model project aimed at social implementation of renewable energy has been developed (Ryukoku University website A; LORC website). Ryukoku University has two campuses in Kyoto Prefecture and one in Shiga Prefecture and can be regarded as a regional university.

The reasons for this selection are as follows.

(1) It is an initiative aimed at social implementation of the university's research seeds back into the local community.

(2) It is an initiative involving local financial institutions.

(3) It is an initiative that aims to contribute to the local community and solve social issues facing the local area.

(4) It is an initiative that involves a diverse range of actors.

For these reasons, this study aims to examine this case and obtain insights for future regional revitalisation through regional private universities and regional venture companies.

### 10.3.3.1　Analysis Case

Since this study focuses on the regional university and the regional venture company, "the community-contributing mega solar power generation business model" which the university is working on, was chosen as the case study, as an initiative that has already been implemented in society to solve social issues and revitalise the local community.

First, the mechanism of the "community-contributing mega solar power generation business model" will be introduced. Then, the mechanism of the "Ryukoku Float Solar Park" will be introduced as an actual example of social implementation. And then, a semi-structured interview conducted with Mr. Masataka Fukao, one of the originators of "the community-contributing mega solar power generation business model," the planner of the "Ryukoku Float Solar Park" project, and a coordinator connecting the university and local communities, the university and financial institutions, the university and trust companies, etc., is analysed and discussed. A semi-structured interview was also conducted with Mr. Irisawa, the current Executive Director and President of Ryukoku University, and the results of this discussion are also showed.

10.3.3.1.1　Mega Solar Power Generation Business Model for Contributing to Local Communities

This section explains the newly developed trust scheme by PLUS SOCIAL Co., Ltd. based on Ryukoku University website B. PLUS SOCIAL is a stock company-type NPO established by Mr. Fukao with the intention of solving social issues. The background of its establishment was "the need for a mechanism to connect the social nature of the community and those in need to social business," he stated in an interview. PLUS SOCIAL, as an intermediary support organisation, acts as an intermediary, connecting trust banks and regional financial institutions with public interest corporations, educational institutions, small and medium-sized businesses, and individuals who are expected to be investors. The funds from investors are used to install solar power plants and sell the electricity generated to local power companies, and PLUS SOCIAL makes a profit from the sale of electricity through an independent trust account, which is then donated and returned to the community through a local community foundation established to contribute to the community.

In this scheme, PLUS SOCIAL can be positioned as an intermediary or an intermediate support organisation that connects investors, local communities, and financial institutions through the installation and operation of mega solar power plants that generate renewable energy.

10.3.3.1.2 "Ryukoku Solar Park" Business Model (case of Awaji City, Hyogo Prefecture)

The business model is described as follows (Ryukoku University website A).

"PLUS SOCIAL Co., Ltd. as the business company and PS Sumoto Co., Ltd. (hereinafter referred to as PS) will work in collaboration with financial institutions and others to install mega solar power plants on land owned by the local government, using funds invested by the university as part of socially responsible investment (SRI), and sell the electricity generated using the feed-in tariff system. The profits, after deducting necessary expenses from the revenue, will be provided as support funds for community contribution activities and civic activities in the areas where the panels are installed, as well as in Kyoto. Additionally, these profits will be donated to the university as funds for social contribution activities and will be utilized to promote the university's social collaboration initiatives."

10.3.3.1.3 "Ryukoku Solar Park" Business Model (case of Inami Town, Wakayama Prefecture)

According to the Ryukoku University Extension Center website, the actors involved in this project are Ryukoku University, Inami Town, Wakayama Prefecture, Kyocera Solar Corporation, PLUS SOCIAL, and Transvalue Trust Co., Ltd. These actors worked together to launch the Ryukoku Solar Park in November 2011 as the nation's first mega solar power plant that contributes to the local community. The purpose of the project is "to contribute to the local community by returning the profits from solar power generation to the revitalisation of the local community. The profits from the sale of electricity will be used as activity funds for local activities and volunteer activities in Wakayama and Kyoto through a public interest incorporated foundation" (Ryukoku University Extension Center website).

### 10.3.3.2 Perspective of Analysis

Since this study focuses on the regional university and the regional venture company, it was decided to analyse the case study from both perspectives. Therefore, in conducting the case study, the interview was conducted with the following perspectives in mind.

(1) Applicability of social investment projects conducted by universities to regional universities
(2) Key persons in decision making at the university
(3) Significance of regional venture companies that aim to become social businesses

### 10.3.3.3 Interview Guide

The interviewee was Professor Masataka Fukao (Faculty of Policy Studies), one of the originators of the business model described above, and the current Vice President of Ryukoku University, as well as the Representative Director of PLUS SOCIAL.

And the second, Professor Takashi Irisawa is the current President of Ryukoku University and was involved in the decision-making process regarding the implementation of the project at Ryukoku University as the dean of the Faculty of

Letters and a member of the board of trustees, and has been one of the key players in promoting the Ryukoku Solar Park Project as the President and Executive Director since 2017.

The dates and times of the interviews are shown as follows.

Mr. Masataka Fukao: Semi-structured interview conducted on 1 Dec. 2023, 10:00-11:00 at Fukao Lab, Fukakusa Campus, Ryukoku University.

Mr. Takashi Irisawa: Semi-structured interview conducted on 21 Jul. 2024, 13:50-14:20 at his home.

### 10.3.3.4 Interview Survey Items

The interview questions for Mr. Fukao were sent by e-mail in advance and the handling of personal information was explained to him before the semi-structured interview was conducted. And the interview questions for Mr. Irisawa were explained to him before the interview and the handling of personal information was explained to him before the semi-structured interview was conducted.

For the analysis of the interview content, co-occurrence network analysis was conducted as a content analysis using the KH coder (Higuchi, 2020). The KH coder was used because it is a tool that enables quantitative analysis of qualitative data, mechanically counts words and is not limited by the subjective ideas of the user (Higuchi, 2020, p.102).

The following is a summary of the interview questionnaire survey items for both respondents.

10.3.3.4.1 Interview questions asked of Mr. Fukao
- Background to the establishment of PLUS SOCIAL and challenges in establishing it.
- Why did Ryukoku University participate in the nation's first community contribution mega solar power plant project as socially responsible investment, and what were the challenges in making decisions regarding the implementation of the project, and how were they resolved?
- How is the social implementation of these research results returned to education?
- How was the business model of the "Ryukoku Solar Park" planned and

designed? And who were the key players?

- What specific role did financial institutions play? How do financial institutions view social investment?
- What specific benefits have been brought to the region through regional revitalisation? How do the residents of each region feel about the contributions being made to the region? Furthermore, what role does each government play?
- What are the factors behind the increasing number of companies being certified under the Social and Sustainable Standard Scheme.
- How is the company value assessed using non-financial information rather than just financial information? Also, what is the purpose of the application of companies certified as social companies and what are the specific effects.
- Situations in which entrepreneurship is considered to have been demonstrated.
- What skills and knowledge are required with regard to the exercise of entrepreneurship? Additionally, what is the necessity of entrepreneurship education at universities?

10.3.3.4.2    Interview questions asked of Mr. Irisawa

- What are your thoughts on the Buddhist SDGs and the various projects you are developing, especially in terms of solving social issues? What were the factors that enabled your university to make decisions in carrying out these projects?
- What actors are important for the socially responsible investment projects centred on the Ryukoku Solar Park?
- What role does Ryukoku University play as an intermediary or as an intermediate support organisation? Furthermore, what is needed for it to function as an intermediary support organisation?

## 10.4   Results and Discussion

A semi-structured interview was conducted with Professor Masataka Fukao, the creator of the "Ryukoku Solar Park" business model, who is also the actual person in charge at Ryukoku University. **Figure 10.1** shows the co-occurrence network resulting from the content analysis using the KH coder (Higuchi, 2020) after converting the interview content into text. A co-occurrence network is "a network of words with similar patterns of occurrence, i.e., words with a strong degree of co-occurrence, connected by lines" (Higuchi, 2020, p.182), and "the area of the circle is proportional to the number of times a word appears" (Higuchi, 2020, p.185). And Figure 10.1 classifies the co-occurrence network into five groups from A to E based on the connection of frequently occurring words, each of which is analysed and discussed based on the perspectives shown below. Basic information about the texts used in the interviews is as follows: the total number of words (used) was 13,221 (4,306), the number of different words (used) was 1,521 (1,226), the

**Figure 10.1** Relationship Between Regional Universities and Value Creation by Diverse Local Actors (Co-occurrence Network)

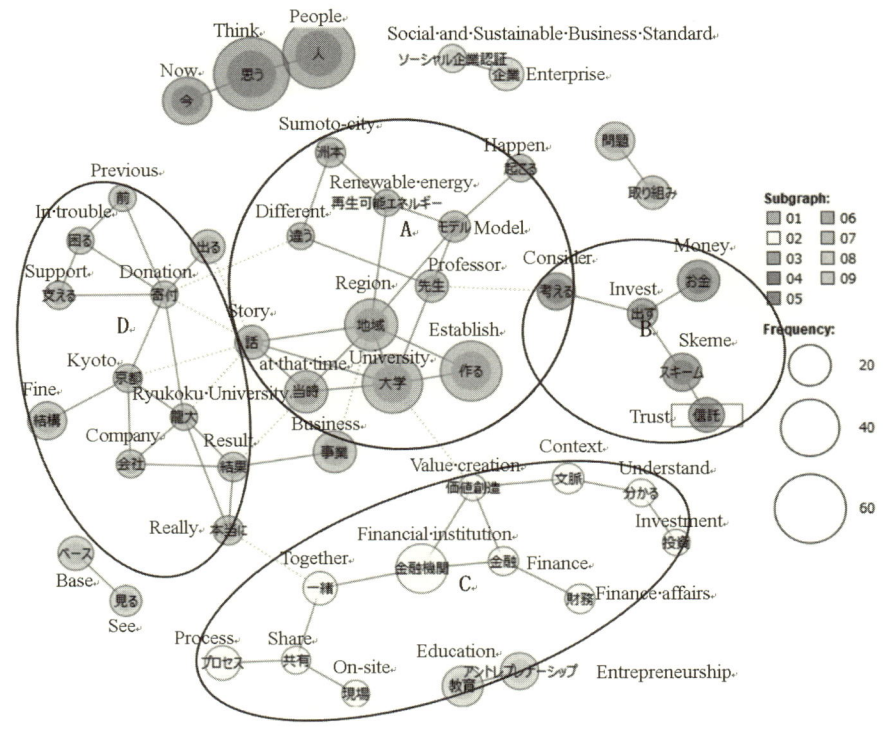

Source: Created by the author using KH Coder

average number of occurrences was 3.51, and the standard deviation of the number of occurrences was 10.26.

### 10.4.1 Social Implementation Scheme Connecting Regions and Universities (Renewable Energy)

In Group A, the following can be inferred from the words and phrases that appear and their connections. In addition, what can be said from the content of the interviews is also discussed. The parts bracketed by " " indicate words and phrases that appear in the co-occurrence network. Group A represents a group of co-occurrence networks related to the "Region" and the "University". This co-occurrence network represents the business "Model" of the Ryukoku Solar Park. In this co-occurrence network, the "Region" and the "University" are connected, and the "Renewable energy" and the "Model" that are socially implemented in the "Region" of "Sumoto-city" are connected. The Ryukoku Solar Park "Sumoto" is a social implementation model "established" with the participation of local government agencies, local financial institutions, and local residents as diverse local actors. The "University" is positioned as an intermediary and intermediate support organisation for this model.

In relation to RQ:"What functions can regional universities fulfill as intermediary support organisations to solve social issues (regional issues)?", the following comment was made in the interview.

> "In the case of Sumoto, there is the regional-academic collaboration that I mentioned earlier, so the use of revenues is very local-managed with local people spending money on issues they have and things they want to do or revitalise. This is a model for providing money while collaborating with the government. Local people are coming up with more and more interesting proposals, which are then supported by the revenues of the Ryukoku Solar Park."

It can be said that this co-occurrence network shows the *"The key individual actors and stakeholders"* and *"Their actions and activities within the public service ecosystem"* (Osborne, 2021, p.117, Table 5.1) of the components of the PSE.

### 10.4.2   Trust Scheme Thinking and Attitude Change toward Value Creation

In Group B, as in Group A, what can be inferred from the words and phrases that appear and their connections is as follows. In the same way, what can be said from the content of the interviews is also supplemented. Group B represents a group of co-occurrence networks related to the "Trust" "Scheme" shown in Figure 10.1. In this co-occurrence network, "Invest" and "Money" are connected, and "Money," "Scheme" and "Trust" are connected. The business model shown in Group A is based on the trust scheme. Mr. Fukao himself is not a finance professional, and he had many difficulties in how to raise "Money" and how to install solar panels. At such a time, there was a finance professional who appeared to solve the problem. This was a connection that resulted from Mr. Fukao's personal network and connections with other people. It is clear from the interview that this person resonated with Fukao's concept and worked hard with him to "Consider" the "Trust" "Scheme" that would become the core of this business model.

On the other hand, the interviews confirmed that the key department at the university was the finance department. Usually, departments related to community contributions take some initiative to revitalise the community. However, the finance department played a major role in creating a new value for the university by developing this "Trust" "Scheme" as a business model for the university. In this case, the finance department played a role in transforming the existing concept of university value within the dual structure of corporations and education in universities, not just "Invest" "Money."

In this group, it can be seen that Fukao's personal thoughts were conveyed to the people involved and moved the finance department. In other words, it can be said that of the components of the PSE shown by Osborne (2021), *"Their personal beliefs/philosophies, prior experiences",* as well as *"further expectations of these key actors"* (p.117, Table 5.1) are shown.

### 10.4.3   Involvement of Regional Financial Institutions in Value Creation

In Group B, as in Group A/B, what can be inferred from the words and phrases that appear and their connections is as follows. In the same way, what can be said from the content of the interviews is also supplemented. Group C represents a group of co-occurring networks of regional "Financial institution" related to the "Process" of "Value creation" for regional revitalisation. In this co-occurrence network, "Financial institution" and "Value creation", "Financial institution" and "Together" and "Share" are connected, and this connection is at the heart of this network. When this business model was first conceived, regional financial institutions were initially skeptical about participating in this business model, as it was an initiative in which they had no experience. However, this initiative was a "Value creation" business model with social impact, and the creation of social impact led to the discovery of a new role for "Financial institution". It could be said that this was the moment when new roles and functions of regional "Financial institution" were born.

In the interview, Mr. Fukao commented that it was a game-changing moment. "Financial institution" are now actively involved in investing in social businesses, which are business models that generate renewable energy to solve social issues "On site" "Together", in addition to the general lending business they have been engaged in up to now. In the same way as above, it can be said to be a moment that led to a change in the mindset of regional "Financial institution."

This organisation, a financial institution, is an organisation that provides the resource of "Finance," which Osborn (2021) indicates as the component of the PSE: "organisations supporting their work or supplying resources" (p.117, Table 5.1).

### 10.4.4 Value Creation Networks through Community Contribution Businesses

In Group D, as in Group A/B/C, what can be inferred from the words and phrases that appear and their connections is as follows. Group D represents a group of co-occurring networks related to the establishment of a regional contribution business model of "Donation" between the regional venture "Company" and "Ryukoku University" in "Kyoto." Group D is also connected to Groups A and C. The core concept of the "Donation" business model is connected to the words "In trouble" and "Support," "Kyoto," "Ryukoku University" and "Company". It can be said to represent a network of value creation through a business model in which

"Ryukoku University" in the region of "Kyoto" first engages a diverse range of local actors, including financial institutions in "Kyoto," and then "Support" those "In trouble" through "Donation" made through various relationships.

Behavioral changes in local actors can be seen in Group A, in Group B in the university itself, and in Group C in the attitudes and behavioral changes of local financial institutions. These changes in awareness and behavior are strengthening the relationship with various local actors. It can also be said that donations from the profits generated by the sale of renewable energy have created a kind of culture of mutual support to solve local issues and build a network for the creation of new value.

As Osborne (2021, p.116) identifies "process" as one of the factors that he points to as being key to functioning in the value dimension, the processes of awareness and behavioral change that can be found in these groups are considered to be important factors for value creation.

### 10.4.4.1　Specific Examples as Regional Contributions (solutions to regional issues)

In the interviews, the following examples of how donated money from these business models was used to solve specific regional issues and revitalise local communities were presented.

- The money donated is used for initiatives identified by the local community to revitalise the area, in collaboration with the local government.
- Many interesting proposals led by the local community are supported by the revenue from the Ryukoku Solar Park.
- Local festivals and events, which are increasingly difficult to fund through government sources, are supported by this revenue, including fireworks displays and the development and promotion of local specialty products.
- Donations are utilized to enhance community building and the sustainability of local life.

In this way, donations are being used to solve local issues at the initiative of local actors. The mechanism for guiding the initiative of local actors will also be important.

### 10.4.5  Implications from the results of the interview with the President of Ryukoku University

After analysing and discussing the results of the interview with Mr. Fukao, I decided to conduct an interview with Mr. Irisawa, the current President of Ryukoku University, with the view to complementing these discussions. The following suggestions related to this case study were obtained from Mr. Irisawa.

#### 10.4.5.1  Decision-making factors in implementing social investment projects

The determinants of decision-making in implementing this social investment project, the first of its kind in the country, include the following. The university should consider what they should do when they are trying to make a concrete contribution to the local community and solve regional issues. Specifically, when considering such new schemes, the university should return to the perspective of whether they will contribute to the local community and solve regional issues, which is the original mission of the university.

#### 10.4.5.2  Actors involved in socially responsible investment projects centred on the Ryukoku Solar Park.

In implementing these projects, there are limits to what the university can do on their own. From now on, "collaboration" will become important. The government, the industry and the financial sector are each key actor, and they need to work together as a whole to form a powerful scrum to solve regional issues.

#### 10.4.5.3  Ryukoku University's role as an intermediary or intermediate support organisation

To initiate some kind of business, it is very important to have "some kind of philosophy." Whether a company can trust the university as a partner, for which the university is required to have educational and research outcomes. To try to solve some social issue, it is necessary for the university to take a multifaceted approach rather than to work alone. The university's unique "perspective," or "eye for the essence," on the viewpoints from the industrial and financial sector is the role of the university. These will ensure the sustainability of the relationship of trust between the three parties.

#### 10.4.5.4 Functioning as an intermediate support organisation for the university to connect between actors for regional revitalisation

To maintain its function as an intermediary support organisation, it is important to sustain a sense of "connection". In the case of the university the main focus should be on the relationship between the university and the community, the university and the students, and the "connection". It is important to live in a way of life that is aware of society, i.e. to be aware of "connections with society".

## 10.5  Conclusion

In this case study, the research questions "What functions can regional universities fulfil as intermediary support organisations to solve social issues (regional issues)? How can regional venture companies involve diverse local actors to solve social issues? What kind of the ecosystem is needed to achieve this?" were clarified through content analysis of the semi-structured interview results with Mr. Fukao.

Specifically, in the case of the university in this case study, in addition to social implementation of research results, the university has become an investor to solve regional social issues. In other words, the university is an intermediary support organisation that connects the local community, financial institutions, local residents, and business companies.

On the other hand, it is clear that the regional venture company, which was established to solve social issues, has an indispensable function and role as a core entity that forms an ecosystem, connecting local communities, financial institutions, electric power companies, and solar panel manufacturers through regional universities.

The results of the interview with Mr. Irisawa also provided the following insights.

- When the university make decisions on implementing social investment projects, the university should return to the original mission of the university.

- There are limits to what the university can do on their own to solve regional issues, and strong cooperation between the industry and the financial sector is required.
- The role of the university as an intermediary or intermediary support organisation requires it to have a unique "perspective," i.e. an "eye for the essence." To maintain this support function, it is also important to sustain a sense of "connection."

As indicated in the previous section, it was possible to confirm the "ecosystems and assumed internal components" set out in the research design as a perspective for analysis based on the PSL concept and the PSE framework. As for "Specific value creation as societal impact," in the case of Inami Town, Wakayama, it was possible to identify value creation as societal impact, such as the organisation of local events by young people to revitalise the area, and the marketing and commercialisation of local products.

From the above, it can be interpreted that, as the core of the service ecosystem pointed out by Osborne (2021), a regional university or regional venture company plays a key role in promoting value co-creation, either as an intermediary support organisation or as a coordinator. The ecosystem formed in this case study can also be described as the ecosystem that connects the government and the private sector based on the PSL concept. It would also be possible to say that this case study forms the PSE with the regional university and the regional venture company as intermediaries (intermediate support organisation).

## 10.6 Limitations of this Study - Future Issues

Kobayashi (2021) asks the following questions as emerging issues in social impact investment: "How to we measure social and environmental impact, and whether it is possible to standardise this measurement? How to verify the intention to create social and environmental impact? Whether is it possible to reflect the results of social and environmental impact in corporate accounting and auditing reports?" (pp.2-3).

As one solution to these issues, social impact evaluation in the social and sustainable business standard implemented by Ryukoku University in collaboration with Kyoto Shinkin Bank and others (Social Enterprise Certification Organisation website) is expected. Currently, the system is at the diffusion level and seems to have reached the point of developing more specific evaluation indicators, but in the interview, they are considering visualization of sociality and social impact as the next level, and a higher level of certification.

In this way, further empirical research on how to measure and visualize the output as social impact through case studies is desirable.

## ●References

GIIN website, What you need to know about impact investing; https://thegiin.org/publication/post/about-impact-investing/#what-is-impact-investing. (Date of access December 4, 2024)

Higuchi, K. (2020). *Quantitative Text Analysis for Social Researchers: A Contribution to Content Analysis*, Nakanishiya Shuppan.

Kobayashi, T. (2021). Impact toushi no hatten to kenkyujyo no kadai 〔Development of Impact Investment and its Research Agendas〕 (in Japanese), *Journal of economics & business administration*, 224(1), 1-16.

Matsumoto, T. (edi) & Mizuguchi, T. (2005). *Shakaitekisekinintoushi(SRI) no kisochishiki* 〔Fundamental knowledge of Socially Responsible Investment (SRI)(in Japanese), Japanese Standards Association.

MEXT website (2023). Houdou Happyou reiwa 5 year 20, December 〔Press release 20 December 2023〕 (in Japanese); https://www.mext.go.jp/content/20230823-mxt_chousa01-000031377_001.pdf. (Date of access July 14, 2024)

MEXT, Higher Education Bureau (2020). Chiikirenkei platform kouchiku ni kansuru guidline 〔Guidelines for the Establishment of Regional Collaboration Platforms - Toward Higher Education that Contributes to and is Supported by the Community〕 (in Japanese); https://www.mext.go.jp/content/20201029-mext-koutou-000010662_01. pdf, 1-43. (Date of access July 12, 2024)

Omuro, N. & Ohira, S. (2013). DIFFUSION OF SOCIAL INNOVATION AND SOCIALLY RESPONSIBLE INVESTORS, *Journal of Business Management*, 31(0), 39-49.

Osborne, S. P. (2021). *Public Service Logic Creating value for public service users, citizens, and society through public service delivery,* Routledge.

Petrescu, M. (2019). From marketing to public value: towards a theory of public service ecosystems, *Public Management Review*, 21(11), 1733–1752.

Promotion and Mutual Aid Corporation for private schools of Japan (2023). Reiwa5 (2023) year shiritudaigaku·tankidaigakutou nyugaku shigan doukou 〔Trends in applications for admission to private universities and junior colleges in 2023〕 (in Japanese); https://www.shigaku.go.jp/files/shigandoukouR5.pdf, 1-80. (Date of access July 14, 2024)

Ryukoku Research Centre for the Local Public Human Resources and Policy Development (LORC) website, About; https://lorc.ryukoku.ac.jp/about/. (Date of access July 15, 2024)

Ryukoku university website A, Ryukoku Solar Park; https://www.ryukoku.ac.jp/about/solar/. (Date of access July 15, 2024)

Ryukoku University website B, Daigakuhatsu mega solar hatsudensho de chiikikeizai o hatten 〔Developing the local economy with university-based mega solar power plants〕 (in Japanese); https://retaction-ryukoku.com/83. (Date of access July 4, 2024)

Ryukoku University Extension Center, Zenkokuhatsu chiikikoukengata mega solar "Ryukoku Solar Park" kadou 〔First in the Nation, Community Contribution Type Mega Solar "Ryukoku Solar Park" Operation〕 (in Japanese); https://rec.seta.ryukoku.ac.jp/area04/data/topic1.pdf. (Date of access July 15, 2024)

Social Enterprise Certification Organisation website, social kigyouninsyouseido S ninsyou towa 〔Social and Sustainable Business Standard: What is S-Standard〕 (in Japanese); https://besocial.jp/. (Date of access July 17, 2024)

Strokosch, K. & Osborne, S. P. (2020). CO-experience, co-production and co-governance: an ecosystem approach to the analysis of value creation, *Policy & Politics*, 48(3), 425-442.

Tanimoto, K. (2006). *CSR kigyou to syakai wo kangaeru* 〔CSR - Thinking about business and society〕 (in Japanese) , NTT Publishing.

Vargo, S. L. and Lusch, R. L. (2017). Service-dominant logic 2025. *International Journal of Research in Marketing*, 34 (1), 46-67.

# Afterword

This book is the result of a joint research project "Value Research in Business Studies" (FY2022-2023) conducted by the Institute for Industrial Research at Kwansei Gakuin University, and is now published as "Sanken Sosho 48".

Joint research, one of the main research activities of the Institute for Industrial Research at Kwansei Gakuin University is an interdisciplinary research activity conducted by joint research project teams consisting of faculty members from the faculty and research institute, as well as researchers and practitioners from outside the university. Research themes are selected from the fields of economic, social, industrial, and corporate research, regional research, and so on. Research meetings are held during the three-year activity period, and the research results of each project are published and made public at the end of the activity.

In the "Sanken Sosho" to date, we have studied regional issues and proposed solutions through collaboration with industry, government, and academia. Specifically, we have published "Community Business in a New Era" (2006), "The Economics of 'Village Attractiveness' " (2009), "Public Infrastructure and Regional Development" (2015), "Structural Analysis of the Kansai Economy" (2018), "Evidence-based Unraveling the Future of the Region" (2022), "Economic Analysis of Regional Revitalization" (2023), and "Regional Economy and Industry in the Post-Corona Era" (2023), among others, and this book is an addition to the series.

The current project focuses on the concept of value in business administration. Value is a very important concept not only because it is used to evaluate the effectiveness of businesses and transactions, but also because it is the basis for decision making and performance measurement in the management of organizational bodies.

Part 1 reviews concepts analogous to the concept of value and examines some interesting performance measurement issues using the concept of value, such as what is the value of design thinking and what value is created by a family business. Part 2 focuses on several Japanese phenomena related to value and analyzes these on a theoretical basis. The uniqueness of this project is that it adopts the perspective of the "integration of adjacent sciences" and examines "integration" of value research in business administration. We hope that this book, which summarizes our findings, will further advance the study of value in business administration.

We would like to express our sincere gratitude to Professor Ishihara of Kwansei Gakuin University and the other authors for serving as co-research representatives for this publication.

We are grateful to Chuo Keizai-sha, Inc. for their support in publishing this book in spite of the difficult publishing conditions. I would especially like to thank Mr. Kazumasa Tanabe for his editorial work.

December 2024
Takayuki Yamaguchi,
Director, Institute for Industrial Research, Kwansei Gakuin University

関西学院大学産研叢書(48)

# Value Research in Management Studies

2025年3月31日　第1版第1刷発行

| | |
|---|---|
| 編著者 | Toshihiko Ishihara |
| 発行者 | 山　本　　　継 |
| 発行所 | ㈱中央経済社 |
| 発売元 | ㈱中央経済グループ パブリッシング |

〒101-0051　東京都千代田区神田神保町1-35
電　話　03 (3293) 3371 (編集代表)
　　　　03 (3293) 3381 (営業代表)
https://www.chuokeizai.co.jp
印刷／三英グラフィック・アーツ㈱
製本／誠　製　本　㈱

© 2025 関西学院大学産業研究所
Printed in Japan